grow vegetables

Penguin
Random
House

US Consultants Lori Spencer, Fern Marshall Bradley
Editor Katie Dock
Senior Designer Rachael Smith
Designer Andrew Milne
US Editor Kate Johnsen
US Senior Editor Shannon Beatty
Managing Editor Anna Kruger
Managing Art Editor Alison Donovan
DTP Designer Louise Waller
Picture Research Mel Watson, Lucy Claxton
Production Controller Mandy Inness

First American Edition, 2008
This edition published in the United States in 2016 by
DK Publishing, 375 Hudson Street, New York, New York 10014

Copyright © 2008, 2016 Dorling Kindersley Limited
DK, a Division of Penguin Random House LLC

Text copyright © 2008, 2016 Alan Buckingham

16 17 18 19 10 9 8 7 6 5 4 3 2 1

002–288667–Feb/2016

A catalog record for this book is available from the Library of
Congress

ISBN 978-1-4654-4486-8

DK books are available at special discounts when purchased in bulk
for sales promotions, premiums, fund-raising, or educational use.
For details, contact: DK Publishing Special
Markets, 345 Hudson Street, New York, New York 10014
SpecialSales@dk.com

Printed and bound in China

A WORLD OF IDEAS:
SEE ALL THERE IS TO KNOW

www.dk.com

grow vegetables

ALAN BUCKINGHAM

Specialist consultant JO WHITTINGHAM

CONTENTS

Why grow your own?

A word of warning: growing your own vegetables is not only seriously addictive but will also completely change your attitude about what you eat. Once you've tried freshly dug new potatoes or tomatoes picked straight from the vine, or bitten into a ripe cob of sweet corn still warm from the sun, nothing will taste the same again. Equally, nothing will match the simple satisfaction of eating food you've raised from seed, planted, watered, fed, and tended until it's reached that moment when it's ready for harvesting. There's no looking back: you'll be hooked.

Seasonal and local

We all share a growing concern about the food we eat. Where has it come from, how was it produced, and what has been done to it before it reaches us? Increasingly, we see the common sense in eating what's in season and what's grown locally, not what has been shipped halfway around the world, at an unacceptable ecological cost. Growing your own food is a very real answer to such concerns. How can anything be fresher, more seasonal, or more local than if you've only just picked it yourself?

Organic or not?

This book does not insist on an organic approach. However, the chances are that if you care about the food you eat, you'll probably want to avoid artificial fertilizers and pesticides as much as possible. In the end, it's your decision. Whether you choose to go organic or not, at least when growing your own, you're in control; nobody apart from you is going to spray your plants with chemicals.

Pea flowers are delicate and wonderfully colored—proof that many vegetables can be as attractive as garden flowers.

For freshness and flavor, what can compete with homegrown beans picked, cooked, and eaten straight from your vegetable garden?

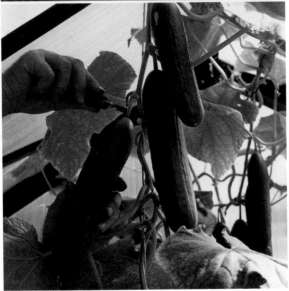

(top) **A container-grown salad bowl** planted with a mixture of tomatoes, lettuces, and herbs is ideal for small gardens and patios.

(bottom) **Homegrown cucumbers** have an intensity of flavor that makes their store-bought cousins seem watery and tasteless in comparison.

Choice and variety

Look through almost any seed catalog and one thing will be immediately apparent. Growing your own gives you access to a much richer choice of vegetables, salads, and herbs than you can buy in even the best-stocked supermarket. And if you join one of the many seed-sharing societies, you'll discover a huge range of rare, heritage varieties that are no longer available for sale.

Healthy and natural

Eating food that you've grown yourself is extraordinarily satisfying. Partly, it's the simple pleasure we all take in having done something ourselves, but there are other feel-good factors, too. Being outdoors, getting regular exercise, staying in touch with the seasons, really noticing the weather—all these things add up. They all contribute to the magic of serving up homegrown vegetables, freshly picked and freshly cooked. They're high in natural vitamins and minerals, and full of natural flavor.

One thing is for sure. Once you've grown your own, you'll never feel quite the same about the shrink-wrapped pack of washed and trimmed green beans or the plastic bag of prepacked salad that you drop into your shopping cart at the supermarket.

Unusual varieties may be easier to grow than to buy. Why not try one of these? (clockwise from top left) **Basil 'African Blue', sweet pepper 'Atris', calabrese 'Romanesco', beet 'Detroit Tardel'**

Vegetable Grower's Know-How

There's a mystique about the art of cultivating vegetables. It's rich in old sayings, anecdotes, strange customs, and closely guarded potting-shed secrets. There are a lot of old wives' tales, too. Should shallots really be planted on the shortest day of the year and harvested on the longest? Do parsnips really taste better if you delay harvesting them until after a frost? As a beginner, it seems there's a lot to learn. Yet it's not nearly as difficult as it looks. Learning by imitation is a good way to start. If you have a community garden, there's no harm in copying your neighbors if they grow plenty of healthy, good-looking vegetables. And don't be shy about asking for guidance. No one objects to being asked for advice—particularly old gardeners. It's what they live for!

There's not much know-how needed here. Anyone who can remember to water should be able to grow a selection of vegetables in containers.

Starting a vegetable plot

The history of vegetable gardening is littered with unkempt, overgrown plots started with the best of intentions, but abandoned when the time to maintain them can't be found. There's no way of divorcing how much space your vegetable garden occupies from how much time you will have to spend on it. To put it bluntly, the bigger your patch, the more time it will take. So don't kid yourself—be honest about how much time you can devote. A few hours a week is fine for a small plot or a corner of the garden, but a large one will demand a lot more time. Remember that traditional, working kitchen gardens once had full-time staff.

Labor-intensive chores

In a large vegetable garden, weeding is likely to represent the biggest demand on your time. As the weather warms up in spring, weeds get into gear. Left unchecked, they'll grow faster than you would believe possible, and will quickly colonize whole areas of ground.

The trick is to tackle them before they take hold—lay lightproof mulches of plastic sheeting or old carpet, apply weedkiller if you must, or simply hand-weed. It's far easier and quicker to eradicate weeds when they're seedlings than when they've taken root and established themselves. Thereafter, weed little and often to keep them under control.

At certain times of the year, watering can be particularly time-consuming. This is the case in periods of drought, certainly, but also when you've just planted out seedlings, when you're trying to stop plants from bolting, or when vegetables are plumping up ready for harvesting. Be smart about watering: spread mulches to help retain moisture, use seep or drip hoses, and don't think you have to water all of your plants all the time.

Strangely enough, it seems to be much easier to find time for sowing seeds, planting out seedlings, and, of course, harvesting. They feel a lot less like chores!

Small is beautiful

If you're short on time or tight for space, think small. Don't attempt to grow vegetables that need a lot of room (globe artichokes, asparagus, or cauliflower) nor ones that need a lot of fussy care and attention (tomatoes, for example). There are plenty that can be planted and then left more or less to themselves.

Pots and containers take up little space and are ideal for growing baby or "patio" varieties. Keep in mind, however, that although pots are great for small spaces, they usually need to be watered more frequently than crops growing in the ground; you shouldn't go away and leave them unattended for several days on end.

(clockwise from top)

A large plot like this needs an investment of time to maintain; don't underestimate how much.

Vertical gardening makes sense in small urban spaces—if you can't spread out, spread up.

Pots and containers are easy to plant and economical on space, but pick crops young, before they grow too large.

Location and climate

There's little you can do about your local climate. If you garden in far northern latitudes, you'll struggle to grow Mediterranean vegetables such as tomatoes, peppers, and eggplant. You need to understand your climate and the conditions it produces throughout the year to help choose varieties you can grow successfully. Find out the average date for the last frost in your region—often later than you think—to avoid planting out tender seedlings too soon. Then come to grips with what you can control: the factors that create your yard's "microclimate."

Microclimates

It's surprising how conditions in one part of a vegetable garden can be completely different from those in another part, even in a small yard. A south-facing plot is always warmer than a north-facing one, of course, but the path the sun takes across the sky at different times of year is also important. A north-facing spot thrown into shade by buildings for most of the year may suddenly get the sun when it is at its highest in May, June, and July. And a west-facing bed may benefit from the lingering warmth of late-afternoon and early-evening sun.

Open, exposed areas will almost certainly get more light and sun, but may suffer from lack of shelter if you have strong prevailing winds. On the other hand, low-lying corners sheltered by walls and hedges may be sun traps in the summer but frost pockets in winter.

Frost pockets

Frost pockets occur where cold air—which is heavier than warm air—collects in dips in the ground or at the base of walls. If the cold air can't escape and is not warmed by the sun, it is likely to produce frost.

A wall of sunflowers acts as a tall hedge to provide a natural windbreak for more vulnerable plants growing in raised beds.

Sun traps

Solid brick walls that face the sun can act rather like storage heaters. They absorb heat during the day and reflect some of it right away, but retain the rest and release it slowly throughout the course of the evening. This can raise the overall temperature in the garden quite dramatically, and creates the perfect spot for vegetables such as tomatoes, cucumbers, eggplant, and peppers for which you might otherwise need a greenhouse.

Windbreaks

Sadly, wind is not the vegetable gardener's friend. Apart from the damage that storms and strong gusts can do—blowing over stakes and wigwams, knocking down climbing beans, peas, Brussels sprouts, or artichokes, and tearing plastic and fabric cloches—it can reduce the overall temperature and increase the rate at which water is lost through evaporation. All this puts plants under stress.

Plants grow better and tend to crop more generously on sheltered sites. Traditional kitchen gardens were surrounded by high brick walls. Today, fences or hedges are likely to be a more realistic option. In fact, hedges have an added advantage of being semipermeable. Stopping wind dead can cause turbulence on the leeward side, while a hedge softens the wind's effect.

(from top)
Gardening close to the ocean can present certain problems. Sites may be very exposed, and winds may carry damaging salt.

Greenhouses let you create and control complete microclimates.

South-facing walls are often natural sun traps, absorbing and retaining heat.

Plot layouts and bed systems

The layout of your plot is important. Since it's an area in which you are going to spend a good deal of your time, you want it to be as easy and efficient to work as possible. You want it to provide all your crops with the best growing conditions. You want a certain amount of built-in flexibility so that you are able to rotate the crops from one year to the next. And, of course, you may also have requirements that aren't strictly concerned with horticulture—your garden or plot may also provide a kids' play area, a place for a barbecue, or simply a spot where you can sit and relax on warm summer evenings.

Apple stepovers—single cordons bent over horizontally at about knee or waist height—are a space-saving approach to growing apples on your plot.

Raised beds keep you off the soil. If they are not too wide, you can do everything from sowing to harvesting from the paths, so you never stand on the soil and compact it under your weight.

Designing your plot

Find a pencil and paper, measure the overall dimensions of your plot and sketch it out. Now block in the features that are going to stay in one place, at least for the foreseeable future: boundaries and paths, sheds and compost bins, fruit trees and fruit cages, and long-term perennial crops such as asparagus beds or rhubarb patches. Are they in the right place, or do you want to move them?

The next thing is to decide is whether you want rows or beds. Traditionally, plots were planted in neat, parallel rows or patchwork squares interspersed by trodden paths. It's an efficient use of space and because nothing is permanent, it is completely flexible. However, constantly walking up and down over soil compacts it, which is bad for its structure.

The bed system

Laying out a permanent pattern of beds and paths will keep you off the areas that you are cultivating. The beds are solely for growing crops, not for walking on, and should be small enough for you never to have to stand on them. Likewise, the paths are always paths—so you can grass them or lay down paving slabs, gravel, or bark chips, if you wish.

If you regularly add organic material to your beds, the soil level will in time become higher than that of the paths. For this reason, raised beds are edged with boards, bricks, concrete blocks, or even tiles and slates to retain the soil. Deep beds are the same as raised beds, but without the edging.

Grass paths dividing up beds undoubtedly look good, but they need mowing and edging regularly to stop the grasses from self-seeding and to keep the paths neat.

THE "NO-DIG" SYSTEM

This approach does away with the need for digging—at least it does once it's up and running. The aim is to create beds full of well-structured soil that are "topped up" each year with a surface layer of fertilizer and organic material. This suppresses weeds and is incorporated into the soil by earthworms and other organisms, rather than by digging it in. For the system to succeed:

- Begin by thoroughly digging the bed to open up the soil and improve drainage.
- Carefully remove all perennial weeds.
- Each year spread a surface mulch of well-rotted compost or manure.
- Disturb the soil as little as possible at harvesting.
- Use a sheet mulch if necessary to suppress any persistent weeds.

Kitchen garden tradition

There was a time when every reasonably sized household would have had an area of land dedicated to growing vegetables, fruit, and herbs—perhaps even flowers for cutting, too. Whatever its size, the kitchen garden was a source of fresh, seasonal produce. It was inexpensive and, often literally, right on the doorstep. Traditions arose for how such vegetable gardens were designed and laid out. Though there were certainly no rules, a few tried and tested ways of doing things arose that gave traditional kitchen gardens their distinctive quality.

The kitchen garden

A traditional kitchen garden intended to provide for the needs of the family and staff of a large house often had a separate area, walled off from the rest of the yard. The layout would have been ordered and workmanlike. There would probably have been permanent structures such as greenhouses and cold frames, potting and storage sheds, and bins for manure and compost. Elsewhere, most vegetables would have been grown in long parallel rows in large beds. The same style can still be seen in many vegetable gardens today.

Potagers

In France, the kitchen garden evolved into something more stylized and formal. Called a "potager" (literally, a vegetable stew or soup) it served the same purpose of producing food, but was more elaborate. The area was usually divided geometrically into many small square, rectangular, or triangular beds, each bordered by a low hedge and separated by immaculate paths. Plantings were highly decorative—in contrasting colors, for example.

(top) **Close planting** is the order of the day, as peas, chives, cabbages, lettuces, and more jostle for space.

(bottom) **Criss-cross rows** of red and green lettuces divide triangles of onions, shallots, and carrots in a decorative potager.

Organized chaos

Not everyone is blessed with a yard large enough for a full-scale kitchen garden or potager. Equally, not everyone has the sort of temperament that's drawn to extreme formality and symmetry. For such gardeners, a vegetable plot is likely to be a much more relaxed, informal affair. It tends to evolve haphazardly, with a generous amount of improvisation. Plants are squeezed into every available inch of space, and the effect is one of overflowing profusion. There's often a degree of planning underneath it all, but it's unlikely to be apparent.

The cottage vegetable garden

Cottage gardens are by their very nature humble. They're usually small, and in the past would have produced a large harvest of vegetables, herbs, and fruit. Geometric beds with neat edging, wide gravel paths, and purely decorative plants would have been an unaffordable luxury. Flowers would have been squeezed in among crops, unless there was another reason for growing them.

To create a modern vegetable garden of this kind is not hard. In spite of the informal look, it needs a plan and a structure—but probably one based on narrow, curved paths, irregularly shaped beds, tightly grouped plantings rather than neatly organized ranks, and rustic features like tepees or arches made from hazel or willow poles. Forethought in terms of maintaining it is required, too—if nothing else, to ensure regular crop rotation.

Mixed plantings

Without the space for separate flower and kitchen gardens, vegetables, fruit, and flowering plants must be grown together. There's no harm in this; indeed, the effect can be charming. Sweet peas winding through climbing beans or cucumbers look wonderful, as do globe artichokes, ruby chard, or fennel planted among perennials in a flowering border. Flowering plants will also attract birds and insects, which help to keep vegetables healthy and pest-free. Dig some organic matter into the soil before sowing or planting, though, since vegetables require fertile soil. Beware of competition from the roots of nearby trees and shrubs, too.

Peas climb up a garden fence
while nasturtiums scramble over a low framework of stakes; cabbages, lettuces, and other vegetables occupy the beds.

Your soil

All soil is made up of tiny particles of weathered rock plus water and organic matter from the rotted-down remains of plants and animals. The size of the rock particles is important. Tiny particles produce clay soil, which can be dense and heavy. Larger particles produce sandy soil, which is lighter and grittier. The amount of organic matter is also important. The more there is, the more fertile the soil and the better your plants will grow in it. In addition to this, soils vary in their degree of acidity or alkalinity, a quality to which some plants are very sensitive.

Clay soil

If your soil is heavy and sticky and can be formed into a ball that keeps its shape, it's probably clay. Clay is often full of nutrients and is therefore fertile, but water doesn't drain freely through it, making it turn muddy in winter and bake to a crust in summer. It is also prone to compaction, so avoid stepping directly on it wherever possible; use planks to spread your weight. The composition can be improved somewhat by adding organic matter and sand.

Sandy soil

Sandy soil is harder to form into a ball. It will probably run through your fingers, and you may be able to feel the gritty particles. It is lighter and easier to dig than clay, warms up faster in spring, and often drains more freely. However, this means not only that it dries out quickly in hot weather, but also that nutrients wash through it after heavy rain or watering. It is therefore less fertile, and needs plenty of well-rotted manure, compost, or any other organic material added to it.

(top) **Clay soil** can be squeezed and formed into shapes when damp—not unlike dough.

(bottom) **Sandy soil** is composed of larger particles—more like fine salt—and tends not to form clumps.

Spread powdered lime thinly over the soil with a spade, then rake it in evenly. Avoid windy days on which lime may be blown around, and always wear gloves and a mask when applying it.

Other soils

Silt is somewhere between clay and sandy soil. It feels smoother and silkier than a sandy soil but not as heavy and sticky as clay.

Limestone or chalky soils are pale-colored, often full of stones, and tend not to be very deep. They are reasonably fertile but, being full of calcium, are very alkaline.

Peat soils contain a lot of organic plant matter that has not yet fully rotted down. They retain lots of moisture, so may be prone to waterlogging, and they are very acidic.

SOIL ACIDITY AND ALKALINITY

The pH of a soil is a measurement that tells you whether it is acidic or alkaline. The pH scale runs from 1 (very acidic) to 14 (very alkaline). A pH of 7 is neutral; most garden soils have a pH that lies somewhere between 4.5 and 7.5.

Although most vegetables are fairly tolerant, some are unhappy in soil that is too acidic, while others dislike soil that is too alkaline. A pH of 6.5 is generally regarded as optimal. A higher figure suits cabbages and other brassicas since the alkalinity discourages clubroot, and a lower figure is fine for acid-tolerant plants such as rhubarb, radishes, or sweet potatoes.

To find out whether soil is acidic or alkaline, use a test kit (*see below*), taking samples from different parts of the vegetable patch. It's fairly easy to make acidic soil more alkaline. Simply add lime (calcium carbonate) or a lime-rich material such as mushroom compost. Don't add it at the same time as manure: they will react chemically with each other. Leave it to become absorbed for a few months before planting. It's harder to make an alkaline soil more acidic, although it will happen over time due to the natural effects of rainfall and weathering.

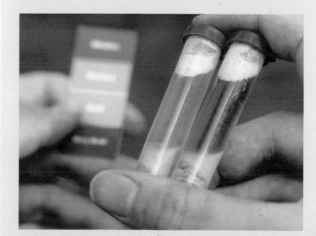

Compost, manure, and other fertilizers

Vegetables take a lot more out of the soil than do the flowering plants and shrubs in a regular garden, and you will only get consistently good crops from a vegetable plot if you work at putting the goodness back in. If you feed your soil, you'll help to keep it healthy and fertile. And healthy, fertile soil means healthy, productive plants.

A vegetable patch needs feeding in two ways. The first is to add various forms of well-rotted manure or compost. This not only enriches the soil, it also radically improves its composition or structure. The second is to apply fertilizers—either organic or inorganic ones—in order to top off the nutrients that plants need for strong and healthy growth.

Manures and composts

These are natural organic materials derived from decomposed or rotted plant matter and animal waste. They are usually bulky and, when dug into the soil, they enrich it with nutrients, make it more water-retentive, and break up compacted masses so that air can circulate. All of these factors encourage plants' roots to grow deeply and spread without restriction.

Barnyard and **stable manures** are ideal, if you can find a source for them. They are usually a mixture of straw and animal dung. Avoid any manure that contains too high a proportion of wood shavings or sawdust. Let animal manures rot down for at least six months before using them, or the ammonia they contain may scorch young plants.

Compost is decayed plant matter, which might come from your vegetable garden, your yard, or even your kitchen. Inside a compost pile, tiny microorganisms are hard at work breaking down the rotting, organic material and transforming it into a rich, dark substance not unlike soil.

For the process to work, the pile needs air, warmth, and moisture. If you get the balance right, your compost should feel pleasantly crumbly or "friable," and it will smell good. Too much water or not enough air, and it will be wet and slimy and smell disgusting.

Spreading a mulch of well-rotted compost or manure around growing plants after watering helps increase moisture retention.

A couple of alternatives to garden compost are leaf mold and mushroom compost. You can make **leaf mold** yourself by gathering up dead leaves and piling them up in wire cages, or by combining them with a little soil in plastic bags punctured with holes. They can take a long time to rot down, though. **Mushroom compost**, which is the medium left after growing mushrooms commercially, can be purchased from most garden suppliers.

Applying manures and composts

There are two ways of doing this: either dig it into the soil, or spread it over the ground as what's called a surface mulch.

Digging in manure or compost is usually a job for the late fall. That way it will rot down fully and become thoroughly incorporated during the winter months, ready for sowing or planting in the spring. It's particularly beneficial for heavy clay soil or ground that has become hard and compacted.

On light, sandy soil a mulch of manure or compost 2–4 in (5–10 cm) thick can be simply spread over the surface and left there over the winter. Much of it will be carried down into the soil by worms, and anything that's left can be dug in lightly in the spring.

(top) **A homemade compost bin** constructed from hollow wire-netting walls filled with straw.

(middle) **The bottom layers** of a compost pile generate heat as they rot. A covering of plastic keeps the heat in and the rain out.

(bottom) **Plastic compost bins** have snugly fitting lids and a door at the bottom for removing material that has rotted down.

The joy of compost

Making your own compost is so easy and so beneficial that, if you're not already doing it, you should start immediately. The principal is very straightforward. Make or buy a compost bin, set it up somewhere convenient, and then simply fill it with garden prunings and clippings, dead plant material from your vegetable patch, grass cuttings, and certain kitchen waste.

Keep your pile covered with plastic or old carpet: the hotter it gets, the quicker it will decompose. And remember to turn the compost every now and then to allow air to circulate throughout it. Within months you'll have earned your eco-credentials as a home composter, and your vegetable garden will love you!

What to add

■ Do add vegetable peelings and unwanted fruit from the kitchen.
■ Do add grass clippings, but not in thick layers—mix them up so that air can circulate.
■ Do add water when necessary—but never so much that the pile is waterlogged.

What not to add

■ Don't add perennial or annual weeds that have already produced seed—they will survive.
■ Don't add any diseased plants—you should discard or burn them instead.
■ Don't add thick woody stems or twigs—they take too long to rot down.
■ Don't add meat, fish, or cooked food from the kitchen—it will attract mice and rats.

Green manure

If you have an area of your vegetable patch that you plan to leave empty for six weeks or more, grow a crop specifically designed to be dug back into the soil—known as "green manure." Legumes such as clover, vetch, and lupine absorb nitrogen from the air and incorporate it into the soil. Other green manures—which include alfalfa, mustard, rye, borage, and comfrey—will break up heavy soils with their roots, as well as adding organic matter when they are dug back in.

In all cases, it is important that green manures are cut and dug in before they become woody or set seed, or they may take a long time to break down, and could become weeds.

Fertilizers

These are more concentrated sources of soil nutrients than manures and composts. They're often processed, in liquid, powder, granule, or pellet form, and may be organic or inorganic in origin. **Organic** fertilizers come from plants or animals. They include kelp extracts, pelleted chicken manure, bone meal, hoof and horn, fish meal, dried blood, and fish, blood, and bone meal. **Inorganic** fertilizers are extracted from minerals or manufactured using industrial-scale chemical processes.

All fertilizers contain at least one of the three key soil nutrients: nitrogen (N, added in the form of nitrates), phosphorus (P, added in the form of phosphate), and potassium (K, added in the form of potash). Many contain all three, and some contain more—including essential trace elements such as manganese, molybdenum, boron, and so

on (*see pp.334–337*). But processed fertilizers come at a price. Although more concentrated and faster-acting than natural manures and composts, they are expensive and don't add anything to the soil's structure.

Applying fertilizers

Adding fertilizer to soil before seeds are sown or seedlings planted is called **base dressing**. Mark out areas of the ground with string or stakes to help calculate quantities, sprinkle or scatter the fertilizer over the surface, then rake it. If the ground is dry and there is no rainfall over the following few days, water it in.

Topdressing involves sprinkling soluble fertilizer around plants; as the fertilizer dissolves and is absorbed into the soil, nutrients reach the plants' developing root systems. Liquid fertilizers are dissolved in water before being applied, and foliar fertilizers are sprayed directly onto the leaves. In all cases, wear gloves, and handle fertilizers with care, as they can be toxic.

(far left) **Green manure** will add nutrients, increase fertility, and improve soil structure. Cut down plants that reach 8 in (20 cm) in height, let them wilt for a few days, then dig them into the soil.

(left) **Red worms** are a type of earthworm particularly adept at converting garden and kitchen waste into rich, fertile worm compost.

Tools and equipment

Gardening tools are deeply seductive. Wander around a well-stocked garden center or flip through a beautifully produced mail order catalog, and it's very easy to convince yourself that you can't live without a colinear hoe, a corkscrew weeder, or a thumb waterer. The truth is that you can probably manage perfectly well without them. At best, such tools fall into the category of "nice to have" or "may come in handy from time to time." At worst, they'll just gather dust. In fact, there are very few gardening tools that are genuinely essential.

Essential tools

A fork, a spade, a hoe, a rake, a trowel and hand fork, and a pair of pruners—these are the few tools you simply have to have. Buy the very best you can afford. The higher the quality, the easier and more comfortable they will be to use, and the longer they'll last. Look for high-carbon steel or stainless steel, and for handles made of ashwood or aluminum. Keep your tools in good condition, too. Clean them after every session, dry them off to prevent them from rusting, and rub them with an oily rag to keep rust at bay if you are going to be storing them for a while.

Standard forks usually have four prongs and a head that measures about 8 in (20 cm) wide and 12 in (30 cm) deep. Border forks are smaller and lighter. The prongs or "tines" are generally square in shape, although special potato forks are available with flat tines. Fork and spade handle grips may be D-, Y-, or T-shaped.

Standard spades have a rectangular blade 8 in (20 cm) wide and 11 in (28 cm) deep. If you're planning heavy or extensive digging, these are what you need. They are, however, pretty heavy. Border or lady's spades are smaller and lighter. Don't be put off by the less than macho name; for many tasks, they are much easier to use.

The push or Dutch hoe is the most useful kind of hoe. It has an angled flat blade that is held parallel with the ground. Use it to weed carefully around plants and slice the tops off shallow-rooted surface weeds using a push-pull action.

Standard garden rakes have metal heads 12–15 in (30–38 cm) wide with 12–16 evenly spaced teeth. They are used for leveling the ground and breaking soil into a fine, smooth tilth ready for planting. Wider wooden rakes are useful for working large areas.

Trowels are used for digging holes and planting out, either straight into the ground or into containers. They may have a standard-sized scoop-shaped blade, or a narrow one for tight spaces. Hand forks are used for breaking up soil and weeding. If you find bending down uncomfortable, buy a trowel or hand fork with a long handle.

Pruners have many uses: cutting, snipping, trimming, pruning, and more. Some gardeners even wear them in a holster like a gunslinger. Bypass pruners, with curved blades, are probably the best. They should be strong enough to cut woody stems as thick as your little finger; keep them sharp so they make clean cuts.

Additional tools

Here are some tools it would be nice to have but it's quite possible to do without.

Dibber

Essentially, dibbers are little more than sticks for making planting holes. But they do have two advantages: first, they are pointed or tapered so that they're easy to push into hard ground; and second, superior models may have rings marked around them to indicate planting depth.

Pronged cultivator

Hand cultivators usually have three or five sharp, angled prongs. They are dragged through the ground to break up the soil, to loosen weeds, or to mix in a topdressing of fertilizer or compost.

Draw hoe

Weeding with a draw hoe employs a chopping or dragging action, rather than the push-pull of a Dutch hoe. Draw hoes are also useful for earthing up soil (over potatoes, for example) and for making seed rows—flat-bottomed ones using the base of the blade, or V-shaped ones using a corner of the blade. Small, short-handled draw hoes are called onion hoes.

Loppers and pruning saws

These are for pruning jobs that are too big for pruners. Generally, that means trees and shrubs— which may or may not be a feature of your vegetable patch. They are also useful for cutting down Jerusalem artichokes or the tough stumps of Brussels sprouts and cabbages.

Ridger

This is a surprisingly useful tool, and once you've tried one, you may not want to give it up. It's similar to a draw hoe but has a blade shaped like a reverse-facing plow. You drag it toward you to create furrows in the ground for planting or to earth up soil into ridges.

Essential equipment

There are a few items it's difficult to do without. **Watering cans** are essential, though it doesn't really matter whether they are made of plastic or galvanized steel. Perhaps it makes the most sense to have at least two: a large plastic one, and a smaller, long-necked one that will deliver a fine spray for watering delicate seedlings. **Sprayers** are useful, too, though you may need three: one for weedkiller, one for insecticide, and one for fertilizer.

A **wheelbarrow** is invaluable on all but the smallest of plots. Use it to move soil, compost, and manure, and to collect weeds and plant debris. **Sacks** and carrying bags perform the same function. A trug is a bit of a luxury but can end up being used almost continuously, when both harvesting and weeding.

Gloves are a must, not just to keep your hands warm in winter but also to protect them. Buy a pair of thick suede or leather ones for heavy jobs and a pair of thinner cotton ones for lighter jobs in warmer weather.

Other equipment that should come in very handy when growing vegetables includes a good selection of bamboo canes, sticks, stakes, and other supports; some strong garden twine or string, rolls of wire, and plant ties; and a range of plant labels and markers. Apart from cloches, frames, fabric, and netting (*see pp.40–41*), that's about it. Everything else can be considered optional.

(clockwise from top left)
Ridger, dibber, wheelbarrow, watering can

Sowing seeds and raising seedlings

Vegetables are almost always grown from seed. A few are cultivated by planting tubers (potatoes and Jerusalem artichokes) or bulbs (onions and shallots); others can be propagated by division or from cuttings (rhubarb and certain herbs). But growing from seed bought from reputable seed suppliers has its advantages. First, seeds are guaranteed to be viable, so they should germinate successfully. Second, they will be true to type: the cultivar will be what is described, not a hybrid variation created by cross-pollination. And third, growing from seed is a relatively cheap way of producing your own vegetables. You can even grow vegetables from seeds you save yourself, though there are risks (*see pp.52–53*).

Sowing inside

Why sow seeds indoors instead of outside, directly into the soil? Quite simply, it's easier to control the temperature, humidity, soil type, and amount of fertilizer and water when working indoors, in a greenhouse, or under cover than it is in the garden. Many seeds need a constant minimum temperature to germinate. Keeping them in a cold frame or under a cloche should suffice, but in certain cases, they'll need a heated greenhouse or propagator.

Certain vegetables have a long growing season—tomatoes, eggplant, peppers, and okra, for example. To ripen fully by the end of the year, they may need to be started off inside before it gets warm enough outside for them to be planted out.

Moreover, plants raised from seeds sown inside, in carefully controlled conditions, tend to be stronger, healthier, and more resistant to pests and diseases than those raised outdoors.

If you don't have an outside area at all, don't underestimate the value of windowsill space—there are a few vegetables that can be grown in pots indoors without ever needing to plant them out (*see pp.46–47*).

Young seedlings growing in module flats and pots on a greenhouse shelf, with potatoes chitting underneath.

(top) **Sowing seeds** in a seed flat.

(bottom) **Biodegradable pots** made of paper decompose when planted out, so seedling roots are not disturbed.

Pots, trays, and modules

Terra-cotta pots look better, but plastic ones are cheaper and easier to keep sterile. Tube-shaped biodegradable pots can be planted directly into the soil with young seedlings inside. They are ideal for plants that develop deep roots—fava beans, sweet corn, or tomatoes, for example. Over time, the pots rot away naturally.

Modules are flats divided into separate cells. Seeds are sown in each cell, and seedlings are transplanted by pushing them out from beneath; the root ball and the plug of potting mix remain undisturbed.

Propagators

The simplest propagator of all is a clear plastic bag tied over a plant pot or seed flat. Its job is to create the kind of warm, humid microclimate in which seeds germinate best. Specially made propagators are plastic flats with close-fitting clear lids. Some have a heating element in the base and a thermostat for regulating temperature.

Propagators create microclimates: vents at the top can be opened to keep excess humidity from causing seedlings to rot.

Seed-starting and potting mixes

Specially formulated growing mediums for sowing are a consistent mix; if you buy them fresh each year, they should be sterile and free of pests, viruses, and other soilborne diseases. Soilless mix doesn't contain any soil; it's made of a bulking material such as coir or peat and sand. It contains no nutrients, as germinating seeds don't need any. Potting mix is used once seedlings are repotted; it may or may not contain soil, but certainly has more nutrients, which seedlings need once they've rooted.

Pricking out

Once seedlings have developed a couple of leaves, move them into individual pots or modules. This is known as "pricking out." Use a dibber or a pencil to pry them very gently out of the soil, taking care not to damage the delicate roots. Always handle seedlings by the leaves, not the stem. Once replanted, they will develop their own root system without crowding or competition from neighbors.

Sowing outside

Most vegetables sown outdoors go into the ground in the position where they will stay—brassicas, leeks, and root vegetables, for example. A few are sown in temporary seedbeds to start them off, and then transplanted to final growing locations, but with today's prevalence of biodegradable pots and plastic module flats, this is less common than it once was.

Warming the soil

There is no point in sowing too early; most seeds need a minimum temperature to germinate, and if the soil is too cold they will simply sit there until it warms up—or, worse, rot or be eaten by predators. Beets, for example, will probably germinate when the soil temperature reaches about 45°F (7°C), so you can plant them in early spring, but green beans need at least 54°F (12°C). It doesn't sound like much of a difference but it can be critical.

Lend a helping hand by warming up the soil artificially. Use cloches or frames, or cover with sheets of black polyethylene (*see pp.40–41*). This will not only allow heat to build up, it will keep off rain and prevent waterlogging.

(far left) In wet conditions sprinkle some sand in the base of the row and sow seeds on top of it.

(left) In dry conditions water the base of the row to moisten the soil before sowing seeds.

(above) Cover broadcast seeds by carefully raking soil back over them and then watering with a fine spray.

Preparing the soil

Let's assume you dug over the soil last fall or winter, and that you incorporated plenty of well-rotted organic material. The task now is to produce a fine tilth: soil that is fine and crumbly, with no large clods. This is achieved by hoeing to remove any new weeds and then raking backward and forward until you have broken down the soil into fine particles. If it is dry and dusty, water it. And if it sticks to your shoes when you walk on it, wait for it to dry out a little more.

Sowing methods

Seeds are sometimes sown in a drill, a shallow trench marked out in the soil with a hoe, or scattered over a prepared area of ground (known as "broadcasting"). They are then covered with soil and watered. When seedlings appear, they usually need thinning so that they are not overcrowded.

Planting out

Before long, young seedlings that have been raised under cover in pots and modules will need to be transplanted into their final growing locations. Deciding exactly when to do this is a bit of an art. If you do it too early, the ground may not yet be warm enough or there may still be a danger of frost. On the other hand, if you do it too late, the seedlings may outgrow their containers and their roots can become potbound. However, timing is less critical for plants that have been raised in a nursery seedbed.

Hardening off

Seedlings raised indoors or under cover get used to a warm, sheltered microclimate. If you suddenly move them outdoors into the cold, they'll probably experience a dramatic shock. To avoid this, they should be acclimatized slowly by being hardened off. Either put them outdoors during the day and bring them in at night, or keep them in a cold frame with a lid you can open and close. Alternatively, plant them out but cover them at night with cloches.

Transplanting from pots and modules

Seedlings should be planted out once they have four to six true leaves and before their roots fill their pots. Before you start, soak both the seedlings and the holes in the ground into which they are being planted. Carefully remove the seedlings from their pots or modules, holding them by their leaves rather than their stems or roots, and retaining as much of the potting mix as possible. Drop them into their planting holes and gently firm soil around them.

(top) **Plug plants** bought via mail order arrive in special plastic packs. Plant them out immediately.

(bottom) **Cutting a hole in a plastic mulch** allows you to plant a cucumber seedling in a biodegradable pot straight through it.

Transplanting from a seedbed

Don't transplant in full sun. Seedlings already under stress from being uprooted will only wilt further in the heat. Instead, choose a day when the weather is gray and overcast. Give your plants a thorough soaking before attempting to lift them, then dig them out with a hand fork or trowel, keeping as much soil intact around their roots as you can. To keep them damp, put them in a clear plastic bag or a bucket with an inch or so of water in it. After watering the planting holes, carefully insert the seedlings, drawing the soil around them, then firming it down.

Mulches

A layer of organic or inorganic material spread over the surface of the soil is called a mulch. It might be a sheet of plastic that you've been using to warm up the ground; if so, you can cut holes in it and plant through it. Alternatively, it might be well-rotted manure, compost, or grass cuttings. It's best to apply mulches after watering newly planted seedlings but not when the soil is either very wet or very dry.

Mulches serve a number of purposes. They keep the soil warm. They retain moisture by preventing water from evaporating. They can act as organic fertilizers if they contain nutrients that will be absorbed into the soil. They inhibit weed growth. And they may also—depending on the material—deter pests and parasites such as slugs, snails, and certain insects.

(top) **Marking out a rough grid** in the soil will help you plant out module-grown seedlings such as these lettuces equidistantly.

(bottom) **Grass cuttings** spread over a layer of newspaper make an effective mulch for a chard seedling.

Crop rotation

With the exception of one or two perennials that occupy a permanent location (artichokes, asparagus, or rhubarb, for example), vegetables are sown or planted fresh each year. It's smart to grow them in different places from one year to the next. That way, you will prevent your soil from becoming exhausted by the same crop continually taking the same nutrients out of it. You'll also reduce the risk of pests and diseases establishing and becoming difficult to eradicate. There are numerous crop-rotation systems, which all group together crops belonging to the same family or sharing the same needs.

FIVE-YEAR CROP ROTATION

Large vegetable plots are big enough to be divided into numerous, different-sized beds or planting areas. If so, you might like to try this longer-term rotation plan, which means that it will be five years before any one crop is grown again in the same place.

- Year 1: brassicas
- Year 2: peas and beans
- Year 3: potatoes and fruiting vegetables
- Year 4: the onion family
- Year 5: root and stem vegetables

It's not so critical to rotate vegetables such as zucchini and squashes, or leaves such as lettuce, spinach, and other salad greens; they may be slotted in as part of any rotation group.

THREE-YEAR CROP ROTATION

YEAR 1: peas, beans, and fruiting vegetables

Peas and beans are all legumes and share an important characteristic. They absorb nitrogen from the air and store, or "fix", it with the help of bacteria in small nodules on their roots. If you leave those roots in the soil after harvesting, the crops that you grow there next year can benefit from the nitrogen left behind. Along with legumes, this group includes fruiting vegetables like eggplant, cucumbers, peppers, sweet corn, and tomatoes.

YEAR 2: brassicas

This rotation group includes related crops such as broccoli, Brussels sprouts, cabbages, cauliflower, kale, and Asian greens—as well as the lesser-known brassicas such as kohlrabi, radishes, rutabagas, and turnips. Moving them around a plot from one year to the next is particularly important because they are all susceptible to the soilborne fungal disease clubroot. Brassicas are all nitrogen-hungry, so grow them in the section in which last year's peas and beans were grown.

YEAR 3: roots, onions, and leaves

Root crops, for example beets, carrots, and parsnips; and tubers, such as Jerusalem artichokes, potatoes, and sweet potatoes, don't have a particularly high requirement for nitrogen. They're therefore ideal for following in an area after brassicas, where the nitrogen levels in the soil will have been depleted. This rotation group may also include crops from the onion family, such as garlic, leeks, and shallots, and salads and leafy vegetables, for example lettuce, spinach, and Swiss chard.

(far left to right) **Year 1 vegetables** could include eggplant, green beans, tomatoes, soybeans, sweet peppers, and fava beans. You could also grow peas, snow and snap peas, lima beans, chilies, okra, sweet corn, as well as cucumbers, pumpkins, and squashes.

(far left to right) **Year 2 vegetables** could include cauliflower, cabbages, Brussels sprouts, rutabagas, kale, and radishes—both summer and winter varieties. You could also grow calabrese, sprouting broccoli, kohlrabi, and turnips, as well as Asian brassicas such as Chinese cabbage, choy sum, mustard greens, and bok choy.

(far left to right) **Year 3 vegetables** could include onions, beets, carrots, parsnips, sweet potatoes, and potatoes. You could also grow garlic, shallots, green onions, celery, Florence fennel, Jerusalem artichokes, leaf beet, spinach, and Swiss chard, as well as chicory, endive, lettuce, and other salad leaves.

War on weeds

Here's an alarming statistic: it's estimated that in every square yard of soil there are probably 100,000 seeds. This is why regular weeding is inescapable. Resign yourself to the fact that it's going to be a constant battle. Weeds are invasive and competitive—they drink the water and absorb the nutrients you want your vegetables to have; they crowd them for space, hogging the light. And they can be a home to all kinds of pests and diseases.

Annual weeds

Regular hoeing will control annual weeds such as chickweed, speedwell, shepherd's purse, and hairy bittercress, which spring up between rows of plants. Don't let them flower, or they will generate a new crop of fresh seeds. Keep your hoe sharp, slice off weeds just below the surface, and clear away the remains if it is wet.

Perennial weeds

These are harder to eradicate, and will probably need digging out by hand. Remove every last bit of root or rhizome; perennial weeds can regenerate from tiny segments, so using a rototiller rarely works. More effective is a sheet of thick black plastic or carpet laid over the ground. It deprives weeds of light, weakening or even killing them. You may even be able to plant crops through it.

Weedkillers

Restrict the use of chemical weedkillers to heavily overgrown plots that need clearing. Tenacious perennials that are simply too deeply rooted to dig up are best tackled using a systemic weedkiller. Wear protective gear when applying, and spray on a still day to prevent it being blown onto nearby plants.

(left) **Loosen large weeds** with a fork before carefully pulling up the entire rootball by hand.

(right) **Skim annual weeds** by using a spade to slice off the layer of soil in which they are growing and flip it upside down.

Bindweed creeps or climbs and has white trumpet-shaped flowers. Its roots must be completely dug out intact.

Couch grass spreads aggressively via underground rhizomes; they look like white roots but have sharp, pointed tips.

Creeping buttercup throws out horizontal runners. A new plant forms at each node, so dig the whole bunch up.

Creeping thistle has spreading horizontal roots and long, deep taproots. Systemic weedkiller may be needed.

Dandelion flowers turn into "clocks" made of tiny parachutelike seeds. Pick off the heads or cut them down before this stage.

Dock plants have long taproots when fully grown. Pull them up intact or they will regrow. Don't let them go to seed.

Ground elder is a perennial. It spreads via underground rhizomes and will regrow from the tiniest fragment.

Goosegrass ("cleavers") spreads widely and has sticky green leaves. Dig it up (don't pull) to avoid it breaking and regrowing.

Stinging nettles can deter aphids, but both annual and perennial forms are invasive and are best hoed or dug up.

Growing under cover

Though we might dream of growing our own vegetables in a custom-built greenhouse or a full-size, walk-in polytunnel, the chances are that lack of space won't allow it, especially in urban areas. Yet cold frames, cloches, and other improvised plant covers can offer the same benefit: a protected microclimate in which you can sow seeds and raise seedlings earlier than you would out in the open. There are other advantages, too. Plants grown under cover are easier to protect from predators such as birds, mice, butterflies, moths, and other insects while they are still small, tender, and at their most vulnerable.

Cold frames

Traditional cold frames were essentially boxes in which to grow plants. They had low brick walls and transparent glass lids or "lights" that could be opened or closed. They were often built on the sides of greenhouses as a sort of halfway house between indoors and outdoors. If necessary, plants could be moved out of the greenhouse into the cold frame to be hardened off (*see p.34*) before being transplanted into open ground.

The same principle holds today, though modern cold frames are more likely to be constructed from aluminum or plastic. Alternatively, they can be homemade—using old window frames, for example. It's important that they are securely anchored and draft-free to ensure good insulation, and that they can be opened or closed to allow sufficient ventilation.

Cloches

Cloches can be moved from one part of the vegetable patch to another. The word "cloche" is French for "bell"; early designs were often bell-shaped, originally made of glass but now more often clear plastic. Other designs are barn-, tent-, or lantern-shaped. If you'd rather recycle, small cloches for covering individual plants can be improvised from plastic bottles.

Cloches are useful at the beginning and end of the year. At the start of the season, they warm the soil before sowing or planting, then maintain the temperature as seeds germinate and seedlings develop. At the end of the season, they offer extra protection while late-harvesting crops ripen (such as outdoor tomatoes). They provide some protection from pests, but not from those in the soil. Like cold frames, cloches need vents to prevent the vegetables from rotting.

Tunnel cloches

Sometimes called low continuous polytunnels, tunnel cloches are made from clear plastic film or fabric stretched over wire hoops. Heavy-gauge plastic that has been treated with an ultraviolet inhibitor will last the longest. The material can be pinned down at the sides and tied in a knot at each end.

(clockwise from top left)
Traditional cold frame, homemade bottle cloches, small garden greenhouse, horticultural fabric tunnel cloche

Training climbers

Some vegetables are natural climbers—most beans and peas, for example, as well as certain squashes and cucumbers. They therefore need something to climb. Without it, they'll still grow, but they will sprawl, and crops trailing on the ground risk being damaged or eaten. In most cases, a few sticks or poles and some garden twine will provide any support required, but with a little ingenuity it's possible to construct frames, tepees, obelisks, and tunnels that are not only sturdy and effective but are also architectural wonders.

Sticks and stakes

Peas are traditionally supported by twiggy peasticks, usually made of hazel or birch, upended and pushed into the ground. Pea tendrils shoot out, find the peasticks, and coil around them tightly. Wire or plastic netting will also do the job but isn't nearly as attractive, especially if you are growing semi-leafless varieties that don't have enough foliage to disguise the net. Strictly speaking, fava beans are not climbers, but they tend to get top heavy when laden with ripening pods and need some support to prevent them from falling over. A line of stakes or short poles on either side of each row, with a couple of lengths of strong garden twine strung between them, will help them stay standing.

Canes and tepees

Climbing green and runner beans can grow to heights of 10 ft (3 m) and more, so they need some serious support structures. A long line of beans is best supported by a double row of poles crossed over and tied at the top.

For only a few bean plants, a tepee will suffice. Hazel, willow, and sweet chestnut poles make attractive, rustic alternatives to poles. Whichever type you use, it's worth erecting the structures early in the season, before the beans are planted; if you leave it until summer, the ground may be too hard to push the stakes or poles deep enough into the soil.

Most climbing beans will find their own way up, spiraling around the poles as soon as they get a grip, but tie them in with string if they look as if they need some initial encouragement.

Tunnels and trellises

Climbing squash and cucumbers put out tendrils, like peas, to help them climb. But unlike peas, when their fruits are fully grown, they can be very heavy indeed, and they'll need much stronger supports.

Trellises are sufficiently sturdy, and can be made from wood or from a combination of wooden poles and rope, in vertical or fan shapes. Arches and tunnels are certainly attractive but they have a practical purpose, too. It's much easier to harvest crops when they are hanging down around you as walk underneath them!

(from far left) **Fava bean stakes, tepee, fan trellis for squash, tying in peas, bean tunnel**

Crops in containers

Flats, modules, biodegradable tubes, and seed and seedling pots are all used at the start of a plant's life. They are for sowing and germinating seeds, planting cuttings, and growing on seedlings. Thereafter, when the plants reach a certain size, they move on.

Yet not all transfer to a home in the ground. Some remain in containers for their whole lives. In situations where space is at a premium, entire vegetable gardens can be cultivated in pots, tubs, troughs, planters, window boxes, hanging baskets, and growing bags. And almost any kind of container can be used for growing vegetables. The one inviolable rule is that there must be a hole or holes in the bottom, to allow drainage and prevent waterlogging.

Terra-cotta versus plastic

Clay or terra-cotta pots are authentically traditional and weather beautifully. They are heavy and solid, so they may be less likely to tip over if plants become top heavy, but they are breakable and may crack or flake in a hard frost. Plastic pots are less expensive. They are also lighter, so they are much easier to move around, and they are impermeable, so the soil inside them will not dry out as quickly.

Growing bags

Growing bags have their uses—there's no doubt that successful crops can be grown in them. But they dry out quickly and need regular watering, and may require special frames to support climbing plants. The volume of soil can be increased by inserting bottomless pots into the bags, then planting directly into the pots.

(left) **Drill holes** in the base of pots to ensure that excess water drains away freely.

(opposite page, clockwise from top left)
Modern metal planters are available in a wide variety of striking colors.

Fat-bellied terra-cotta pots look lovely, but it may be hard to remove plants without damaging the roots or breaking the pot.

A container-grown herb garden is perfect for a sunny location close to the kitchen door.

Growing bags produce a good crop, but it is difficult to make them look attractive.

Hanging baskets

Wire or wicker hanging baskets are usually planted with decorative flowering plants, but they can make an equally good home for herbs, salad leaves, and tomatoes. A number of bush tomato varieties have small, cherry-sized fruits and the plants are natural trailers. They are ideal contenders for hanging baskets, although they are notoriously hungry and thirsty.

Line the basket with mock moss made from wool, coir, or other recycled materials (as traditional sphagnum moss is no longer considered to be eco-friendly) in order to retain soil or potting mix, and water and fertilize regularly. This may mean watering twice a day in hot weather. If you let the basket dry out completely, it's hard to get it to hold water again.

Window boxes

Vegetable plots don't get much closer to the kitchen than on the windowsill. Just lean out and pick a handful of salad leaves or a few sprigs of an herb—what could be fresher?

Cut-and-come-again salads are perfect for window boxes: they germinate easily from seed, need little care, and replenish themselves in summer. Green onions, radishes, chili peppers, tomatoes, and baby carrots and beets are well-suited, too. Window boxes need drainage holes to prevent waterlogging, and frequent watering so the soil doesn't dry out. Unless you're on the ground floor, remember what's underneath while you're watering.

Indoor vegetables

Most herbs are easy to grow indoors; if you don't have a greenhouse, a windowsill is a great substitute when raising seedlings. Either sow your own seeds, propagate from existing plants by taking cuttings, or buy plants from a garden center or other supplier. Place pots somewhere bright but out of direct sunlight, and you'll have created an indoor herb garden. Other crops that need little space indoors are sprouting seeds such as mustard and cress, mung beans, alfalfa, chickpeas, and fenugreek. All you'll need is a flat, jar, or sprouting bag, some water, and a few days' patience (*see pp.188–189*).

(clockwise from top left)
Cut-and-come-again salad mixes are the perfect crops for window box kitchen gardens.

Herbs such as parsley and mint can be sown and raised outdoors, then potted up, brought indoors, and placed on a windowsill.

Chilies need heat, so it's a good idea to grow them on a sunny, south-facing windowsill.

Hanging baskets are a smart way of employing unused wall space, but they are heavy and need strong supports.

"There are plenty of quick-growing, shallow-rooted vegetables that will be **perfectly happy** in small containers."

Ecogardening

A green approach to growing vegetables involves more than rejecting chemical fertilizers, weedkillers, and pesticides. It's also about conservation, reuse, and employing resources intelligently. There are numerous ways to encourage a healthy garden in which plants will thrive. You could recycle organic material to return nutrients to the soil, or follow a crop-rotation plan to reduce the risk of disease. Even something as simple as encouraging beneficial wildlife into your yard should reduce the need to resort to chemical controls.

A chemical-free vegetable patch

It's really not hard to do without artificial fertilizers. Your soil will get many of the nutrients it's likely to need—and you'll improve its structure and composition—if you regularly dig in plenty of well-rotted organic material such as kitchen and garden compost, barnyard or stable manure, leaf mold, or mushroom compost (*see pp.22–24*).

There are alternatives to synthetic pesticides and weedkillers, too. Pyrethrum and insecticidal soaps are effective against certain insects and are all derived from plant extracts. Weeds that can't be dug up can usually be killed off by covering the ground with plastic or by using a flame weeder.

Biological controls

Some of the creatures you might initially think of as pests are in fact the very opposite: they're natural predators. And they can be employed to tackle the bugs that really threaten your crops.

A combination of mixed planting and leaving a few areas of your plot less than immaculately neat will help attract bees, ladybugs, hoverflies, lacewings, and other beneficial insects. You could dig a pond to provide frogs and toads with a home. You might even try introducing some specialty contract killers yourself—slug-destroying nematodes, for example (*see pp.338–339*).

(top) **Composting kitchen waste**
(bottom) **Dried-grass earwig trap**

(clockwise from above)
**Rain barrel, water-efficient soaker hose,
household gray water**

Conserving water

Water is a precious commodity. It makes sense
to save it, recycle it, and use it wisely. Not all
plants need the same amount of water, and
some need it only at key points during their
development—so prioritize young seedlings,
new or recent transplants, and plants growing
in pots. When you water, soak the soil rather
than the plant foliage, and if possible use
soaker hoses. Mulching cuts down water loss
due to evaporation and helps keep the soil
moist. Collect rainwater in rain barrels, and
reuse household gray water, though not on
food plants if it has soap, detergent, or oil in it.

Harvesting and storing

Some vegetables are best eaten as soon as possible after harvesting. Peas and sweet corn, for example, start to convert their sugars to starch the moment they're picked, so from that point on the clock is ticking on how long they will stay super-sweet. Lettuces, Asian salad greens, and spinach quickly wilt, too. They are best picked in the early morning or evening, not in the heat of the day. However, many other vegetables will keep for a long time if stored carefully.

Storing vegetables

Onions, shallots, garlic, pumpkins, squash, cabbages, potatoes, and other root vegetables should last into winter if stored. Eat or discard damaged produce, because it won't keep. Store dry potatoes in paper sacks or bags—not plastic, which will make them sweat. Hang onions, shallots, and garlic somewhere cool, dry, and well-ventilated, and put cabbages in nets or on straw-lined shelves. Store root vegetables like carrots and parsnips in wooden boxes packed with damp sand.

Freezing

Green beans, runner beans, fava beans, peas, cauliflower, broccoli, and Brussels sprouts are all suitable for freezing. Wash, trim, and blanch them in boiling water for a few minutes, then bag them up and freeze them right away. Tomatoes and zucchini can be frozen, but they may turn mushy when defrosted.

Pickling and preserving

Oils and vinegars can be flavored with garlic, chili peppers, and herbs. And vegetable chutneys and pickles—which combine vinegar, sugar, and salt as preservatives—traditionally contain onions, tomatoes, peppers, carrots, beans, cauliflower, or eggplant.

(left) **A mid-fall harvest** of squashes, field mushrooms, celery root, sweet potatoes, parsnips, and other root vegetables.

(top right) **Harvest dwarf runner beans** young and often to prevent pods from becoming tough and stringy.

(bottom right) **Homemade rosemary- and chili-flavored oils**

Free food

The idea of propagating your own vegetables is very tempting. It means food for free, after all. But it's worth sounding a note of caution. Although most vegetables are grown from seed, not all are worth attempting to propagate from seed you save yourself. Beans, peas, onions, tomatoes, squashes, and certain herbs are the most likely to be successful, while others are difficult or unreliable. However, a few vegetables can be propagated using methods such as dividing established rootstocks and certain herbs by taking cuttings.

Which seeds to save

Don't attempt to save seeds from what are called F1 hybrid plants. They are the offspring of two inbred parents, crossed to produce a cultivar with very specific characteristics. Their seeds will not breed "true," which means they are unlikely to inherit the same uniform qualities. Even ordinary seeds, those allowed to form naturally, without hybridization, may get accidentally cross-pollinated in your garden or in your vegetable patch, and may produce offspring with nonstandard variations. For this reason, grow plants from which you intend to save seed well away from other cultivars.

How to collect seeds

Allow tomatoes and squashes to ripen fully before collecting seeds, and leave pea and bean pods on the plants until they have withered and dried. To collect seeds from onions, shallots, and leeks, leave a few healthy plants in the ground in winter and let them produce flowerheads the following spring. When they turn to seedheads, cut them down and dry them.

(opposite page, clockwise from top left)
Hanging up chili peppers to dry, drying fennel seedheads, dividing an asparagus crown, rooting sweet potato slips

Propagation by division

Perennial vegetables like asparagus, globe artichokes, and rhubarb are best propagated by digging up existing plants, dividing them, and replanting on a fresh site. You get three or four new, vigorous plants from one single parent.

Propagating bulbs and tubers

Potatoes or onions left in the ground often sprout the next year—they can be propagated this way. However, this isn't advisable, since they tend to become diseased. It's safer to buy new, virus-free seed potatoes and onion sets.

Collect seeds from tomatoes only when the fruit is very ripe. Cut it in half, pry out the seeds, and leave to dry on paper towels.

Cabbages & Leaf Vegetables

Cabbages, Brussels sprouts, calabrese, broccoli, cauliflower, and kale are all members of the family known as brassicas. They share a number of characteristics. Most of them take a long time to mature, so it's worth thinking carefully about where you plant them—wherever you put them, they're going to be there for many months. They're large, too, so you'll need to give them plenty of space. Sadly, they also share a vulnerability to certain pests and diseases; clubroot and cabbage root flies are among the worst, although birds and caterpillars left by visiting butterflies can also cause damage. But don't be discouraged from growing them. A few simple precautions such as brassica collars, netting, and regular crop rotation should help prevent serious problems—and, if you're smart about what and when you plant, you can have fresh crops almost year-round.

Ornamental kale, sometimes called flowering cabbage, has beautiful, vividly colored, highly textured leaves, and is grown for both decoration and eating.

1 **Cabbages** take up lots of space, so plant just a few of each group for a crop throughout the year.

2 **Napa cabbage** looks like a tall, cylindrical lettuce with tightly packed, pale green-white leaves.

3 **Bok choy** grows very quickly—within a month of sowing, you can usually harvest the first leaves.

4 **Brussels sprouts**, picked young and small, taste sweeter and nuttier than you might think.

5 **Spinach** is highly nutritious and can be picked almost year-round.

6 **Kale** is easy to grow, generally trouble-free, and should survive the harshest, most severe winters.

7 **Swiss chard** is grown for its vibrantly colored leaves, which can be eaten like spinach.

8 **Cauliflower** varieties are grouped according to the time of year at which they can be harvested.

9 **Broccoli** can be harvested almost year-round, and has a reputation for being rich in healthy antioxidants.

Cabbages

Cabbages can be classified according to when they are harvested. Spring and summer cabbages are smaller, and are eaten right after picking. Fall and winter types have denser heads, can be left in the ground for longer, and can be stored. Varieties include Savoy cabbages, with crinkly leaves; white Dutch cabbages; red cabbages, which come in summer and fall varieties; and spring greens, which are either loose-leaf cultivars or regular spring cabbages harvested before heads have formed. Related vegetables include collards, grown as winter greens, and broccoli rabe or rapini, which is used in Italian and Chinese cooking.

	spring			summer			fall			winter		
	E	M	L	E	M	L	E	M	L	E	M	L
Spring cabbages												
sow				▪	▪							
plant out							▪	▪				
harvest	▪	▪	▪									
Summer, fall, and red cabbages												
sow	▪	▪	▪									
plant out				▪	▪							
harvest							▪	▪	▪	▪		
Winter cabbages												
sow		▪	▪									
plant out				▪	▪							
harvest	▪								▪	▪	▪	▪

Where to plant

Cabbages don't mind full sun or partial shade, but they do like fertile soil that will retain moisture and is slightly alkaline—a pH of at least 6.8 (see p.21).

Most importantly, the soil must be firm. Bear in mind that the roots and stems have to support heads that may grow very heavy. Light, sandy soil can be improved by adding either compost or manure during the previous season.

Crop rotation is important, too: avoid planting cabbages where you've grown them in the last three years.

Savoy cabbages, with deeply veined and intricately textured leaves, look as good as they taste.

Sow in flats and transplant seedlings when they have formed three or four leaves.

PLANTING OUT CABBAGE SEEDLINGS

Seedlings are ready to transplant when they have about four true leaves. If they've been grown indoors or under cover, harden them off first. After planting, you may want to put brassica collars around the stems to deter cabbage root flies (*see below*).

1 If you're transplanting from a seedbed, water the plants before lifting. Hold seedlings by their leaves to avoid damaging the roots, and keep seedlings damp in a water-filled trench or a pail to stop them from wilting.

2 Make planting holes 6 in (15 cm) deep about 18 in (45 cm) apart in shallow furrows. Water the holes before carefully lowering the seedlings in, then gently firm the soil around them.

When to plant

For a continuous harvest, sow cabbages of different types successively through the year. Start under cover at the beginning of spring for an early harvest of summer cabbages, and sow in late spring and summer for fall and winter harvesting. You can even sow in mid- to late summer for a crop of spring cabbages the following year.

How to sow seeds

It's best to sow all cabbage seeds in flats, pots, or modules—or in a seedbed— and then transplant them to their final location once they're established. Sow thinly and cover with potting mix to a depth of about ¾ in (2 cm).

(far left) **Brassica collars** prevent female cabbage root flies from laying eggs in the soil around seedling stems.

(left) **Net cabbages** to protect them from birds and cabbage white butterflies, which find young cabbages irresistible.

Routine care

Keep seedlings weed-free and water them regularly—daily at first in dry weather, then once or twice a week if there is any danger of their drying out. Earth up the stems to support them as the plants grow, and cut off and remove any dead outer leaves.

Harvesting

Spring or early summer cabbages can be harvested as spring greens once the young leaves appear, but before they form hearts. Otherwise, leave them until they have hearted up and are solid all the way through. Cut off the heads with a sharp knife, and use them immediately. Fall and winter cabbages (such as 'January King') can be harvested later, then stored on shelves or in nets for a few months in a cool place. Winter cabbages are frost hardy and slow to bolt, so don't feel pressured to pick your entire crop if frost is in the forecast.

Shortly after harvesting, lift cabbage roots to prevent the spread of disease; alternatively, simply uproot the whole cabbage when you harvest it rather than just cutting it away with a knife.

What can go wrong
Pests

Cabbage root fly maggots often cause damage—they hatch from eggs laid on the soil, eat the roots, and leave the stumps to rot. Once present, they are impossible to get rid of. To prevent flies from laying their eggs in the first place, use a covering of fabric or fine net, or collars around seedlings. Collars can be purchased, or simply fashioned from squares of carpet pad, cut so they can be slipped around the seedlings. Any eggs laid on the collars will die before hatching.

Cabbage caterpillars burrow into the heart and eat holes in the leaves. The caterpillars of the large cabbage white butterfly are yellow, black, and hairy; the small cabbage white butterfly pale green; and the cabbage moth yellow-green or brown. Pick them off or spray with pyrethrum or an approved pesticide.

Mealy cabbage aphids are so-called because the gray aphids are covered with white wax. They congregate beneath the leaves, suck the sap, and cause yellow patches and leaf curl. Spray with insecticidal soap, pyrethrum, or an approved pesticide.

Other pests include cutworms, flea beetles, leatherjackets, whiteflies, slugs and snails, and birds (*see pp.324–333*).

(top) **Harvest spring greens** while the leaves are still loose, before they form dense heads.

(bottom) **Harvest mature cabbages** when the heads feel firm and solid. Use a sharp knife to cut through the base of the stem.

Diseases

Clubroot is a very serious problem. It's a fungus or mold that attacks roots and, as it kills them, releases spores into the soil. Leaves start to discolor, and the plant becomes stunted and eventually dies. What's worse is that the spores can survive in the soil for up to 20 years—and there is no cure. Preventive measures include systematically rotating crops, burning (not composting) all diseased plants, improving drainage, liming the soil (*see p.21*), and planting out only when seedlings are well established.

Other diseases include downy mildew, powdery mildew, bacterial leaf spot, and white blister (*see pp.318–323*).

Recommended cabbages

SPRING **Duncan, Durham Early, Pixie, Pyramid, Spring Hero**

SUMMER/FALL **Derby Day, Dutchman, Filderkraut, Greyhound, Hispi, Minicole, Savoy King, Serpentine**

WINTER **January King, Kilaton, Tundra, Winter Jewel**

RED **Kalibos, Lodero, Red Drumhead, Red Jewel**

COLLARDS **Georgia, Vates**

BROCCOLI RABE **All Season, Raab**

(opposite page, clockwise from top left)
Serpentine, Red Jewel, Red Drumhead, Spring Hero

Winter cabbages are able to survive surprisingly hard frost or snow, and can be left in the ground until you need them.

Brussels sprouts

Few vegetables polarize people the way that Brussels sprouts do: you either love 'em or you hate 'em. However, even if you have decided you don't like them, perhaps you could give them one more try? Homegrown sprouts, picked when young and small, and cooked while still fresh and tender, are sweet and have a wonderful nutty flavor that might just change your mind. And if you develop a taste for them, you could try one of the unusual red or purple varieties, or even some of the new frilly-leaved "flower sprouts," which are a cross between Brussels sprouts and kale.

	spring			summer			fall			winter		
	E	M	L	E	M	L	E	M	L	E	M	L
sow indoors	■											■
sow outdoors		■	■									
plant out				■	■	■						
harvest	■						■	■	■	■	■	■

Where to plant

Brussels sprouts grow best in fertile soil that has had plenty of well-rotted compost or manure dug into it in the previous season. The ground should then be allowed to settle and bed down. Brussels sprouts grow tall and heavy, and their roots need firm soil to help support them. If necessary, add some lime to the soil in order to increase the pH to at least 6.8 (see p.21), then apply a base dressing of general fertilizer.

As with all brassicas, crop rotation is important. Don't plant Brussels sprouts where you've recently grown any members of the cabbage family.

When to plant

For sprouts that will be ready to harvest in late fall and winter, sow seeds in early or mid-spring, and plant out seedlings in early or midsummer. For sprouts to harvest in late summer and early fall, sow under cover the previous winter and transplant in spring, as soon as the weather is warm enough.

Modern F1 hybrid varieties have been bred to produce regularly spaced, identically sized sprouts.

Earth up the plants about a month after planting them out, by drawing soil up around the stem. This helps prevent them from flopping over.

How to sow seeds

Sow seeds thinly in flats, pots, or modules and cover with potting mix or soilless mix to a depth of about $3/4$ in (2 cm). Keep indoors or under cover until it is warm enough to plant them out. Alternatively, sow seeds directly in the ground, protecting them from frost if necessary, and then transplant them to their final location once they're established.

How to plant out seedlings

Seedlings should be ready to transplant about four or five weeks after sowing—usually from early summer onward. Plant dwarf cultivars about 18 in (45 cm) apart, to produce small, uniformly-sized sprouts. However, space large cultivars at least 24 in (60 cm) apart and plant them deeply; they take up more space and grow taller stems, from which you can pick sprouts successively. Don't be tempted to crowd the plants—they need plenty of light and air to keep them healthy.

Fitting a brassica collar around each seedling's stem will deter cabbage root flies, and covering with netting will keep off birds and butterflies.

(left) **Remove leaves** when they start turning yellow in fall, since they can become infected with fungal diseases. If they remain on the plant, the disease may affect the whole crop.

(right) **Sprouts mature from the base** of the stem, so start harvesting at the bottom and work your way up.

Routine care

Keep young plants well-watered and free of weeds in order to encourage strong root growth; thereafter, water sparingly. Four or five weeks after planting, earth up the stems to give some extra stability, and stake plants that you plan to leave in the ground over winter. Cut off and remove any dead or dying leaves.

At some point in mid- to late summer, it's worth applying a topdressing of a nitrogenous fertilizer such as sulfate of ammonia, or an organic liquid fertilizer.

If you pinch out the plant's growing tip when the sprouts toward the bottom of the stem reach about $1/2$ in (1 cm) in diameter, the others should grow to match them: this will encourage a harvest of sprouts that are approximately the same size.

(from far left) **Maximus, Revenge, Bosworth**

Harvesting

Brussels sprouts are usually ready to harvest about five months after sowing, although with fall and winter crops you could wait until after the first frost, when they tend to taste better. Starting with the sprouts at the bottom of the stems, cut them with a sharp knife or snap them off by pulling downward.

Alternatively, uproot the whole plant and leave the sprouts on the stem until you need them. They will keep for a few days standing in a pail containing a little water or for several weeks if hung in a cool, frost-free place.

The youngest leaves—at the top of the stems—can be harvested as sprout tops and cooked like spring greens. Once you've picked off the sprouts, dig up any remaining plants and smash the stems with a hammer before composting. This helps them rot down quickly and reduces the risk of spreading diseases.

What can go wrong

Brussels sprouts can be afflicted by all the pests and diseases that affect other brassicas (*see pp.61–62*)—including clubroot and cabbage root flies—so take all the standard precautions. Mealy cabbage aphid and whiteflies can be particularly problematic and, although they may not destroy your crop, they're unpleasant and difficult to wash off.

Recommended Brussels sprouts

GREEN Bedford Fillbasket, Bosworth, Cascade, Crispus, Maximus, Revenge, Trafalgar

RED Falstaff, Red Bull, Rubine

FLOWER SPROUTS Petit Posy

Spinach

Spinach is a vegetable that grows best in cool climates. If given the slightest chance, it will bolt and go to seed as soon as the weather becomes hot and dry. Bolt-resistant varieties are available but it can be a battle to prevent even those from flowering during the summer months. It's worth persevering, though. Fresh spinach not only tastes wonderful—either cooked or eaten raw in salads—but is highly nutritious. Traditional spinach varieties have either smooth or wrinkled ("Savoy") leaves. Smooth leaves tend to be thinner, sweeter, and better suited to salads; wrinkled leaves are thicker and retain their texture when cooked. Modern Asian cultivars are darker in color and usually have longer stalks.

	spring			summer			fall			winter		
	E	M	L	E	M	L	E	M	L	E	M	L
sow indoors											■	■
sow outdoors	■	■	■			■	■					
plant out	■											
harvest		■	■	■	■	■	■	■	■			

Where to plant

Spinach is not too fussy about where it is grown. It is slightly unusual in that it will happily tolerate partial shade; in fact, in summer it probably prefers not to be in full sun. It is, however, both hungry and thirsty. It needs fertile, nitrogen-rich soil that retains moisture effectively, so grow it where you have dug in lots of well-rotted compost or manure. If the soil is particularly poor, prepare the ground thoroughly in advance by spreading some compound fertilizer or poultry manure.

When to plant

Seeds of modern cultivars can be sown almost all year—though they may not germinate very successfully in the very hot temperatures of high summer. For a continuous crop, sow seeds every few weeks from early spring right through to late summer or early fall. Early sowings will be ready in spring, and in mild climates, late sowings should last through the winter for harvesting the following spring, although you may need to protect them with cloches in very cold weather.

Asian spinach cultivars tend to have much longer, thicker stems than their Western counterparts.

"As well as being highly **nutritious,** spinach can be picked almost **year round.**"

How to sow seeds

Spinach is best sown straight into the ground. Sow seeds about $^3/_4$ in (2 cm) deep, about 1 in (2.5 cm) apart, and in rows 12 in (30 cm) apart. When they are large enough to handle, thin out seedlings to about 3–6 in (7–15 cm) apart, depending on the size of plants you want. If you're planning a cut-and-come-again crop, sow within wide furrows.

Routine care

Keep plants free of weeds, and water as regularly and copiously as you can. As soon as you let the plants dry out, they are likely to bolt. In midsummer, spinach is much more inclined to produce flowers and go to seed than it is to grow new leaves. If leaf growth seems slow, apply a topdressing of a nitrogenous fertilizer or an organic liquid fertilizer.

Harvesting

Spinach is usually ready for harvesting 10–12 weeks after sowing, although you can start cutting young leaves for salads much earlier. As soon as they are about 2 in (5 cm) in length, take a few of the outer leaves from each plant at a time.

To harvest the whole plant, uproot it completely or cut off the head about 1 in (2.5 cm) above the level of the soil. New leaf shoots should sprout from the stump.

What can go wrong

Apart from premature bolting, downy mildew (*see p.321*) is likely to be the biggest problem. Giving your plants more space, thereby allowing air to circulate freely, is the best solution.

Birds can be pests, too, as they may eat young seedlings. If so, you may have to use netting to keep them off.

Recommended spinach

Bolt-resistant, smooth-leaved varieties are probably the easiest to grow, but it's also worth experimenting with some of the more unusual colors and shapes.

WESTERN **Amazon, Bordeaux, Emilia, Medania, Palco, Reddy**

ORIENTAL **Mikado**

You can pick off the outer leaves about eight weeks after sowing. Alternatively, remove the whole plant by cutting it just above the soil level.

(top) **Palco** (bottom) **Bordeaux**

NEW ZEALAND SPINACH

This is actually a different species but is grown and used in the same way as regular spinach. The great benefit to growing it—apart from the fact that it tastes good—is that it is much happier than normal spinach when grown in high temperatures, since it will tolerate dry conditions and is less likely to bolt. Soak seeds in water beforehand to encourage germination, then sow outdoors in late spring after the last frost, and thin out the seedlings so they are about 18 in (45 cm) apart.

You can usually begin picking the young, fleshy leaves as early as six weeks after sowing (*see below*). They will keep regrowing, so treat the plant as a cut-and-come-again crop that should last right through summer to the first frost in fall.

Kale

Kale is a real survivor. The most ancient of all cabbages, it's one of the toughest, hardiest vegetables of them all, and its tall, ribbed leaves can be seen standing in the ground in the harshest, most severe winters, at temperatures as low as 5°F (–15°C). Indeed, in some climates it may be the only fresh vegetable available during the coldest months. Some varieties will also tolerate high temperatures and are therefore equally happy in hot summers. Unlike cabbage, kale doesn't form a dense heart. Instead, the leaves spread out from the central stem. They may be green, purple, red, or black, and either tightly curled or broad and loosely crinkled.

	spring			summer			fall			winter		
	E	M	L	E	M	L	E	M	L	E	M	L
sow indoors		■	■	■								
sow outdoors			■	■	■							
plant out				■	■	■						
harvest	■	■							■	■	■	■

(left) **Harvest young leaves** by pulling a few from the center of each plant. Leave healthy outer leaves in place.

(right) **Pull up plants** when you've finished harvesting leaves in order to reduce the buildup of diseases such as clubroot.

Where to plant

Some kale varieties grow up to 3 ft (90 cm) in height and 24 in (60 cm) in spread, so they need a site where they have plenty of room. They like fertile, well-drained soil that's firm and well-compacted. Don't allow the soil to become waterlogged in winter.

When to plant

Sow in early spring for a summer crop, and in late spring or early summer for fall and winter harvests.

How to sow seeds and plant out seedlings

Sow to a depth of about ¾ in (2 cm) in modules, or outdoors in a seedbed, and protect them from frost. Transplant seedlings around 6–8 weeks later, being careful to disturb the roots as little as possible.

For early cut-and-come-again salad crops, seedlings can be planted quite closely—about 3–4 in (8–10 cm) apart. Seedlings intended to grow into full-sized plants should be spaced 18–24 in (45–60 cm) apart.

Routine care

Keep plants free of weeds, and water sparingly. If leaves are yellow or growth seems slow, give plants an organic liquid fertilizer in early fall.

Harvesting

For summer salads, pick individual leaves or cut young plants when they are 4–6 in (10–15 cm) tall. They should resprout. Full-grown leaves can be cut and cooked throughout the winter.

What can go wrong

Kale is a brassica, so in theory it is at risk from all the usual pests and diseases that affect cabbages, cauliflower, and Brussels sprouts (*see pp.61–62*). However, it is generally trouble-free and is certainly less prone to clubroot.

Watch out for whitefly infestations, though, and if you get them, wash leaves thoroughly in salt water before eating them. Butterflies and birds seem attracted to some varieties but not others, so you may have to use netting.

Recommended kale

Black Magic, Black Tuscan (Cavolo Nero), Dwarf Green Curled, Fizz, Redbor, Red Russian, Reflex, Scarlet

(far left) **Redbor** (left) **Red Russian**

Swiss chard and chard

Both these vegetables are related to beets, and are therefore often known collectively as leaf beets. In one crucial way, however, they are the exact opposite of beets: they grow large edible leaves and have small inedible roots. Swiss chard is the better-looking of the two. With its dark- or yellow-green leaves and vibrant white, red, yellow, or purple stalks and veins, it is so dramatic that it is often grown as much for ornament as for food. Chard has smaller leaves and narrower green stalks. Both can be cooked and eaten like spinach.

	spring			summer			fall			winter		
	E	M	L	E	M	L	E	M	L	E	M	L
sow outdoors		■	■	■	■							
harvest	■	■	■		■	■	■	■	■			

Growing chard in containers is possible, though remember that leaves will become large unless harvested regularly when young.

Where to plant

Chard grows best in rich, moisture-retentive soil. Dig in plenty of well-rotted compost or manure if possible; if not, simply apply a base dressing of general fertilizer or poultry manure. The soil should have a neutral or slightly alkaline pH (*see p.21*).

When to plant

Sow in spring and early summer for crops that will last through to mid- or late fall, and sow in mid- or late summer for harvesting in spring the following year.

How to sow seeds

Sow seeds thinly directly into the ground at a depth of 1 in (2.5 cm), in rows 18 in (45 cm) apart. Thin seedlings to 4 in (10 cm) apart for young salad leaves, and 12 in (30 cm) for full-grown plants. To get ahead when the ground is still cold, sow seeds in modules under cover. Transplant them once there is no risk of frost.

Routine care

Keep plants weed-free, and water in dry spells. Regularly cutting back flower shoots will encourage plants to keep cropping. Any plants you plan to leave in the ground until the end of the year may benefit from a topdressing of a nitrogenous fertilizer or an organic liquid fertilizer in late summer. Overwintering plants tend to fare better under cloches than those exposed to the elements.

Harvesting

Pick young, tender leaves as soon as they are large enough for salads. Early plantings should mature 8–10 weeks after sowing. As they become ready, harvest alternate plants in each of your rows to leave more space for those that you leave behind. Continue to cut full-grown leaves as and when you need them until the plant finally bolts and goes to seed.

What can go wrong

Very little can go wrong with these leafy plants. Chards are generally healthy and resilient.

Recommended Swiss chard and chard

Beware: the different names applied to Swiss chard and chard can be confusing. Both may be referred to as leaf beets. Swiss chard is sometimes known as seakale beet. And chard may be called spinach beet, perpetual beet, or perpetual spinach.

Bright Lights, Bright Yellow, Lucullus, Rhubarb Chard, White Silver

(below left) **Mulching** around young plants discourages weeds and helps to keep the soil moist.

(below right) **Harvest** Swiss chard as a cut-and-come-again crop. New leaves will grow to replace those you've picked.

(top right) **Perpetual Spinach**
(bottom right) **White Silver**

Asian greens

In recent years, an increasingly wide range of Asian brassicas has become available from garden centers, specialty nurseries, and via mail order, either to grow from seed or as ready-to-plant plug plants. Some are best picked when they are still young and their leaves used in salads (*see pp.178-9*). Others, such as those here, can be left to grow larger, harvested in late summer and fall, and then steamed or stir-fried. Protect them with fabric or cloches at the end of the season and they should provide fresh greens into early winter.

Napa cabbage

Napa cabbage

Most types of napa cabbage, or Chinese cabbage, look like tall lettuces, with cylindrical-shaped heads of densely packed leaves. They are crisp, with a mild cabbage taste.

They need a sunny, sheltered location and rich soil. Sow in modules from mid-spring onward and keep under cover to keep cold temperatures from causing them to them bolt. Sow outdoors only from late spring or early summer once the weather is warmer. Water regularly, and harvest within eight to ten weeks of sowing, from midsummer until the first frost.

	spring			summer			fall			winter		
	E	M	L	E	M	L	E	M	L	E	M	L
sow under cover		■	■									
sow outdoors			■	■	■							
plant out				■	■	■						
harvest					■	■	■	■	■			

Bok choy and tatsoi

Useful as a late summer and fall crop, bok choy (sometimes spelled pak choi) has large, rounded green or purple leaves. Its close relative, tatsoi, has spoon-shaped leaves that splay out in the shape of a rosette. Both can be quickly stir-fried so that they retain their crunch and preserve their delicate flavor.

Choose a warm, sheltered site with fertile soil that won't dry out. Like napa cabbage, plants tend to bolt if temperatures are low. It's therefore best not to sow directly into the ground until summer. To start earlier, sow bolt-resistant varieties under cover to keep them warm until you plant them out.

	spring			summer			fall			winter		
	E	M	L	E	M	L	E	M	L	E	M	L
sow under cover		■	■	■								
sow outdoors				■	■	■						
plant out				■	■							
harvest					■	■	■	■	■			

Bok choy

Choy sum

Choy sum is a generic name for Chinese flowering greens or flowering cabbage. The plants are in fact flowering forms of bok choy, and they are best harvested and eaten leaves, stems, and all, just after the flowering shoots have formed but before the yellow flower buds open.

Sow indoors under cover or outdoors direct in the ground only when you can guarantee a reliable temperature of 68°F (20°C).

	spring			summer			fall			winter		
	E	M	L	E	M	L	E	M	L	E	M	L
sow under cover			■									
sow outdoors				■	■	■						
plant out				■	■							
harvest					■	■	■	■	■			

Chinese broccoli

Like choy sum, Chinese broccoli, or Chinese kale, is grown for its flowering stems, which taste similar to sprouting broccoli. The whole plant can be eaten: stems, leaves, and white or yellow flowers buds.

Sow seeds under cover in spring or outdoors in summer. Too cold and plants will bolt. Grow in rich, fertile soil, and water regularly in dry weather. Harvest before the flower buds open or the stems may be tough and taste bitter.

	spring			summer			fall			winter		
	E	M	L	E	M	L	E	M	L	E	M	L
sow under cover		■	■				■	■	■	■	■	■
sow outdoors		■	■	■	■							
plant out				■	■	■						
harvest							■	■	■	■	■	

Cauliflower

With a bit of planning, it's not difficult to have a constant supply of cauliflower throughout the year. The secret is to plant the right varieties at the right time: fast-growing cultivars sown in spring should give you a harvest through the summer and fall; slower growing ones will produce cauliflower to pick in winter and even, in frost-free areas, the following spring. Most cauliflower have creamy-white heads or "curds," but lime-green and purple varieties are also available. The trickiest thing about growing them is to prevent them from bolting. Given half a chance, they'll do so and start to produce seed.

	spring			summer			fall			winter		
	E	M	L	E	M	L	E	M	L	E	M	L
Early summer cauliflower												
sow indoors											■	
sow under cover								■				
plant out	■											
harvest				■								
Summer/fall cauliflower												
sow indoors	■	■										
sow under cover	■	■	■									
plant out			■	■	■							
harvest						■	■	■	■			
Winter/spring cauliflower												
sow			■									
plant out						■						
harvest	■	■	■							■	■	■

Where to plant

Cauliflower grows best in fairly rich, moisture-retentive soil that has had plenty of well-rotted compost or manure dug into it a couple of seasons beforehand. If necessary, add some lime to the soil to increase the pH to at least 6.8 (*see p.21*), and apply a base dressing of general fertilizer.

Allow the soil to settle and don't fork it over before you start planting—cauliflower needs firm ground that will help to support its weight.

As with all brassicas, crop rotation is important. Don't plant cauliflower where you've recently grown any members of the cabbage family.

Cauliflower curds are actually masses of flower buds that haven't yet opened.

Sow early summer types under cloches—seeds won't germinate at low temperatures.

BLANCHING AND FROST PROTECTION

1 During the summer, sun may cause the cauliflower's white curd to yellow, while in winter, the curd is prone to frost damage. Both of these problems can be dealt with by carrying out a simple task.

2 To blanch the curd in summer, fold a couple of leaves over the top like a headscarf. And to protect the curd from frost in winter, wrap the leaves around the head and tie them with string.

When to plant

For cauliflower that will be ready to harvest in early summer, sow seeds the previous fall or winter, keep seedlings under glass or in a greenhouse, and transplant in early spring. For summer- and fall-harvest cauliflower, sow in spring, and transplant in early summer. Sow seeds for winter- and spring-heading cauliflower in later spring, and transplant in late summer. Protect them from frost if they are going to overwinter.

How to sow seeds

Sow seeds thinly in flats, pots, or modules and cover with potting mix to a depth of about ¾ in (2 cm). Seeds usually need a temperature of about 70°F (21°C) to germinate, so keep them in a heated propagator or outdoors under cloches or in a cold frame until it is warm enough for them to be transplanted. Alternatively, sow seeds in a seedbed, protecting them from frost if necessary—although if you do this, remember to harden them off before transplanting them out.

How to plant out seedlings

Seedlings should be transplanted before they get any taller than 2 in (5 cm). If you leave them any longer than this, you may damage the roots and cause them to bolt. In general, the later in the year cauliflower seedlings are transplanted, the bigger they'll grow and the more space you'll need to give them. As a rule of thumb, plant early summer and summer/fall cauliflower about 24 in (60 cm) apart. Winter- and spring-heading varieties may need a little more room, so plant them about 28 in (70 cm) apart. Err on the side of more rather than less space, because light and air help keep the plants healthy.

A brassica collar around each seedling stem will deter cabbage root flies, and netting will keep birds and butterflies at bay.

Routine care

Keep plants free of weeds, and water regularly throughout the growing season. If you let the plants dry out, their growth will be interrupted and they are likely to bolt. Winter- and spring-heading cauliflower can be given a topdressing of a nitrogenous fertilizer or an organic liquid fertilizer in late winter or early spring—but no earlier, or it will weaken their resistance to the cold—in order to encourage new growth before harvesting.

Harvesting

Harvest all cauliflower while the curds are still firm and tight. Unless you're going to eat them immediately, don't cut off all the leaves around the heads; leaving a few in place will help protect them. Summer cauliflower can be stored for a few weeks if you hang them upside down in a cool place and spray them from time to time with water. Fall and winter varieties may keep for longer, since they will have stopped growing by the time you harvest them. It's also worth bearing in mind that all types of cauliflower freeze well.

What can go wrong

Cauliflower may be affected by all the pests and diseases that attack other brassicas (*see pp.61–62*)—including clubroot and cabbage root flies—so take all the standard precautions. Downy mildew (*see p.321*) can be troublesome. So, too, can deficiencies of magnesium, boron, and molybdenum—the latter produces thin, deformed leaves, a condition called "whiptail."

Recommended cauliflower

EARLY SUMMER **Candid Charm, Mayflower**

SUMMER/FALL **All-The-Year-Round, Clapton, Goodman, Graffiti, Snowball, Sunset, White Step**

WINTER/SPRING **Aalsmeer**

To grow mini cauliflower, reduce the planting distance to 6 in (15 cm). The overcrowding will produce stunted growth. This technique works best with fast-growing early-summer varieties.

Purple-headed cauliflower, such as Graffiti (left), don't always retain their color when cooked, though they are less likely to fade if steamed rather than boiled.

Broccoli

There are two slightly different vegetables here—though they come from the same family group of brassicas. One is *calabrese*, which grows a large, green cauliflowerlike head and is what we usually just call "broccoli." The other is *sprouting broccoli*, which grows many small florets instead of a single head and is available in purple or white varieties. Traditionally, calabrese was the one that you harvested during summer, and sprouting broccoli was a valuable source of fresh produce during winter and through to late spring. However, modern cultivars have extended the seasons for growing both types.

	spring			summer			fall			winter		
	E	M	L	E	M	L	E	M	L	E	M	L
Calabrese												
sow outdoors	■	■	■	■	■							
harvest					■	■	■	■	■			
Sprouting broccoli												
sow indoors	■	■	■									■
sow outdoors	■	■	■	■	■							
transplant under cover	■	■										
plant out						■	■					
harvest	■	■		■	■	■	■	■	■		■	■

Where to plant

All broccoli likes a sheltered site and fertile, well-drained soil packed down firmly to give it sufficient support. If necessary, add some lime to the soil to increase the pH to at least 6.8 (*see p.21*). You can apply a base dressing of general fertilizer before planting sprouting broccoli, but calabrese doesn't usually need it.

Crop rotation is important to help prevent clubroot. Don't plant broccoli where you've recently grown any members of the cabbage family.

When to plant

Calabrese seeds are best sown from mid-spring through early summer. You can also sow in fall for a crop the following spring if you keep the plants in a cold frame or greenhouse in winter. Sow traditional sprouting broccoli in spring and leave the plants in the ground until harvesting in late winter or even early the following spring. Sow new cultivars at any time from late winter onward for harvesting through the summer and fall.

Late Purple Sprouting

Support broccoli stems using stakes, or earth them up to help increase the stability of plants.

HARVESTING CALABRESE

1 Cut the main central head while it is still firm and the flowers are tightly budded, before it gets much bigger than 4 in (10 cm) in diameter.

2 Sideshoots should develop once the central head is gone. They can be harvested later.

How to sow seeds

Calabrese seedlings don't like being transplanted, especially in warm weather, so it's best to sow seeds directly into the ground, in succession to avoid having them all mature at once. Sow three seeds to a hole, $3/4$ in (2 cm) deep, about 12 in (30 cm) apart, and in rows 18 in (45 cm) apart. Thin out the two weakest seedlings and leave the strongest to grow on.

For calabrese that you plan to overwinter, sow in modules in mid-fall and transplant seedlings in early winter to a growing site protected by a cold frame or inside a greenhouse.

Sow sprouting broccoli seeds in flats or modules, or outdoors in seedbeds—in both cases to a depth of about $3/4$ in (2 cm). Keep them covered until there is no longer a risk of frost.

How to plant out seedlings

Transplant seedlings as carefully as possible. They don't like any kind of root disturbance. Space calabrese about 12 in (30 cm) apart in rows 18 in (45 cm) apart. Sprouting broccoli takes up more room when fully grown, and should therefore be spaced at least 24 in (60 cm) apart in rows also 24 in (60 cm) apart.

Routine care

Keep seedlings weed-free and well-watered until established. After that, water calabrese regularly but don't overwater sprouting broccoli—it will survive the winter better if you avoid this.

As the heads or florets develop, the plants have a tendency to become top-heavy, so earth up their stems to support them. Stake sprouting broccoli when fall arrives, especially if it is exposed to wind.

Harvesting

Most calabrese varieties are fairly fast-growing, and you should be able to harvest them within three or four months of sowing. With any luck, sprouting broccoli should give you a continuous crop that lasts for up to two months. Snap off the flowering shoots when the flowers are in bud but before they open, when they're about 6 in (15 cm) long. The more you pick, the more new shoots will grow.

What can go wrong

Although broccoli can be affected by problems that afflict other brassicas (*see pp.61–62*)—including clubroot—it's usually fairly trouble-free. The most irritating pests are likely to be birds (especially pigeons) and caterpillars left by visiting butterflies. You may need to cover your plants with netting to keep them out.

Recommended broccoli

CALABRESE Aquiles, Belstar, Marathon, Romanesco

SPROUTING BROCCOLI Cardinal, Claret, Early Purple Sprouting, Early White Sprouting, Red Arrow, Rudolph, Summer Purple

(clockwise from top)
Romanesco, Claret, Early White Sprouting

Root & Stem Vegetables

This group of vegetables includes two major types: roots such as potatoes, carrots, beets, and turnips (which all grow underground); and stems such as celery, fennel, onions, and leeks (which grow above the surface). In the case of some stem vegetables, it's quite clear that what you're eating are the stalks or stems—celery, green onions, and leeks, for example. In the case of others—celery root, kohlrabi, and even bulb onions—it's not so obvious; they look more like roots than the swollen stems that they actually are.

   Almost all the vegetables in this group share a valuable characteristic: they can be stored after harvesting and eaten during the winter months, when other fresh foods are scarce. The exceptions are celery, Florence fennel, and green onions; they are best eaten soon after being picked.

Fertile, well-prepared soil is the key to growing healthy, well-formed root vegetables such as these freshly pulled carrots.

1. **Potatoes** are classified as early, main, or storage, depending on when they will be ready to harvest.

2. **Sweet potatoes** need a long, hot summer if they're to be grown successfully outdoors.

3. **Beets** are best eaten when young and small; that's when they're at their sweetest and tastiest.

4. **Carrots** are easy to grow, take up little space, and are available in a wide choice of unusual varieties.

5. **Parsnips** benefit from a cold snap before harvesting—a sharp frost intensifies flavor and sweetness.

6. **Turnips** are grown for their roots and their leaves, the latter ("turnip greens") being eaten cooked.

7. **Rutabagas** are not the easiest or fastest vegetable to grow but are useful for storing throughout winter.

8. **Celery** stays fresh and crisp for longer if you water your plants well shortly before digging them up.

9. **Celery root** tastes much better than it looks, and is delicious eaten either cooked or raw.

10 **Kohlrabi** produces bulbous, turnip-shaped globes that sprout cabbagelike leaves.

11 **Florence fennel** produces large bulbs that are in fact swollen, overlapping leaf stems.

12 **Onions** are easy to grow—search out unusual varieties that are harder to find.

13 **Shallots** are best grown from "sets"—they divide to produce a handful of new bulbs.

14 **Green onions** are essentially junior, immature onions grown for harvesting while young.

15 **Garlic** is famous for its flavor, medicinal properties—and its power to ward off vampires.

16 **Leeks** fill a gap by coming into their own when the season's onions have been harvested.

Potatoes

A handful of new potatoes dug up straight from the ground, rinsed under the faucet, quickly boiled or steamed, and served up with a pat of butter and a couple of sprigs of mint. Can there be any more persuasive argument for growing your own? The same goes for the fluffy potatoes destined to be baked, roasted, mashed, sautéed, or French fried.

Potatoes are traditionally classified according to the length of time they take to mature. New potatoes or "early" are ready for harvesting first, then come "main," and finally "storage." Growing from seed is almost unknown. Instead, it's standard to buy specially cultivated seed potatoes or, in the case of specialty heritage varieties, "microplants" (see p.95).

	spring			summer			fall			winter		
	E	M	L	E	M	L	E	M	L	E	M	L
plant	■	■	■									
harvest				■	■	■	■					

Where to plant

Choose an open, well-drained site, and if possible dig in some bulky organic material such as well-rotted manure or compost during the preceding fall or the winter months. Ideally, the soil should have a pH level of 5–6 (see p.21).

Don't plant potatoes in the same place from one year to the next, or you'll increase the risk of disease. Devise a crop-rotation plan and move on to a new site—but not one where you've just grown onions or other root vegetables. In an ideal situation, you should choose one where you have grown beans or peas the previous year.

When to plant

Plant seed potatoes outdoors in early or mid-spring when the soil has warmed up to at least 45°F (7°C) and, if possible, when there's no longer a chance of a severe frost. In order to speed up the time between planting and harvesting, get ahead by "chitting" or sprouting your seed potatoes before they go into the ground.

Plant a mixture of early and maincrop varieties, and you could harvest from summer through to mid- or even late fall.

Potato flowers are usually a sign that the moment for harvesting has arrived. A trial excavation will confirm whether your potatoes are ready for digging.

All potatoes taste better homegrown and freshly dug from the ground.

CHITTING SEED POTATOES

Seed potatoes are commercially grown tubers that can generally be relied on to be disease-free. They are usually available for sale in midwinter.

1 Lay the potatoes out in single layers in egg cartons or seed flats, so that the ends with the most eyes are pointing up. Keep in a cool, light place; soon the eyes will begin to sprout into strong, dark chits, about $\frac{3}{4}$ in (2 cm) long. If it's too warm or too dark, chits may be pale, weak, and long.

2 Just before planting, some people pick off all but three of the chits. This may give you larger potatoes but will probably also produce a lower overall yield. Dig a furrow about 6 in (15 cm) deep, and within it place the potatoes with their chits uppermost.

3 Use a rake to push the soil back over the potatoes to a depth of at least 1 in (2.5 cm).

How to plant seed potatoes

Dig a shallow trench about 6 in (15 cm) deep down the length of your row, and, if you wish, sprinkle in some general-purpose fertilizer. Place your seed potatoes in small holes, standing them up so that the "rose" (the end with the greatest number of chits) is pointing upward. Space earlies 12–14 in (30–35 cm) apart in rows about 18 in (45 cm) apart. Give main and storage varieties slightly more room: plant them 15 in (38 cm) apart in rows about 30 in (75 cm) apart. Cover them carefully with at least 1 in (2.5 cm) of soil.

Routine care

Keep early plantings watered and free of weeds, and cover young plants if there is any danger of a late frost. Later main and storage varieties don't need watering until the tubers have started developing.

As your plants grow, they need "earthing up" to ensure that the potatoes themselves remain underground, out of the light. Otherwise, they will turn green and become inedible. When the stems reach about 9 in (23 cm) tall, rake or draw soil up around them, leaving about 4 in (10 cm) of foliage above the surface to keep growing. You may need to repeat the process once or twice more throughout summer.

Giving potatoes an organic liquid fertilizer or applying a topdressing of nitrogenous fertilizer may help increase the yield.

Harvesting

Earlies should be ready to harvest 100–110 days after planting, mains within 110–120 days, and storage in 125–140 days—although the exact timing depends on the cultivars you're growing, the weather, soil conditions, and any number of other factors. Flowers can give you an indication, too: you should be able to lift potatoes when, or just before, they flower. However, the only way to be certain is to scrape back some of the soil from a plant and take a look.

Of course, you can leave storage potatoes in the ground longer, provided they're lifted before the first frost arrives. Just how long is something of a gamble. The upside of leaving them is that they'll continue to grow larger. The downside is that they're more likely to be attacked by slugs, worms, and scab. Whatever you decide, it is wise to cut off the stems (known as "haulms") as they begin to die down in fall.

If you plan to store your potatoes, preferably lift them when it's not raining, and leave them

Earth up potatoes regularly by drawing soil up around the stems, or the crop will turn green and become poisonous.

Cut off the stems in early fall as they die. Trim them off at about 2 in (5 cm) above the ground.

Store potatoes in a clean, dry paper bag, and fold it over to shut out light. Don't store any damaged tubers.

to dry in the sun for a few hours. Set aside any damaged tubers for immediate use and store the remainder in double-layered paper bags. Stack them in a cool, dry, and well-ventilated place, making sure you cover them to keep out the light. Alternatively, make a special "clamp" for storing them outdoors (*see p.112*).

What can go wrong
Pests
Potato cyst eelworms attack potato roots. Each tiny cyst is the body of a female worm and may contain 600 eggs. When the eggs hatch, they absorb all the nutrients from the plant, causing it to shrivel and die. The worms also tunnel into the potatoes themselves. Unhatched eggs can lie dormant in the soil for many years. There is no cure: it's best simply to employ meticulous crop rotation.

Colorado potato beetles are black-and-yellow-striped beetles that are a major pest of potato crops in most areas of the United States. They are resistant to most pesticides, so for a small plot, pick them off by hand, place in a container of soapy water, and discard.

Other pests include cutworms, wireworms, and slugs (*see pp.324–333*).

Diseases
Potato blight will start as brown patches on the tips and edges of leaves, sometimes with a fluffy white fungus growth underneath as well. The leaves wither and die, while stems or haulms develop dark brown patches and collapse. The potatoes themselves may have dark patches, beneath which the flesh will turn reddish-brown, slimy, and smelly before rotting completely. Potato blight is a fungus, and its spores are spread by wind and rain. Copper-based fungicides such as traditional Bordeaux mixture are no longer available to amateur gardeners, so choose blight-resistant varieties and earth up plants well.

Potato common scab produces rough, brown, corky patches on the skin of potatoes. This isn't fatal, but the tubers must be scraped or peeled hard to remove discoloration. Scab is less of a problem in acidic soils containing a lot of organic matter, but tends to be exacerbated by hot, dry weather.

Potato powdery scab (a fungus), **potato black leg** (which is bacterial), and any general potato viruses are best treated by removing and destroying affected plants. Prevent them by practicing crop rotation and by buying certified disease-free seed potatoes.

Recommended potatoes

Potatoes are usually chosen according to whether they're early, main, or storage, but of course it's just as important to consider their texture and taste. If you like fluffy potatoes ideal for baking and roasting, try 'King Edward' or 'Maris Piper'. If you prefer waxy salad potatoes, you should probably go for 'International Kidney', 'Roseval', 'Charlotte', 'Belle de Fontenay', or the wonderful knobby 'Pink Fir Apple'.

For many years, traditional "heritage" or "heirloom" cultivars (*see panel*), long neglected by the major commercial horticultural conglomerates, have been hard to track down or were simply not available at all. Fortunately, interest in them has survived among amateur gardeners, and as a result, many are now being rediscovered and reintroduced by specialty seed suppliers.

EARLY **Arran Pilot, Casablanca, Foremost, International Kidney, Pentland Javelin, Red Duke of York, Rocket, Swift**

SECOND EARLY **Anya, Charlotte, Kestrel, Nicola, Picasso, Ratte, Roseval, Vivaldi**

MAINCROP **Belle de Fontenay, Cara, Desiree, King Edward, Maris Piper, Maxine, Pink Fir Apple, Sharpo Mira**

(clockwise from top left)
Foremost, Red Duke of York, Maxine, Charlotte

HERITAGE POTATOES

Some are quite exotic, with bright red, purple, or black skins and, in the case of 'Salad Blue', alarming vivid blue flesh. They're sometimes sold not as seed potatoes but as "microplants," potted seedlings ready for planting in pots or growing bags. They produce a few tubers in their first year, some for eating and others to be saved as seed potatoes for the next year.

Recommended heritage potatoes

Arran Victory, Highland Burgundy Red, Mr Little's Yetholm Gypsy, Salad Blue, Shetland Black

(top) **Highland Burgundy Red** (bottom) **Salad Blue**

Sweet potatoes

Sweet potatoes actually have nothing to do with potatoes at all. They're relatives of the bindweed or morning glory family—evident when you see their trailing foliage. They produce underground tubers with sweet-tasting white or orange flesh. Sweet potatoes are originally tropical and subtropical plants, so although they can be grown in temperate climates, they will only produce a good crop during warm summers, or indoors in a greenhouse. They can be raised from seed, but it's easier to buy—or grow your own—rooted cuttings, otherwise known as "slips," and plant them out directly in the ground. Because sweet potatoes need deep, rich soil, they're often grown in earthed-up ridges.

	spring			summer			fall			winter		
	E	M	L	E	M	L	E	M	L	E	M	L
sow indoors	■	■										
transplant			■	■								
plant slips out			■	■								
harvest								■	■			

Beauregard

Where to plant
Sweet potatoes take up a lot of space, and they need a warm sheltered site that has very fertile, sandy soil high in nitrogen and with a pH of 5.5–6.5 (*see p.21*).

When to plant
If you're attempting to grow sweet potatoes from seed, sow them indoors in early or mid-spring. If you're growing from slips, plant them out in late spring once the soil has warmed up.

How to sow seeds
Sow seeds in flats or medium-sized pots at a depth of about 1 in (2.5 cm). Harden off the seedlings when they grow to a height of about 4–6 in (10–15 cm) and transplant them.

(far left) **To plant slips,** construct wide ridges 12 in (30 cm) high and 30 in (75 cm) apart. Cover with black plastic to warm the soil before planting—this will also help discourage weeds.

(left) **Sweet potato leaves** can be cooked and eaten like spinach.

How to plant slips and seedlings

Earth up a raised ridge in the soil about 12 in (30 cm) high. If you're making more than one row, space the next at least 30 in (75 cm) away from the first. Plant out seedlings 10–12 in (25–30 cm) apart along the top of the ridge. Plant slips in holes 2–3 in (5–8 cm) deep the same distance apart.

As an alternative, plant slips or seedlings in growing bags and place them in a warm, sheltered spot in the garden, or just keep them in a greenhouse.

Routine care

Sweet potatoes are thirsty, so keep them well watered. They need fertilizer, too, certainly in their early growing phase, while the tubers are forming. Use a general-purpose fertilizer every two to three weeks.

The foliage grows and spreads rampantly. Either trim the growing shoots to keep them neat, or train them up wire supports.

Harvesting

Sweet potatoes should be ready to harvest by early fall. Of course, the longer you leave them in the ground, the larger they'll grow, but you should lift them if the leaves start to turn yellow and certainly before the first frost. Use a fork to dig them out, taking great care not to split or damage them.

They can be stored indoors in flats for a few months, but first they should be "cured"—left out in the warm sunshine for four to seven days to harden their skins slightly.

What can go wrong

Outdoors, aphids (*see p.326*) are likely to be the biggest problem, though plants may also be affected by general fungal diseases and viruses. Indoors, watch out for spider mites (*see p.331*) and whiteflies (*see p.333*).

Recommended sweet potatoes

Beauregard, Carolina Ruby, Centennial, O'Henry

Beets

There are many, many more varieties of beets than most of us realize. Of course, we all know the standard, round purple beets sold in supermarkets and the small pickled kind in jars. But farmers' markets and specialty stores are now starting to introduce us to bright red, orange, golden-yellow, white, and even pink-and-white-striped varieties. Even the shapes range from round to oval or long, and on to tapering varieties as well.

Whatever their shape and color, all beets are best eaten young, when they're at their sweetest and tastiest, and when they're smaller than the ones that are normally available to buy at the store. That alone is certainly reason enough to buy a packet of seeds and grow your own.

	spring			summer			fall			winter		
	E	M	L	E	M	L	E	M	L	E	M	L
sow under cover	■	■	■									
sow outdoors			■	■	■							
harvest					■	■	■	■	■			

Where to plant

Beets will grow pretty much anywhere, but they do best in a sunny location, in light, sandy soil; if possible, dig plenty of rich well-rotted manure into the soil in advance. They prefer neutral or slightly acidic soil—a pH of 6.5–7 should be perfect (*see p.21*).

When to plant

Try to sow beets successively through the year so that you have a regular, continuous supply. Start in early spring by sowing seeds indoors or under cover, and use bolt-resistant varieties. In late spring, when the risk of frost has passed, and on into summer, sow directly into the ground outdoors.

"They are best eaten **young,** when **sweet** and **tasty.**"

Slice through a Chioggia beet
to see its remarkable red and white concentric rings.

Using biodegradable seed tape
when sowing beet seeds helps guarantee regular spacing and reduces the need for thinning.

Thin out seedlings when they have about four leaves: pinch out the weaker plants, leaving the others at 3–4-in (7.5–10-cm) intervals.

HARVESTING BEETS

1 In fall, before the frost becomes severe, pull up any beets still in the ground. Be careful when doing so, since they will bleed if their skins are pierced.

2 Remove the tops either with a knife or by simply twisting them off. Store them in a wooden box along with some moist compost or vermiculite.

How to sow seeds

Beet seeds can be difficult to germinate. Soak them in warm water for half an hour before sowing in order to soften them and wash off any germination inhibitor.

For early sowings under cover, sow two seeds per pot or module at a depth of 1 in (2.5 cm). Thin out the weakest, and transplant the strongest from each pot when it is 2 in (5 cm) tall, being careful not to disturb the roots.

If you're not starting the plants under cover, wait until the soil has warmed up to at least 45°F (7°C) before sowing directly into the ground. For standard-sized beets, sow about 4 in (10 cm) apart in rows about 12 in (30 cm) apart. For smaller pickling beets, sow more closely: about 2 in (5 cm) apart in rows only 6 in (15 cm) apart. If necessary, thin out any extra seedlings that appear by nipping off the tiny leaves and leaving the roots undisturbed.

Routine care

Once the plants are established and the roots are starting to swell, water moderately unless conditions are very dry. Overwatering will only encourage leaf growth, while underwatering will cause the outer leaves to turn yellow and the roots woody. Keep your rows well weeded, and spray the growing plants once or twice with a foliar, kelp-based fertilizer to help boost nitrogen, manganese, and boron levels.

Harvesting

If you sow your seeds in successive batches, you should be able to harvest beets all through the summer and fall. Start picking the first beets when they are about the size of a golf ball and pull them from all along the length of your rows, as if you were thinning out. This will give the remaining roots more space to grow. Young leaves can be harvested, too.

What can go wrong

Beets are generally resilient and easy to grow, and you'll be unlikely to have major problems. That said, they can be attacked by black bean aphids and cutworm (*see pp.327–328*), or suffer from damping off and fungal leaf spot (*see pp.320–321*). Birds can be troublesome, too; if so, net your plants.

Recommended beets

Bolt-resistant, smooth-skinned varieties are probably the safest choice, but it's also worth experimenting with some of the more unusual colors and shapes.

Action, Albina Vereduna, Boltardy, Burpee's Golden, Chioggia, Cylindra, Detroit 2 Crimson Globe, Moneta, Pablo, Red Ace

(clockwise from above) **Boltardy, Action, Red Ace**

Carrots

A bewildering array of different types of carrots are available for home growing. Bear in mind that you don't need to stick to the regular-shaped orange ones that we're all so used to, since a wealth of others are available. There are round ones, short and stubby ones, and conical ones; in addition to this, traditional heritage cultivars are being rediscovered and reintroduced as well; these may be white, yellow, scarlet, or purple. The simplest way to classify carrots is to divide them into early varieties (sown in spring) and main crops (sown from late spring to early summer). However, within these categories there are Amsterdam types (small, narrow, and cylindrical), Nantes (slightly broader and longer), Chantenay (short and conical), Berlicum (long and large), and Autumn King (the longest of all).

	spring			summer			fall			winter		
	E	M	L	E	M	L	E	M	L	E	M	L
sow under cover	■											
sow outdoors		■	■	■	■	■						
harvest					■	■	■	■	■	■	■	

Where to plant

Carrots grow best on an open, dry site in light soil that has had plenty of rich, well-rotted compost or manure dug into it during the previous fall. Importantly, the soil should be as free from rocks as possible and not compacted—otherwise roots may fork or suffer from constricted growth. Raised seed beds are ideal.

Crop rotation is important, too. Don't plant carrots where you grew potatoes, beets, parsnips, celery, eggplant, tomatoes, or peppers the previous year (*see pp.36–37*).

When to plant

For a continuous harvest, sow carrots successively throughout the year. Start under cover during early spring in order to produce an early summer harvest, or delay sowing until late spring or early summer for fall harvesting. You can even sow in fall or winter for a crop the following spring if you protect the plants under fabric or cloches.

Homegrown carrots, freshly pulled, rinsed under the faucet, and eaten raw, are sweeter, crunchier, and more concentrated in flavor than you can imagine.

"Traditional **heritage cultivars** may be yellow, white, scarlet, or purple."

THINNING AND HARVESTING

1 When thinning carrot seedlings, nip off the leaves and remove them instead of pulling out the whole root. This will limit the smell that is released, and will reduce carrot rust fly attack.

2 Early varieties can often be harvested just seven weeks after planting; these are perfect for salads or crunchy stir-fries.

How to sow seeds

Carrot seeds are best sown directly into the ground, since they don't transplant well. Sow seeds thinly, 1 in (2.5 cm) apart and at a depth of 1/2–3/4 in (1–2 cm). If the weather is still cold, protect them under cloches, frames, plastic film, or fabric. When the seedlings appear, thin to about 2 in (5 cm), increasing to 4 in (10 cm) as the roots are harvested. The exception to the direct-sowing rule is to use modules; they allow round-rooted varieties to be planted out in well-spaced clumps and left unthinned.

Routine care

Weed regularly and carefully while seedlings appear. It's a precise job to be done by hand rather than with a hoe, but once carrots develop their own foliage, it will help keep rival weeds down. Water if the soil shows signs of drying, but don't overdo it. If you overwater them, carrots produce too much leaf growth.

Harvesting

Early varieties may be ready for harvesting seven weeks after sowing, at which point they should be at least 1/2 in (12 mm) in diameter. Pull a few and leave the rest to continue growing. Maincrop varieties should be ready to lift 10–11 weeks after sowing. Most carrots can be pulled out by hand, but use a fork if the soil is compacted or if they have very long roots.

You can leave carrots in the ground over winter, as long as the soil isn't too wet, the weather isn't too cold, and you protect them with a mulch of straw. But the longer you leave them, the more likely you are to risk an attack of carrot rust flies or damage from frost. It's best to lift and store them in sand-filled boxes.

What can go wrong

Carrot rust flies are the one problem you don't want to encounter. Once your carrots have been hit, you have no choice but to pull up all affected crops and destroy them. The female flies find carrots by following their smell and lay eggs in the soil around the plants. Once these hatch, the white maggots tunnel into the roots and eat them, causing the carrots to rot.

One way to deter carrot rust flies is to minimize the carrot smell— thin seedlings and harvest crops in the evening, disturbing the ground as little as possible. You can even confuse the flies' sense of smell by intercropping carrots and onions.

Careful timing can also reduce the chance of attack. Delay sowing until after late spring and you should avoid the first generation of newly hatched larvae; in addition, if you pick your crop before late summer you should miss the second, as they tend to attack late-harvest varieties.

Watch out for aphids (*see p.326*), and diseases such as downy mildew, powdery mildew, and violet root rot (*see pp.321–323*).

Recommended carrots

Carrots are easy to grow and take up very little space, so why not try a few of the unusual ones as well as your favorites?

EARLY **Amsterdam Forcing, Atlas, Early Nantes, Flyaway, Nandor, Parmex, Primo, Resistafly**

MAIN CROP **Autumn King, Bangor, Berlicum, Chantenay Red Cored, Eskimo, James Scarlet Intermediate, Nantes, St Valery, Sugarsnax**

COLORED **Purple Haze, Rainbow, White Satin, Yellowstone**

To deter carrot rust flies, fence them out. Erect a barrier of clear plastic, cardboard, or fine woven mesh netting, and earth up the soil at the base. Female carrot flies seem incapable of flying any higher than about 18 in (45 cm), so make the barrier 2 ft (60 cm) high or more.

(top left) **White Satin**
(bottom left) **Purple Haze**
(middle) **Bangor**
(right) **Parmex**

Parsnips

Parsnips are one of the archetypal vegetables of fall. There's nothing like the distinctive sweet, earthy taste of roast parsnips to signal the onset of the winter months. And really, parsnips are so easy to cultivate that, provided you have the space, there's no excuse not to grow them. The seeds are always planted directly into the ground. Once that's done, there's very little to do beyond the occasional watering and weeding other than wait for them to mature.

	spring			summer			fall			winter		
	E	M	L	E	M	L	E	M	L	E	M	L
sow outdoors	■	■										
harvest	■							■	■	■	■	■

Where to plant

Parsnips grow best in an open sunny location, in light, sandy soil enriched by digging well-rotted manure into it the previous fall. Since the roots can grow quite long, deep soil is an advantage. Ideally, parsnips like a very slightly acidic pH of 6.5 (*see p.21*).

When to plant

The seeds can be slow to germinate, but don't be tempted to sow too early. Unless the weather is unusually warm, wait until mid- to late spring or your seeds may not germinate at all.

How to sow seeds

Sow seeds directly into the ground, either thinly along the length of the row, or 2–3 together in case some fail to germinate.

When the seedlings are established and each has four leaves, they can be thinned out if necessary to a spacing of approximately 4–6 in (10–14 cm) apart for medium-sized roots or 12 in (20 cm) apart for larger, late-harvest ones.

Sow three seeds at each point, since parsnip seed germination is notoriously erratic.

A hard frost is said to intensify a parsnip's flavor and sweetness.

Intersow parsnips with radishes—the radishes will come up before the parsnips germinate, marking out the row. The radishes will be ready to harvest long before the parsnips are.

Routine care

Weed carefully until your parsnips have established themselves. Water regularly until seeds have germinated but thereafter only if conditions become so dry that the soil is in danger of drying out. If you let the ground dry out, there's a chance the roots will split when you finally do water them.

Provided your soil is rich enough, parsnips don't usually need feeding, but it won't hurt to give them a liquid fertilizer if you think they need it.

Bear in mind that the leaves of parsnip plants die down in winter, so it's a good idea to mark the location of your rows before it happens. Otherwise, locating parsnips for harvesting may prove problematic.

Harvesting

Parsnips usually take about four months to mature, so depending on when you planted them, they may be ready to harvest any time from late summer onward. Many people, however, prefer to leave them until after the first frost. In fact, in all but the coldest climates, they can remain in the ground throughout the winter, to be lifted only when you need them. If the weather turns very severe, it's worth giving them the extra protection of a 6-in- (15-cm-) thick covering of straw or bracken.

What can go wrong

Carrot rust flies sometimes attacks parsnips almost as mercilessly as they do carrots, so try to deter them using the same preventive measures (*see pp.104–105*).

Parsnip canker is particularly unpleasant. It's a fungus that produces rough red-brown, orange-brown, or black growths on the roots, eventually causing them to rot, sometimes because it's provided an entry point for carrot rust fly maggots. There's no cure, so remove and destroy all affected plants. Try to avoid it by practicing crop rotation, choosing modern, resistant cultivars, and not letting the ground become waterlogged. Parsnips planted later in the year and grown closer together seem less susceptible.

Other potential problems include downy mildew (*see p.321*) if it's damp, powdery mildew (*see p.322*) if it's dry, celery leaf miner (*see p.117*), and violet root rot (*see p.323*).

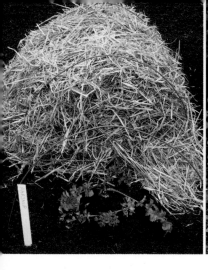

(far left) **Protecting overwintering plants** by covering them with a layer of dry straw held in position by wire hoops or netting.

(left) **Store parsnips after lifting** by laying them flat in shallow wooden boxes packed with moist sand. Then stack the boxes in a cool, dry place where air can circulate freely.

Recommended parsnips

Bolt-resistant, smooth-skinned varieties are probably the safest choice, but it's worth also trying some of the more unusual colors and shapes.

Albion, Gladiator, Javelin, Panache, Tender and True, White Gem

(left) **Tender and True**
(right) **Javelin**

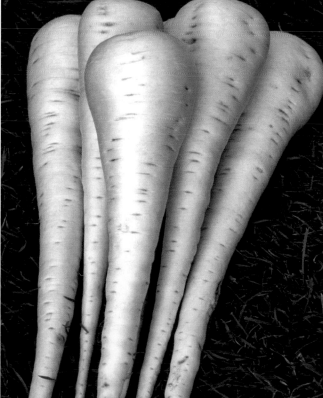

Turnips

Until recently, turnips have suffered from a bit of an image problem: they've been written off as old-fashioned, tasteless, and dull. While this might be true of overgrown, late-season turnips, which can be woody and bitter, it's unfair to judge them all so hastily. Harvested young, when the roots are not much bigger than golf balls, they taste wonderfully sweet and nutty when steamed, roasted, or eaten raw in salads. Modern fast-growing varieties are being introduced, as well as unusual black- and purple-skinned cultivars, and small, round, yellow varieties such as 'Golden Ball'.

	spring			summer			fall			winter		
	E	M	L	E	M	L	E	M	L	E	M	L
sow under cover	■	■										■
sow outdoors		■	■	■	■	■						
harvest				■	■	■	■	■	■	■	■	

Where to plant

Turnips will grow happily in most soils as long as they're reasonably high in nitrogen, have a pH of at least 6.8 (*see p.21*), and have had some well-rotted compost or manure dug in during the previous season.

When to plant

Sow outdoors from early spring once the soil is workable, and protect early seedlings from frost with cloches or fabric. Sow successively—a handful every three weeks or so—to avoid a glut later. Seeds might not germinate as easily in hotter and drier weather toward summer.

How to sow seeds

For a crop of small or even baby turnips, sow in module flats, about four seeds per module. Transplant each group as soon as the seedlings have grown one or two true leaves, before their roots start to develop. Instead of thinning them out, leave each group to produce a cluster of golf-ball-sized roots.

If you're sowing seeds directly into the ground, scatter them thinly and cover them to a depth of about ³/₄ in (2 cm). Rows should be 9–12 in (23–30 cm) apart. Water in, and when seedlings appear, thin them to 4–6 in (10–15 cm) apart.

Routine care

Weed regularly and keep your plants well-watered, particularly in dry weather. Provided the soil is rich enough to start with, turnips don't usually need any additional fertilizer.

Harvesting

Turnips can mature within five or six weeks, so early sowings may be ready for harvesting by the beginning of summer. Harvest when they're 1¹/₂–2 in (4–5 cm) in diameter, and cook and eat them immediately. Leave main crop sowings in the ground for up to ten weeks so the roots grow larger (but not so large that they turn woody), and harvest in late summer and fall.

Don't overlook the leaves, or turnip greens, as they're called. If you pick them when they're still young—no taller than 5–6 in (13–15 cm)—they can be cooked and eaten like spring greens.

What can go wrong

Turnips are brassicas, so they are prone to the pests and diseases that affect fellow members of the cabbage family: cabbage root flies, clubroot, cutworm, flea beetle, mealy cabbage aphids, wireworm, downy mildew, and powdery mildew (*see pp.320–333*).

The list looks daunting, but turnips are rarely attacked so badly that they are impossible to grow.

Recommended turnips

Atlantic, Golden Ball, Oasis, Purple Top Milan, Snowball, Sweetbell, Tokyo Cross

(top) **Baby turnips** can be grown by sowing four seeds in each cell of a module flat, then transplanting the seedlings as groups, letting them grow on without thinning them out.

(bottom) **Harvest** turnips before they become too large. You should be able to pull them from the ground by their stems.

(far left) **Atlantic** (left) **Tokyo Cross**

Rutabagas

Rutabagas are large, yellow- or orange-fleshed roots that are slow-growing, can be difficult to cultivate, and are prone to most of the pests and diseases that affect the brassica family, of which they are a member. Not the most exciting vegetable in the plant kingdom, then. Nevertheless, they do have their uses.

A common ingredient in soups, stews, and casseroles, rutabagas can also be roasted along with other root vegetables, and they are often eaten boiled or mashed. In Scotland, where they are known as "neeps," they are traditionally served with haggis on Burns Night. And, if stored carefully, they will keep through the winter. So, don't write them off entirely.

	spring			summer			fall			winter		
	E	M	L	E	M	L	E	M	L	E	M	L
sow outdoors			■	■								
harvest							■	■	■	■	■	■

Create a "rutabaga clamp" for storing your harvest. In a dry, sheltered spot, spread out an 8-in (20-cm) layer of straw. Stack your rutabagas on top in a pyramid, with necks facing outward. Cover with more straw and, if it is very cold, a layer of soil as well.

Where to plant

Try to plant rutabagas in an open, sunny spot in light soil that is low in nitrogen and has a pH no lower than 6.8 (*see p.21*). If possible, dig some well-rotted compost or manure into the soil at some point during the previous season.

When to plant

Rutabagas take a considerably long time to develop from seed to when they're ready to harvest—this period can be up to six months. Therefore it's a good idea to get them started by sowing at any time from early spring onward, as soon as the soil is warm enough to work. If there is still a danger of frost, protect early seedlings with cloches, frames, or fabric.

How to sow seeds

Sow seeds thinly directly into the ground in shallow drills to a depth of about ¾ in (2 cm). Rows should be at least 15 in (38 cm) apart. Thin out seedlings to about 9 in (23 cm) apart.

Routine care

Weed and water regularly, particularly during dry weather.

Harvesting

Lift rutabagas in fall or early winter, when they are about 4–6 in (10–15 cm) in diameter. They can be left in the ground for longer, but if they are, they're in danger of becoming woody. In very cold weather they will need to be protected with a covering of straw.

Once harvested, rutabagas can be stored by packing them in sand in wooden boxes, but traditionally they are kept in a specially constructed "rutabaga clamp."

What can go wrong

Rutabagas may be afflicted by most of the pests and diseases that attack other members of the cabbage family: cabbage root flies, clubroot, flea beetle, mealy cabbage aphids, and downy and powdery mildews (*see pp.320–333*).

Recommended rutabagas

Best of All, Brora, Helenor, Invitation, Marian, Ruby, Tweed

(top) **Best of All** (bottom) **Marian**

Celery

There are three different kinds of celery: self-blanching and green celery; trench celery (which is planted in trenches and then earthed up or wrapped in collars to keep it white); and leaf or cutting celery (grown for its leaves rather than its stems). In addition, there are cultivars with green, pink, or red stems. Trench celery is labor-intensive and quite difficult to blanch successfully, so it is not grown often these days. Self-blanching—which actually has off-white rather than pure white stalks—is the most commonly seen.

	spring			summer			fall			winter		
	E	M	L	E	M	L	E	M	L	E	M	L
Self-blanching/Green celery												
sow indoors	■	■										
plant out			■	■								
harvest					■	■	■	■				
Trench celery												
sow indoors	■	■										
transplant			■	■								
harvest									■	■		

Where to plant

Celery needs rich soil that will retain moisture, but without being too heavy. Dig in plenty of compost in the season before you plant, and add some lime to the soil if it's too acidic. The pH should be 6.6–6.8 (*see p.21*).

Leaf celery tends to be pretty hardy and should overwinter, but self-blanching celery is prone to frost; if you grow it outdoors, either harvest or cover it by mid-fall.

When to plant

You can start to sow celery seeds sometime in early to mid-spring, but they are notoriously slow to germinate. They need a temperature of at least 59°F (15°C), so use a propagator or keep them in a heated greenhouse if you want to start them early.

Self-blanching varieties with pale green rather than pure white stems are less likely to need earthing up or wrapping in collars to exclude the light.

"Celery tastes better if the stems are **blanched**."

(top) **Plant self-blanching celery** closely in blocks so that those in the middle are protected from the light. Plants on the outside may need collars.

(bottom) **Homemade collars** made from strips of black plastic lined with newspaper are an alternative way to blanch celery. Wrap them around the stems and secure with twine.

How to sow seeds

Sow seeds in pots or modules on or only just below the surface of the soil, as they need light as well as warmth and moisture to germinate. Once the seedlings appear, don't let the temperature drop below 50°F (10°C) or they may bolt.

How to plant out seedlings

Seedlings should be hardened off before transplanting; they are ready once they have four to six true leaves. Plant self-blanching varieties in a block, rather than in rows, at a spacing of about 10 in (25 cm) and deep enough for the crown of the plant to be level with the surface of the soil. Water the seedlings well, and cover them at night if there is still a danger of frost.

Plant trench celery seedlings in a prepared trench that has already had lots of organic matter added to it, about 12–18 in (30–45 cm) apart. Plant leaf celery about 5 in (13 cm) apart.

How to blanch celery

All celery tastes better if the stems are blanched—they're simply more tender. Sadly, self-blanching celery isn't always quite as self-blanching as it sounds, and it may need some help in the form of homemade collars.

Traditionally, trench celery is blanched either by gradually filling up the trench in which it is growing or, if it was planted in a trench already filled to the level of the surrounding ground, by earthing up around the stems as they grow. But this is hard work. There's no shame in using collars for trench celery, too.

Routine care

The most important thing is to keep celery consistently moist. It needs regular watering if its stems are to swell, and if you let it dry out it will quickly start to become stringy. Mulching will help retain moisture in the soil.

If you notice that the leaves are turning yellow, topdress the plants with sulfate of ammonia or give them a liquid fertilizer.

Harvesting

Self-blanching celery should be ready to pick any time from midsummer onward. Don't leave it too late or the stems will become stringy and the leaves will turn yellow. Give your plants plenty of water before you dig them up and they will stay fresh and crisp for longer. Trim off any roots and outer shoots, and keep them in the refrigerator. Snap off, wash, and trim individual stems only just before you use them.

Trench celery can stay in the ground for longer—until late fall or early winter—but will need some protection from frost.

What can go wrong

Slugs and snails are often attracted to celery, as are carrot rust flies (*see pp.104–105*).

Celery leaf miner may cause leaves to develop dried-out, brown patches. These patches are caused by small white maggots eating the insides of the leaves. Pick off the affected leaves before the problem spreads or the celery will become bitter and inedible. There is no other treatment.

Diseases that can affect celery include fungal leaf spots, foot and root rots, and violet root rot (*see pp.321–323*).

WARNING: All celery can cause an unpleasant skin reaction called celery rash. To avoid it, wear gloves and long sleeves.

Recommended celery

SELF-BLANCHING AND GREEN CELERY **Blush, Golden Self Blanching, Loretta, Tango, Victoria**

TRENCH CELERY **Giant Red, Octavius**

LEAF CELERY **Kintsai**

(top) **Harvest self-blanching celery** before the first frost. Use a fork to gently lift the whole plant, roots and all.

(bottom) **Victoria**

Celery root

Celery root is an alarmingly ugly vegetable. It produces large, knobby, misshapen globes that sprout a mass of tangled roots. In fact, it looks like a hairy turnip or rutabaga, though, unlike them, it is not a root but a swollen stem. However, celery root is redeemed by its taste—a mild combination of celery and fennel. It's good peeled and roasted with other winter vegetables, or boiled, combined with potato, and mashed, but can also be eaten raw, grated and mixed with mustard mayonnaise as *celeri remoulade*.

As if that weren't enough, celery root earns its place in the vegetable garden through being very hardy and lasting well into the winter months.

	spring			summer			fall			winter		
	E	M	L	E	M	L	E	M	L	E	M	L
sow indoors	■	■										
plant out			■	■								
harvest	■							■	■	■	■	■

Where to plant
Celery root is not fussy about sun or shade, but it likes moist, rich soil that has had plenty of compost or manure added to it the previous season.

When to plant
Celery root is slow-growing. It needs at least six months to develop bulbs that are worth harvesting, so it's best to get ahead early by sowing seeds under cover in early to mid-spring.

(far left) **Remove split or damaged leaves** as the stems begin to swell up toward the end of summer, and leave the crowns exposed.

(left) **Mulch around the plants** with a layer of straw before the first frost can cause any damage.

How to sow seeds

Sow seeds on the surface of potting mix in pots, modules, or seed flats and keep them in a propagator at a temperature of at least 50°F (10°C). As the seedlings appear, thin or prick them out to one per module or pot, and don't let the temperature drop below 50°F (10°C).

How to plant out seedlings

Harden off seedlings in late spring or early summer, and plant them out at least 12 in (30 cm) apart, in rows 18 in (45 cm) apart. Don't crowd them; they like plenty of light and air. And don't plant them too deep—the crown should be just showing.

Routine care

Water regularly during the growing season—at least twice a week if the weather is dry. If possible, use mulch to help retain moisture within the soil.

As the stems begin to swell up, pull off any split or damaged outer leaves. The tops of the bulbs should begin to stand above the surface of the soil.

Harvesting

You should be able to start harvesting from early fall onward. Use a fork to lift the whole plant and trim off the roots and leaves.

Celery root can be stored if packed in a box of moist sand and placed somewhere cool and dark, but it's better left in the ground until needed. However, if the winter is very cold, spread a 6-in (15-cm) layer of straw around the base of your plants. They should then be able to survive temperatures as low as 15°F (-10°C).

Monarch

What can go wrong

Celery root is very resilient. Pests and diseases that might cause trouble tend to be the same as those that affect celery (*see p.117*).

Recommended celeriac

Brilliant, Giant Prague, Monarch, Prinz

Kohlrabi

Distinctly alien- or prehistoric-looking, kohlrabi produces strange, bulbous, turnip-shaped globes that stand out above the soil surface, sprouting large cabbagelike leaves. Kohlrabi is technically a brassica—a member of the cabbage family—and the green, white, or purple globe is a swollen stem, not a root.

It tastes remarkably good—like a mild, sweet-flavored turnip when cooked. The bonus from a gardening point of view is that it's easy to grow and fast to mature.

	spring			summer			fall			winter		
	E	M	L	E	M	L	E	M	L	E	M	L
sow indoors	■											■
sow outdoors		■	■	■	■	■						
plant out		■	■									
harvest					■	■	■	■	■	■	■	

Where to plant

Kohlrabi will grow in most soils. It's more successful if the pH is high, however, so add extra lime if necessary (*see p.21*).

When to plant

In early spring, sow seeds under cover. As the weather warms up, sow directly into the ground, but not too early or the plants may bolt.

Harvest kohlrabi by pulling the whole plant up or by cutting off the globe just above the roots. Leaving some of the young, central leaves on the globe helps keep it fresh.

Green and white varieties tend to mature more quickly, so plant them first for early harvesting in summer. Plant purple varieties later, since they are slower-growing and will not be ready until later in the fall or winter. If you sow seeds a few at a time, you'll get a steady succession of crops all year in mild climates.

How to sow seeds and plant out seedlings

Sow seeds in pots or modules at a depth of about ¾ in (2 cm) and keep them under cover if the weather is still cold. Transplant seedlings before they grow any taller than 2 in (5 cm) to prevent them from bolting. Leave at least 9 in (23 cm) between plants and, if you plant in rows, set them 12 in (30 cm) apart.

Sow seeds directly into the ground only when you can rely on temperatures above 50°F (10°C) or they may bolt. Sow three seeds at each point, and thin out the two weakest seedlings as soon as you can so as not to disturb the roots of the one you leave in place.

Routine care
You shouldn't have to do much except weed and water regularly throughout the growing season. If kohlrabi dries out, it tends to get woody.

Harvesting
Fast-growing early varieties may be ready five or six weeks after sowing. Bulbs are best harvested when they are the size of a tennis ball, though modern cultivars are still tender and tasty if allowed to grow larger. Slice them off at the root, and cut off all but the youngest leaves. Slower-growing late varieties may take as long as four months to mature and in mild weather can be left in the ground in winter. However, lift them as soon as there is a risk of frost.

What can go wrong
Kohlrabi is a brassica, so it's afflicted by the same pests and diseases as cabbages and Brussels sprouts, particularly clubroot (see *pp.61–62*).

Recommended kohlrabi

Azur Star, Kolibri, Olivia, Superschmelz, White Vienna

Kolibri

Florence fennel

Florence or sweet fennel, as it is sometimes called, is both delicious to eat and wonderfully attractive. With tall fronds of fine, feathery leaves, it looks as good in the garden border as it does in the vegetable patch. Strictly speaking, its large white bulbs are not bulbs at all but swollen, overlapping leaf stems—more like celery than onions. It has a distinctive aniseed taste and can be eaten either raw or cooked. Take note, however, that Florence fennel is not the same plant as the herb fennel (*see p.267*).

	spring			summer			fall			winter		
	E	M	L	E	M	L	E	M	L	E	M	L
sow indoors	■	■										
sow outdoors				■	■	■						
plant out				■	■							
harvest					■	■	■	■	■			

Where to plant
Choose a well-drained site that won't become waterlogged. Fennel likes soil that has been richly manured the previous season and is, if possible, slightly sandy.

When to plant
Fennel seeds will not germinate until they reach 59°F (15°C), so either sow indoors in modules in early to mid-spring, then plant out seedlings, keeping them covered until the weather warms, or sow seeds directly into the ground only after the longest day in midsummer.

How to sow seeds
Sow fast-maturing varieties in modules filled with fresh seed-starting or potting mix. Once the seedlings develop four true leaves, plant out the modules 12 in (30 cm) apart without disturbing the delicate roots. Cover with fabric, cloches, or a cold frame until they have hardened off.

When sowing into the ground, plant three or four seeds close together, 12 in (30 cm) apart and 1 in (2.5 cm) deep. If they're not deep enough, the growing plants may be unstable and could blow over in the wind. As seedlings develop, thin to leave the strongest in each group.

Routine care

Water regularly while the plants are growing. If possible, use mulch to help retain moisture in the soil.

As the plants grow in height, earth up around the stems slightly to prevent them from rocking in the wind and to blanch the bulbs, keeping them white and sweet-tasting.

Harvesting

It will be at least three months after planting before fennel is ready to harvest. The trick is to wait long enough for the stems to swell into good-sized bulbs but not so long that they elongate, start to bolt, and become too tough to eat. When they're just right, cut them off just above ground level with a sharp knife.

If you leave a stump in the soil, it should sprout new shoots that can then be cut and used in salads, and perhaps even additional small bulbs.

What can go wrong

Bolting is the biggest problem. Resistant varieties are available, but even these will bolt if the plants get too dry or too cold. Avoid planting out until the weather has warmed, and keep plants moist.

Rhizoctonia is a fungus that may cause fennel to become stunted, with yellow, red, or dark green-black lesions appearing on the bulbs and stems of the leaves. There's no cure, so dig up the affected plants and destroy them before they rot. And don't grow more fennel—or celery, lettuces, or radishes—in the same spot for a few years. In the future, spraying seedlings with a copper-based fungicide may prevent attacks.

Recommended fennel

Look for varieties that are resistant to bolting. They can be sown or planted outdoors earlier—and will therefore have time to develop larger bulbs. 'Romanesco' reliably produces bulbs weighing up to 2 lb (1 kg) each.

Amigo, Finale, Romanesco, Victorio, Zefa Fino

Zefa Fino

HARVESTING
FLORENCE FENNEL

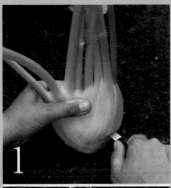

1 To harvest fennel, use a knife to cut the bulb horizontally 1 in (2.5 cm) above ground level, and leave the base in the soil.

2 Feathery leaves should sprout from the stump within the next few weeks—these can be used in salads.

Onions

Onions are among the easiest of all vegetables to grow. You can raise them from seed or from small commercially produced baby onions called "sets." Sets are ideal for novice gardeners, since they are a great deal easier to grow than seeds, although they are more expensive to purchase. Onions don't need a huge amount of attention and, as long as you keep them free of weeds and don't overwater them, especially when they are very young, you should be rewarded with a respectable crop.

	spring			summer			fall			winter		
	E	M	L	E	M	L	E	M	L	E	M	L
sow indoors	■	■										
sow outdoors												
transplant			■	■	■							
plant outdoors				■	■							
harvest					■	■	■	■	■			

Where to plant

Choose an open site where the soil is both well-drained and not too wet, and if possible dig in some well-rotted manure or compost a few months in advance. Onions don't like acidic soils, so add some lime if the pH level is lower than about 6.5 (*see p.21*).

Don't plant onions in the same place year after year, or you'll increase the risk of disease. Check your crop-rotation plan and move to a new area of the vegetable patch—one where you might have grown beans, peas, or tomatoes in the preceding year.

Onions and carrots are often planted next to one another. The smell of onions is thought to deter the carrot rust flies.

When to plant

It's best to sow seeds or plant sets during spring. This should give you onions to harvest in late summer and early fall. However, it is also possible to plant hardy varieties—which were first developed in Japan—in the fall. They will overwinter.

(left) **Onions are ready for harvesting** when their leaves topple over and turn yellow or brown—it's a sign that they have stopped growing.

(right) **Interplanting onions and carrots** is a double whammy: the smell of onions should deter carrot rust flies and the odor of carrots throws any equally unwelcome onion flies off the scent.

PLANTING ONION SETS

1 Mark out a shallow furrow about 1 in (2.5 cm) deep. Push the sets carefully into the soil with pointed ends upward, spacing them 2–4 in (5–10 cm) apart.

2 Draw the soil back around each set so that the tip is only just visible. Gently firm down the soil. Water sparingly if the ground is dry.

Multi-sown onions are grown in clusters. Sow them in module flats, five seeds to each cell. Then transplant the groups of seedlings intact, letting them grow without thinning them out.

How to sow seeds

If you want to grow large onions, sow seeds in midwinter and keep them in a heated greenhouse at a minimum temperature of 50–61°F (10–16°C). This gets them off to an early start and gives them the longest possible growing period. Otherwise, sow them in late winter or early spring, under cover but unheated. Plant them out when the ground is warm enough.

Onion seeds started off under cover should be sown in modules or multiblocks filled with fresh potting mix. Early sowings will need to be transplanted to small pots before hardening off and planting out in mid-spring. Later-sown plants can be transplanted directly into the ground.

In mid- or late spring, when the soil is warmer and drier, plant seeds directly into the ground. Sow seeds thinly at a depth of about ¾ in (2 cm) in rows 12 in (30 cm) apart, and thin them out once they are established. There is no point in sowing outdoors too early; if the soil is cold the seeds won't germinate.

How to plant sets

Rake your soil to loosen it up, and make a shallow furrow the length of your row. Lay out your onion sets about 2 in (5 cm) apart for small or medium bulbs or 4 in (10 cm) apart for larger ones. Press each set gently into the soil, pointed end upward, and draw the soil up around it, leaving the tip just showing. Give them a little water but not so much that you soak them.

(above) **Onion ropes or strings** can be hung up for storage in winter—as long as they are kept dry and well-ventilated.

(right) **Drying onions** Indoors on wooden racks may be necessary if the weather is too wet to leave them outside to dry on the ground.

Routine care

Weed your onion patch thoroughly and regularly, especially in the weeks after sowing seeds or planting sets when competition from other plants is at its fiercest. Take care not to overwater them, though. If onions get waterlogged, they'll take longer to fatten up and may be more prone to disease.

Onions sometimes bolt—they produce a premature flower on top of a tall stalk. If this happens, cut the flower off.

Harvesting

When the leaves turn yellow and start to collapse, your onions are ready for harvesting. For fall-sown varieties, this will be in early to midsummer. For spring-planted bulbs, it will be between midsummer and early fall.

Lift the bulbs gently out of the soil with a fork and either lay them out to dry on the ground for a couple of weeks if the weather is dry and sunny, or bring them indoors if it is wet. Unless you plan to use them in the kitchen right away, onions must be thoroughly dried or they will rot during storage. The best way to keep them is to stack them in single layers in slatted boxes, braid them into ropes, or hang them in nets. Be sure to let air circulate around them.

What can go wrong
Pests

Onion fly maggots might eat roots and bulbs, causing leaves to yellow and plants to collapse during early summer. Onion sets are less prone to attack than plants grown from seed. And covering onion seedlings with fabric will prevent flies from laying eggs.

Onion thrips cause leaves to lose their color and develop rusty stripes or white mottling, especially in hot, dry summers. Keep an eye out for the tiny black or pale-yellow insects. They can be treated with insecticidal soap or pyrethrum.

Allium leaf miner (*see p.326*), **leek moth** (*see p.330*), and **stem and bulb eelworm** (*see p.332*) can also cause problems.

Diseases

Onion white rot causes leaves to turn yellow and wilt; you will also see fluffy white fungus and small black growths around the bulb bases. Onion white rot is very serious. There's no known cure other than to burn the affected plants and avoid growing onions in the same spot for at least seven years, perhaps even longer.

Downy mildew is a fungus that turns leaf tips gray or the tops yellow, and produces a fuzzy gray mold beneath (*see p.321*).

Onion neck rot is a fungus that softens, discolors, and then rots the neck of the bulb, often after harvesting when the onions are in storage. Avoid it by rotating crops, buying good-quality seeds or sets, and ripening and drying bulbs thoroughly.

Recommended onions

Homegrown onions don't taste radically different from those you buy in the supermarket, which are inexpensive and available year-round. Therefore, if you're going to grow onions yourself, it makes sense to choose varieties that are less easy to find, such as red torpedo-shaped onions or large super-sweet Italian ones.

MAIN CROP (SPRING PLANTING) **Ailsa Craig, Bedfordshire Champion, Centurion, Hercules, Marco, Red Baron, Setton, Sturon, Stuttgarter Giant**

OVERWINTERING (FALL PLANTING) **Electric, Hi Keeper, Radar, Senshyu, Shakespeare**

PICKLING **Giant Zittau, Paris Silver Skin**

(from top) **Sturon, Paris Silver Skin, Hi Keeper**

UNUSUAL ONIONS

Welsh onions

These are rather like giant green onions, although they are taller—up to 18 in (45 cm) in height—and grow in clumps. They have green, hollow stems that thicken at the base but don't form large bulbs. The stems are eaten, either cooked or raw in winter salads. Welsh onions planted in spring can be harvested in fall, and those planted in late summer can be cut in the following spring. An additional benefit is that the plant is a perennial, so it will continue to produce year after year.

	spring			summer			fall			winter		
	E	M	L	E	M	L	E	M	L	E	M	L
sow under cover	■	■										
sow outdoors			■	■	■							
plant out				■	■							
harvest				■	■	■	■	■				

Japanese bunching onions

Developed from the Welsh onion, Japanese bunching onions can be grown almost year-round and harvested either young, when they are about the same size as green onions, or when the plants have grown to the size of leeks. They are happy to tolerate poorer soil and colder weather than ordinary green onions, and they are usually grown as annuals.

	spring			summer			fall			winter		
	E	M	L	E	M	L	E	M	L	E	M	L
sow under cover	■	■										
sow outdoors			■	■	■							
plant out			■	■								
harvest				■	■	■	■	■				

Tree or Egyptian walking onions

This strange onion variety produces clusters of small bulblets that appear in midair, sprouting from the top of tall stems in place of flowers. The plants can grow up to 4 ft (1.2 m) tall, and as the stems slowly bow down under their own weight, bulbs that make contact with the soil may take root and produce new plants for the following year. The onions are used for pickling or in cooked dishes.

	spring			summer			fall			winter		
	E	M	L	E	M	L	E	M	L	E	M	L
plant sets		■	■					■	■			
harvest						■						

Tree onions

Shallots

Shallots look much like small onions. They have yellowy-brown or red skins, and vary in shape from round and bulbous to long and torpedolike. Unlike onions, they grow in clumps rather than as single bulbs. Each shallot set you plant will divide and produce a handful of ten or so separate new bulbs. They are worth growing for their distinctive, somewhat sweet, slightly garlicky taste, and for the fact that they can be expensive to buy in the supermarket.

	spring			summer			fall			winter		
	E	M	L	E	M	L	E	M	L	E	M	L
plant outdoors	■											■
harvest					■	■						

Where to plant

Shallots do best in an open, sunny site with light, free-draining, nonacidic soil. If it's too heavy, add some sand or compost, and if it's too acidic, add some lime.

When to plant

Shallots can be grown either from seed or from commercially produced sets that are more likely to be virus-free than bulbs you might have saved from the previous year. Sets are easier to grow and more reliable than seeds. Plant sets in late winter or early spring. Sow seeds under cover in late winter, and transplant them in mid-spring, when the soil has begun to warm up. Sow seeds outdoors, straight into the ground, in mid- to late spring.

(top) **Sets** are easier to grow, but tend to produce a smaller crop.

(bottom) **Seeds** usually produce a larger crop than sets, but take a longer time to do so.

How to sow seeds

Sow seeds at a depth of about 1 in (2.5 cm), and thin to about ¾ in (2 cm) when shoots appear. When transplanting seedlings, space them about 2 in (5 cm) apart.

How to plant sets

Rake the soil to loosen it, and make a shallow furrow the length of your row. Gently press the sets into the furrow about 7 in (18 cm) apart, and draw the soil up around them so that the tips are just showing. Then water them in.

Routine care

Keep your shallots free of weeds if you want them to grow as large as possible. Once they are established, they should need watering only if the weather is very dry.

Harvesting

In mid- to late summer, once the leaves have turned yellow and died down, carefully lift the bulbs out of the soil and lay them out to dry—on the ground if it's not wet, or on wire racks that allow air to circulate.

Once they are completely dry, shallots can be stored indoors for several months. Stack them in single layers in slatted boxes, or braid into traditional strings and keep in a cool, dry place.

What can go wrong

Pests and diseases are the same as those that affect onions (*see p.128*). Downy mildew can be a particular problem.

Recommended shallots

Ambition, Golden Gourmet, Griselle, Jermor, Longor, Red Gourmet, Red Sun, Vigarmor, Yellow Moon, Zebrune

(top) **Red Sun** (bottom) **Golden Gourmet**

Green onions

Green onions—also called scallions, salad onions, or spring onions—are essentially junior, immature onions. They have bright green stems and leaves and small underdeveloped bulbs that are normally white, though occasionally red. Green onions are grown for harvesting while still young and are usually eaten raw in salads, grilled, or added to stir-fries. They can be sown in spring for harvesting throughout the summer, or in fall for harvesting during the following spring.

	spring			summer			fall			winter		
	E	M	L	E	M	L	E	M	L	E	M	L
sow outdoors	■	■	■	■	■	■	■					
harvest	■	■	■	■	■	■	■					

Where to plant

Like all onions, green onions do best in a sunny location in light soil that's not too acidic.

When to plant

Sow seeds directly into the ground at any time from early spring onward. However, don't sow them all at once. If you sow a handful every couple of weeks, you should have a continuous crop that will last throughout the summer.

If you sow seeds late in the summer or in early fall, seedlings will come up before the onset of winter, last through the cold weather, and produce a crop ready to pick in the following spring.

How to sow seeds

Make a shallow furrow in the soil and sow seeds directly into it about ½ in (1 cm) apart. Draw the soil over them so the seeds are ½–¾ in (1–2 cm) below the surface, then water.

Space rows at least 12 in (30 cm) apart to help discourage the spread of downy mildew.

Thinning closely planted green onions when they are still young will actually give you your first crop. Leave the remainder at a spacing of about 1 in (2.5 cm) apart and let them continue growing for a second harvest a few weeks later.

Routine care

Keep your rows free of weeds, and water regularly if the weather is dry. Plants that don't get enough water tend to develop bulbs that become too large.

Young plants grown from seeds sown in fall may need covering with cloches or fabric in cold winters.

Harvesting

Green onions are usually picked when they are about 6 in (15 cm) tall—around two months after planting. They can be left longer, but they will continue to grow and become stronger in taste.

What can go wrong

Pests and diseases are the same as those that affect all other onions (see p.128). Onion flies can be a particular problem.

Recommended green onions

SPRING-SOWN **Feast, Guardsman, Laser, North Holland Blood Red, White Lisbon**

FALL-SOWN **Eiffel, Ramrod, White Lisbon Winter Hardy**

(right, clockwise from top left)
White Lisbon, North Holland Blood Red, Laser

Garlic

Garlic is legendary for its health-giving, medicinal properties, for the unique flavor it gives to food, and (perhaps due to the aroma it imparts to the human breath) for its power to ward off vampires. Could anything be more useful? Moreover, growing garlic is about as easy as it gets. Break a "head" or bulb into cloves, plant them out individually, and in just a few months' time, each one should have grown into a new head of its own.

	spring			summer			fall			winter		
	E	M	L	E	M	L	E	M	L	E	M	L
plant outdoors								■	■	■	■	
harvest			■	■	■	■						

Where to plant

Garlic likes an open, sunny location and light, well-drained soil. If the soil is heavy, bulbs will tend to be small, and if it's too wet they may rot. Lighten heavy soils by digging in a little sharp sand or some well-rotted compost or manure.

When to plant

Garlic needs a cold spell at the start of its growing period, and some wet weather when it starts to develop leaves, so it's best sown in fall for harvesting the following summer. Garlic sown in the spring will grow, but probably not as large.

How to plant

It's better to buy special virus-free garlic from a nursery or garden center than to risk using bulbs bought from a supermarket. Separate the cloves and plant individually, pointed end upward, at roughly twice their own depth and about 7 in (18 cm) apart.

Routine care

Pretty much all you need to do is keep the weeds down and the soil moist. Never overwater the plants.

Some garlic varieties tend to bolt—that is, they try to produce flowers in order to seed themselves. If this happens, the bulbs will be smaller than you want. Prevent bolting by cutting down the flowering stem to about half its height a couple of weeks prior to harvesting.

PLANTING GARLIC IN MODULES

1 Separate a bulb into individual cloves, and remove the loose papery skin. Discard any damaged or diseased cloves.

2 Push one clove into each cell of a module flat and cover with potting mix so the tip is just hidden. Transplant when the cloves sprout.

(left) **Drying garlic bulbs** is essential if you want to store them without their rotting. Spread them out somewhere dry and well-ventilated, or braid them in strings and hang them up.

(right) **Elephant**

Harvesting

As soon as the leaves turn yellow and fade, the bulbs will be ready to harvest. For garlic that was planted in the fall, this will be in late spring or early summer. For spring-planted garlic, harvest between midsummer and early fall. Carefully lift the bulbs and let them dry out thoroughly, outdoors in the sun if the weather is dry or indoors if it is wet. Hang them in traditional braids.

Fresh or "green" garlic can be harvested earlier, before the leaves change color. It has a slightly milder taster but must be used quickly. Because it has not dried out, it will not keep.

What can go wrong

Pests and diseases are the same as those that affect onions *(see p.128)*. Leaves sometimes become discolored with rust, but it shouldn't affect the garlic heads themselves.

Recommended garlic

Softneck garlic does not produce a flower stem, stores well, and is usually milder tasting. Hardneck varieties do produce flower stems (which can be eaten as "scapes") and don't keep as long.

FALL PLANTING **Early Purple Wight, Elephant, Red Duke**

SPRING PLANTING **Picardy Wight, Tuscany Wight**

FALL/SPRING PLANTING **Germidour, Solent Wight**

Leeks

It's tempting to believe that leeks were specifically designed to take over and fill the gap left when the last remaining onions had been harvested. For this reason, they are invaluable in the kitchen garden. Choose the right varieties and, in mild climates, there's no reason why you shouldn't have homegrown leeks readily available from early fall right through winter and into the following spring—conveniently, just before your next crop of onions is ready. Leeks are members of the same family as onions but they differ in that they have longer, thicker stems or "shanks" and almost no bulb. It's the blanched white stems that are cooked and eaten.

	spring			summer			fall			winter		
	E	M	L	E	M	L	E	M	L	E	M	L
sow indoors											■	■
sow outdoors	■	■										
plant out				■	■	■						
harvest	■	■						■	■	■	■	■

Where to plant

Leeks are not particularly fussy, though they grow best in deep soil that has had lots of well-rotted compost or manure dug into it in advance. They also prefer neutral or slightly acidic soil. Don't grow leeks where you grew onions, shallots, or garlic the year before.

When to plant

Aim to sow successively through the year so that you have a continuous supply available. In early to mid-spring, once temperatures have reached a minimum of 45°F (7°C), sow early varieties for harvesting during late summer and fall, midseason varieties for harvesting in winter, and late varieties for the following spring.

Alternatively, you can get started sooner by sowing seeds in modules or multiblocks during the winter and keeping them under cover. Transplant the seedlings in mid-spring.

Harvest leeks shortly before you're ready to use them. Lift them with a fork and trim off the roots, taking care not to get soil in between the leaves.

Planting in deep, narrow holes protects seedlings from the light and produces long, white blanched stems

PLANTING OUT LEEK SEEDLINGS

1 Young leek seedlings growing in a seedbed can be transplanted when they are about as thick as a pencil. If the soil is dry and compacted, water it, then loosen the soil beneath the roots with a fork. Gently pull out the seedlings.

2 Bundle together a handful of seedlings, and with a sharp knife, trim the roots to about 1 in (2.5 cm), and the leaves to 6–8 in (15–20 cm).

3 Mark out a shallow furrow, and use a dibber to make a row of planting holes 6 in (15 cm) deep and 6 in (15 cm) apart. Put one seedling into each hole, ensuring that the roots sit on the bottom and the growing heart tip is level with the soil. Water the seedlings so the soil falls back loosely into the holes, giving the leeks room to grow.

How to sow seeds

Seeds can be sown either outdoors in an area of your garden reserved as a seedbed or indoors under cover. Outdoors, sow seeds thinly at a depth of about 1 in (2.5 cm). Seedlings should be ready to transplant to their final locations after about eight weeks.

Indoors, sow seeds into modules filled with fresh soilless or potting mix and don't let the temperature fall below 50°F (10°C). Harden off your seedlings before planting them out. Toward the end of winter, seeds sown in multiblocks and kept under cover should germinate and grow without extra heating.

Routine care

Water sparingly once plants are established, unless conditions are very dry. To encourage good growth, scatter some high-nitrogen fertilizer around the base of the plants in mid- and late summer, or in late winter. Earth up around the stems to help blanching.

Harvesting

Leeks can usually be harvested about four or five months after sowing, but you can leave them in the ground for much longer if you wish. They don't store well once they've been lifted, so if you need the space they're occupying, you can take them out and temporarily replant them elsewhere (a technique known as "heeling in").

What can go wrong

Leeks can suffer from most of the pests and diseases that afflict onions, shallots, and garlic (*see p.128*).

In recent years, attacks by **allium leaf miners** (*see p.326*) and **leek moths** (*see p.330*) have become more widespread. In both cases, their larvae tunnel into the leaves or stems. Rot sets in and affected leeks may become inedible or even die off completely.

Leek rust is a fungus that produces tiny orange blisters on the outer leaves. When these burst, they produce bright orange powdery spores, like rust. The disease isn't necessarily fatal, and your leeks may still be edible if you cut off and burn the affected leaves promptly. Don't grow leeks in the same spot next year.

Recommended leeks

Early leeks tend to be taller with longer and whiter stems; late-season leeks may be slightly shorter, darker, and tougher. Look for varieties that are resistant to rust.

Below Zero, Cairngorm, Hannibal, Lyon 2 – Prizetaker, Musselburgh, Northern Lights, Oarsman, Porbella, Toledo, Zermatt

(right) **Toledo**

(below) **Leeks that produce flowers** are said to have bolted; they do so in order to produce seed and propagate themselves. Bolting is more likely if a hot, dry fall follows a cool summer.

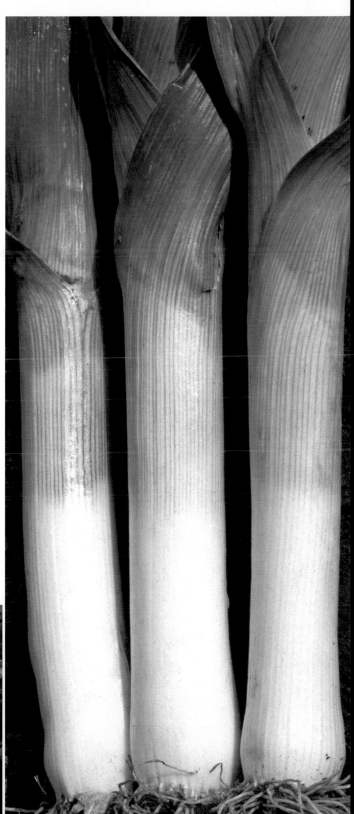

Peas & Beans

Peas, green beans, runner beans, fava beans, and a wide variety of other beans are all members of a family of vegetables called "legumes." They are all grown for their seeds and seedpods, which may be eaten raw when young but are usually cooked. Like many vegetables, peas and beans are at their tastiest and sweetest when eaten fresh—as soon as possible after being picked, before their natural sugars turn to starch. Pods for eating are best harvested when still small, before they turn tough and stringy. However, certain varieties—navy and kidney beans, for example—can also be dried and stored. Historically, this has always made them valuable as a source of food during the lean winter months. All peas and beans freeze well, too.

Runner beans need regular picking—two or three times a week when the harvest is at its peak.

1 **Peas** lose their flavor very quickly after being picked. The swifter the trip from your vegetable garden to your plate, the better.

2 **Green beans** have a bewildering array of different names: snap, string, Kenya, kidney, navy, borlotti, flageolet, and many more.

3 **Runner beans** are notorious for producing a glut, so don't plant too many. Pick them when young, before they turn tough and stringy.

4 **Fava beans** can be sown in the fall for a crop the following spring, or in spring for harvesting in the summer.

5 **Soybeans** are grown like green beans, but they need a warm climate. They produce short green pods covered with downy hair.

1

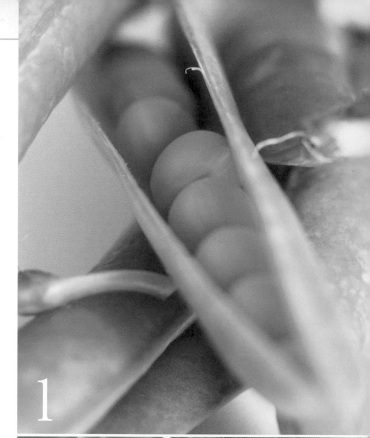

2

Peas

Peas are the perfect vegetable for home growing: they simply don't taste the same if bought from a store. Their flavor starts to deteriorate the moment they are picked, since their natural sugars immediately begin to turn to starch, so it's crucial to delay harvesting until just before you are ready to cook and eat them. The shorter and swifter the trip from vegetable garden to kitchen counter, the better.

Most peas are shelled from their pods before being cooked, but in the case of both snow peas and sugar (or snap) peas, the entire pods are eaten. The young growing shoots or tips are edible, too. In fact, peas can be grown solely for their shoots (*see p.148*).

There are numerous modern cultivars, each with different characteristics: early- and late-harvest varieties, a range of different colored flowers, green or purple pods, and so on. Peas vary in size, as well—from dwarf "petit pois" cultivars just a few inches high to tall climbing varieties that can grow up to 5 ft (1.5 m) or more.

	spring			summer			fall			winter		
	E	M	L	E	M	L	E	M	L	E	M	L
sow indoors									■		■	■
sow under cover							■					■
sow outdoors	■	■	■	■	■							
plant out	■	■	■									
harvest				■	■	■	■	■				

Where to plant

Peas fare best in an open, sunny site, but don't like very high temperatures. The soil should be neutral to slightly alkaline, ideally with a pH of 6.5–7 (*see p.21*), and shouldn't be prone to either drying out or waterlogging. Peas are hungry and need a rich soil, so dig in plenty of well-rotted compost or manure a while before you plant. However, because they have their own system of nitrogen-fixing root nodules—allowing them to convert and use nitrogen from the air—there is no need to treat them with nitrogenous fertilizers.

Crop rotation is important too: don't plant peas where you have grown them (or beans) in the previous couple of years.

Peas are attractive as well as productive, brightening up the vegetable garden with their colorful flowers.

When to plant

Seeds are usually sown successively from early spring through to early summer, either outdoors directly into the ground or in pots, modules, and containers under cover. Sow outdoors only when the temperature reaches about 50°F (10°C); if the soil is too wet and cold, seeds may rot or fail to germinate.

In areas with mild winters, it is also possible to sow in late fall or early winter. Protect plants from the cold with cloches or cold frames for an early crop the following year.

To support growing peas, erect a row of poles to act as fence posts supporting a length of plastic or wire netting. Plant peas in double rows at either side, and tie them in with string to provide extra support if necessary.

SOWING PEAS IN GUTTERS

Forget special seed flats, pots, and planting modules. A few standard lengths of rain gutter offer the perfect way to get peas off to an early start, and make it easier to transplant them straight out into prepared furrows as soon as the weather is warm enough.

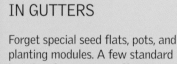

1 Half-fill the gutter with potting mix and sow seeds 2 in (5 cm) apart in two staggered rows. Cover with about 1 in (2.5 cm) of soil, then water, and keep the gutter under cover.

2 When your seedlings are about 3 in (8 cm) tall, dig a shallow furrow in the soil outside, and carefully slide the whole contents of the gutter—seedlings plus potting mix—into the furrow. Firm them down and water them in.

How to sow seeds

Early sowings are best made in pots, modules, or lengths of rain gutter (*see panel*) so that they can be kept under cover. They can then be transplanted outdoors once they've germinated, when the weather is warm enough.

When sowing directly into the ground, plant the seeds in a single row in a narrow furrow or in double rows in a wide furrow. Seeds should be 1½–2 in (4–5 cm) deep and at least 2 in (5 cm) apart; the space between each row should be the same as the eventual height of the plants.

Routine care

Most peas need some kind of support to prevent them from sprawling over the ground and being devoured by slugs and snails. They also need protection to keep off hungry birds.

Apart from some dwarf varieties, peas are natural climbers. They shoot out tendrils that

Pea sticks are an alternative support—once seedlings start to develop tendrils, push them into the ground at regular intervals along the rows. These not only act as a natural hedge for plants to climb, but they look good, too.

Harvest peas about three months after sowing, when you can feel the peas through the pods. To encourage a larger crop, pinch out the top shoot of each plant to stimulate the production of more pods, and harvest regularly.

wrap around whatever support they can find. Traditionally, gardeners have used "pea sticks," usually cut from hazel or birch, for them to climb up, but a framework of poles, string, and wire or plastic netting will do the job just as well, if not quite as attractively. Keep an eye out for cultivars that have been bred to be semileafless: the leaves are replaced by tendrils that mesh together and support the plant, removing the need for staking.

Birds, especially pigeons, love peas. The plants are at their most vulnerable when the seedlings start to show through the soil and while the plants are young. Covering your crop with netting is the only foolproof solution.

Don't overwater peas in the early stages of growth—this will encourage them to produce too many leaves. The time when they really need water is while they are flowering, and to some extent when the pods are fattening up.

Harvesting

Depending on the weather, peas are usually ready approximately three months after sowing, although it is always best to harvest them when they're still young. Use them immediately after you pick them, if at all possible, since the fresher they are, the sweeter they taste. If you do need to keep them in storage for a while, try to carry out all harvesting early in the morning when it is still cool, and put the peas straight into the refrigerator.

Pinching out the top shoot of each plant as soon as the first pods are ready, and then harvesting regularly, will encourage new pods to develop continuously and give you a larger crop overall.

Once harvesting has come to an end, cut the plants down to the ground but leave the roots in place so that the nitrogen they contain is absorbed into the soil.

GROWING TENDER PEA SHOOTS

It's possible to grow peas not just for their pods but also for their tender growing shoots or tips. The thin, delicate leaves and tendrils are crisp and fresh, and taste like snow peas. They can be used in salads or cooked quickly and lightly in stir-fries.

If you have the right conditions for raising them under cover, pea shoots can be grown year-round. They're best sown in large flats, shallow pots or containers, or even wooden fruit or wine boxes, filled with potting mix to a depth of at least 6 in (15 cm). Water the soil, and sow seeds generously, pushing them down 1 in (2.5 cm) beneath the surface.

Cover the containers, put them somewhere warm, and make sure the soil remains moist. Once the peas have germinated, uncover them and move to a cooler and lighter location. Spray them with water regularly and start picking when the seedlings are about 2 in (5 cm) tall. If you leave at least a couple of leaves on the stem of each plant, they should resprout and give you another crop.

What can go wrong

Pests

Birds may eat the young seedlings, and mice the seeds. Netting, wire covers, or a tangle of twigs for the former and setting mousetraps for the latter are the best preventative measures.

Pea moths may lay their eggs on the flowers. Tiny caterpillars with black heads and creamy white bodies then hatch inside the pods and feed on the peas. A serious infestation can ruin a whole crop. They're most prevalent right in the middle of the season, so if you can time your peas either earlier or later, you may avoid them. Alternatively, spray with an approved pesticide just after the flowers form to control young caterpillars.

Pea thrips are tiny black-brown insects that cause the pods to turn silvery brown, stunting their growth or flattening them, so that each may contain only one or two peas. Spray with pyrethrum or another approved pesticide.

Pea aphids inhibit growth and carry viruses. Spray with pyrethrum or another approved pesticide.

Diseases

Powdery mildew (*see p.322*) and downy mildew (*see p.321*) are quite common problems. They tend to get worse as the summer progresses, so sow early crops if you want to avoid them.

Pea leaf and pod spot is a fungal disease that causes brown or yellow markings on leaves and pods, and may kill plants. Fortunately, it is not common. Infected plants must be removed and burned or discarded to prevent the disease from spreading.

Recommended peas

Sow peas successively or plant different varieties to ensure that you have a crop throughout the season.

PEAS **Alderman, Ambassador, Douce Provence, Early Onward, Hurst Green Shaft, Kelvedon Wonder, Onward, Rondo**

SNOW PEAS **Golden Sweet, Oregon Sugar Pod, Shiraz**

SUGAR SNAP PEAS **Delikett, Sugar Ann, Sugar Snap**

(clockwise from top left)
Oregon Sugar Pod, Sugar Snap, Hurst Green Shaft, Kelvedon Wonder

Green beans

Green beans have a bewildering array of different names: French, snap, string, Kenya, kidney, navy, borlotti, and many more. They are actually not French at all: they originally came from the Americas. Some are climbers, some grow as dwarf bush plants, and others are somewhere in between. The pods may be long and thin (as in "filet" or "fine" varieties) or full and fat. They also come in a variety of colors: green, yellow, gold, purple, and red—or, in the case of "borlottis," a multicolored mix of purple, red, and green. The actual beans inside the pods can be a range of colors, too. Half-ripe beans are called or "cannellini" or "flageolets" and are shelled and eaten like peas. Navy and kidney beans are left to ripen fully and when dried can be stored for many months. Green beans are wind-pollinated, so they set seeds more reliably than runner beans, which need insects to pollinate them.

	spring			summer			fall			winter		
	E	M	L	E	M	L	E	M	L	E	M	L
sow indoors	■	■										
sow under cover			■									
sow outdoors			■	■	■							
plant out				■								
harvest					■	■	■	■	■			

Where to plant

Green beans prefer a warm and sunny location—and one that is sheltered from the wind, especially in the case of climbing varieties. They dislike extremes of both heat and cold—and frost will kill them off immediately, at either the start or the end of the season. They need fertile, moisture-retentive soil with a neutral to mild acidity—a pH of 5.5–7 (see p.21). If you've dug in plenty of well-rotted compost or manure before planting, they should be happy. If not, consider digging a "bean trench" (see p.156). Green beans store or "fix" nitrogen in special nodules on their roots, so they do not normally require additional nitrogenous fertilizer.

Follow a crop-rotation plan, and don't plant green beans where you have grown them (or any other beans or peas) during the previous couple of years.

Support dwarf or bush beans by heaping soil around the stems, known as "earthing up."

Tender borlotti beans should only be sown outdoors in late spring or early summer when all risk of frost has passed.

When to plant

Seeds can be sown successively at any time from early spring through to midsummer. However, they won't germinate unless the temperature is at least 54°F (12°C). Early in the year, sow indoors or under cover; later, sow directly into the ground only after the last frost. If necessary, warm up the soil in advance with cloches or plastic sheeting.

How to sow seeds

To start off plants under cover, sow seeds in deep pots or in long, biodegradable-paper tubes. Fill them with soilless potting mix, sow seeds at a depth of about 2 in (5 cm), and keep warm and moist. In early summer, when seedlings are about 3 in (8 cm) tall, harden them off and plant them out.

When the ground is warm enough, sow seeds directly into the soil at a depth of about 2 in (5 cm). Space dwarf plants about 6–9 in (15–22 cm) apart in staggered double rows. Put up supports for climbers, spaced so the plants will be about 12 in (30 cm) apart, and sow one or two seeds at the foot of each stake or pole.

Routine care

Spreading a mulch of organic matter around seedlings will help retain moisture and encourage growth. Climbers should find their own way up poles. Support dwarf or bush plants with twigs, pea sticks, or short poles pushed into the soil, or by earthing up slightly around the stems.

As soon as the flowers appear, give the plants more water, and be careful never to let the soil dry out.

(top) **Erect a simple tepee** support for climbing beans using poles or sturdy sticks and string.

(above) **Beans are best left to dry** on the plant, but in wet weather when there is a risk of rotting, spread them out on wire racks somewhere dry.

(right) **Store dried borlotti beans** in airtight containers after shelling—they will keep for several months.

Harvesting

Green beans should be ready for harvesting within two or three months of sowing. As soon as the pods begin to appear, start picking. The younger and smaller they are the better they taste. Keep picking regularly—two or three times a week. As long as there are still flowers on the plant, the more you pick, the more new pods will set.

The pods of cannellini beans, which are eaten shelled, can be left to grow larger before picking. And beans for drying should be left on the plant until the end of the season.

What can go wrong

Slugs and snails can be a problem and young seedlings should be protected against them (*see pp.324–325*). Blackflies or black bean aphids attack growing tips and young pods, and may need to be sprayed (*see pp.326–328*).

Diseases specifically affecting green beans include halo blight (*see p.322*) and foot and root rot (*see p.321*).

Recommended green beans

CLIMBERS **Blauhilde, Blue Lake, Cobra, Borlotto Lingua di Fuoco (or Firetongue), Helda, Hunter**

DWARF **Amethyst, Delinel, Endeavor, Golden Teepee, Maxi, Purple Teepee, Safari, Speedy**

(top) **Blue Lake**
(bottom) **Speedy**

Runner beans

Runner beans are so easy to grow that it's no surprise many gardeners grow far too many. This produces a glut: more runner beans than anyone can sensibly eat, let alone give away. They compound the problem by failing to pick the pods regularly. The result is a crop of unappetizing, large, tough, stringy beans that end up on the compost pile. The only answer is simply to resist planting very many—a short row or a couple of tepees should be plenty for the average family—and to be sure to harvest all the beans when they're small and young.

There are many varieties available. Most are climbers, although there are dwarf bush plants, too. Cultivars with red flowers (the archetypal "scarlet runner") tend to produce red or purple speckled beans, and those with white flowers produce white beans.

	spring			summer			fall			winter		
	E	M	L	E	M	L	E	M	L	E	M	L
sow indoors		■	■									
sow under cover			■									
sow outdoors				■	■							
plant out				■								
harvest					■	■	■	■				

Many modern runner bean cultivars are bred from both runner and green beans. They are self-pollinating, so their flowers set more reliably, and they produce smooth, stringless pods.

Where to plant

Runner beans like a warm, sunny location. They also need shelter from wind, especially varieties that climb very tall and are prone to becoming top heavy. The most important factor, however, is the soil. Runner beans have deep roots and need very fertile, moisture-retentive soil. Traditionally, they are planted in specially prepared bean trenches (*see p.156*), but any soil that has been well-maintained and fed regularly with well-rotted organic matter should suffice.

Be sure to follow a crop-rotation plan. Don't plant runner beans where you have grown them (or any other beans or peas) in the previous couple of years.

When to plant

It's possible to make two sowings per year—one in mid-spring for a midsummer harvest, and one in early or midsummer for a fall harvest. Seeds need a soil temperature of at least 54°F (12°C) before they will germinate, so don't sow outdoors too early, unless you have warmed up the soil with cloches or a covering of plastic. If you want to get ahead, sow indoors in pots and transplant only when there is no longer a danger of frost.

(above) **Pinch out the growing tips** when plants reach the top of supports to encourage sideshoots lower down.

(below left) **Tie in seedlings** by coiling them gently around the poles and then securing them with string.

(below right) **Construct tepees** from strong poles to stop fully laden bean plants from collapsing under their own weight.

DIGGING A BEAN TRENCH

A traditional bean trench is a great way of creating a super-rich bed for your runner beans—or any kind of bean. It should provide all the nutrients they need.

1 Dig a trench the length of your row. Make it 2–3 ft (60–90 cm) wide and up to 2 ft (60 cm) deep. Loosen the soil at the bottom with your fork so that it is not compacted.

2 Put any well-rotted manure and garden or household compost into the trench, cover with soil, and scatter over some pelleted poultry manure. Leave this to settle for at least two weeks before you begin planting.

How to sow seeds

Runner beans have deep roots, so if you are planting in pots, they must be deep ones. Long, biodegradable-paper "tube pots" are ideal. Fill with soilless mix or potting mix, sow seeds at a depth of about 2 in (5 cm), and keep well-watered and under cover. Harden off seedlings and transplant them in early summer.

Before sowing or transplanting directly into the ground, construct a support structure for your beans to climb. Use strong poles to make circular tepees or double rows crossed over at the top. Plant one seed 2 in (5 cm) deep at the foot of each pole.

Routine care

Mulching around seedlings helps to retain soil moisture and may deter slugs. Encourage seedlings to climb by twisting them gently around the poles. When they reach the top, pinch out their growing tips. As soon as the flowers appear, it's up to insects to pollinate them. Once the flowers have been pollinated you can encourage them to set, or produce pods, by watering generously, two or three times a week if the weather is dry. Letting the roots dry out at this crucial phase is the usual reason for a poor crop. White-flowered varieties are a good choice for later sowings, because they tend to set at higher temperatures.

Harvesting

As a rule of thumb, you can count on runner beans taking at least 100 days before they're ready to harvest. In practice, the most important task is to pick them before they get stringy and tough. And pick them often—twice or three times a week when the harvest is at its height. The more you pick, the more you get.

What can go wrong

Runner beans are usually trouble-free, although slugs (*see p.324*) are capable of stripping the young leaves from a whole row of seedlings overnight, and an infestation of black bean aphids or blackflies (*see pp.326–328*) can disfigure a whole plant. Diseases such as halo blight (*see p.322*) are mercifully rare. Foot and root rot (*see p.321*) can be discouraged through careful crop rotation.

Recommended runner beans

Enorma, Firestorm, Hestia (dwarf), Lady Di, Moonlight, Polestar, St George, Tenderstar, White Emergo, White Lady

(above) **White Emergo** (right) **Lady Di**

Fava beans

Traditionally, there were two different kinds of fava beans: Longpods, which had eight beans per pod, and Windsors, which had only four. It's still possible to find these varieties, but the majority of today's modern cultivars are bred to be somewhere between the two, producing shorter plants with more tender beans. Dwarf varieties are also available; these are ideal for growing in containers.

Like all peas and beans, the sooner you get the pods from your garden to your kitchen, the better they taste. They are sweeter and more succulent the fresher and younger they are. Indeed, if you pick them when they are still very young, then you can either shell the beans and eat them raw in salads, or cook the pods and eat them whole, like sugar snap peas. Remember that harvesting always encourages new growth, so the more frequently you pick, the more beans you'll get.

	spring			summer			fall			winter		
	E	M	L	E	M	L	E	M	L	E	M	L
sow indoors											■	■
sow under cover								■	■		■	■
sow outdoors	■	■						■	■			■
plant out	■	■										
harvest				■	■	■						

Where to plant

Fava beans are not too picky. They like fairly fertile, well-drained soil, and perhaps some shelter from strong winds. It's a good idea to dig in some well-rotted compost or manure before planting, but because the special nodules on their roots store, or fix, nitrogen, they're unlikely to need any extra nitrogenous fertilizer.

Employ a crop-rotation plan. Don't plant fava beans where you have recently grown them (or any other beans or peas).

(left) **For a fall sowing** that establishes quickly and produces an early crop, try growing 'Aquadulce Claudia'.

(right) **Prevent plants from sagging** under the weight of the pods by enclosing them within a ring of strong twine strung between bamboo poles.

(top) **Pinching out the growing tips** discourages aphids and encourages the plant to produce more bean pods.

(bottom) **Once harvesting is over**, cut down plants to just above ground level. But leave the roots in the soil—they are rich in nitrogen.

When to plant

Unless your winters are very cold, grow early fava beans by sowing seeds directly into the ground in late fall. You may lose a few plants to the cold (or to mice) but most should be hardy enough to overwinter and will give you a crop in late spring the following year. Fall sowings are likely to struggle in heavy, wet soil, so make sure your soil is suitable.

Alternatively, sow late varieties in spring—once the temperature reaches at least 41°F (5°C) and the soil becomes workable—for harvesting in summer.

How to sow seeds

Plant seeds about 2 in (5 cm) deep and about 9 in (23 cm) apart. Sow them either in blocks, or in single rows spaced 18 in (45 cm) apart or in staggered double rows 24 in (60 cm) apart. A few extra seeds planted at the end of each row will provide you with some spares that can be used to fill any gaps where seeds were eaten or failed to germinate.

Routine care

Keep the area well weeded and water regularly when flowers appear. Spreading mulch around seedlings will help retain moisture and encourage growth. As soon as the first flowers start to develop pods, pinch out the top growing shoot.

Tall varieties will need some support from stakes or poles and lengths of string. You can prevent dwarf varieties from trailing on the ground by using bamboo poles.

Harvesting

Pick the pods while they are still young, before the beans inside become too large. Harvest the lower beans first, those closest to the central stem; this will stimulate the remaining pods to continue growing. The beans are at their best when the membrane by which they are attached to the inside of the pod is still green or white, not brown or black.

Fava beans can be picked as baby vegetables, when they are no larger than your little finger; at this size, they can be cooked and eaten whole.

What can go wrong

Pests

Pea and bean weevils are tiny gray-brown insects that feed on the plants, leaving distinctive semicircular notches in the leaves. They're unsightly but rarely fatal. Spray with an approved pesticide only if the infestation is very heavy, but not when the plant is in flower or you may harm visiting bees.

Otherwise, blackflies or black bean aphids (*see pp.326–328*) are the most commonly encountered pests. They disfigure the plants and can stunt their growth. Pinching out the growing tips removes the tender young leaves that may attract them. Birds and mice are very partial to fava bean seeds, and you may have to net your plants if you suffer repeated raids.

Diseases

Chocolate spot is a fungus that causes brown spots on the leaves and brown streaks on stems and pods. It's most common on overwintering plants and in damp, humid weather. It can be discouraged by weeding regularly and by placing plants far enough apart to allow air to circulate freely.

Foot and root rot (*see p.321*) may sometimes be a problem.

Recommended fava beans

Aquadulce Claudia, Imperial Green Longpod, Jubilee Hysor, Masterpiece Green Longpod, Red Epicure, Stereo, Robin Hood, The Sutton

(top) **The Sutton**
(bottom) **Red Epicure**

UNUSUAL BEANS

(top) **Lima beans**
(bottom) **Black-eyed peas**

Lima beans

Also known as butter beans, these are flat pods containing large green or white beans. The plants are either dwarf bushes or climbers, and should be grown in the same way as green or runner beans. Bear in mind, though, that lima beans are tropical plants. The seeds will not germinate unless the temperature reaches 64°F (18°C), and they won't really grow well outdoors unless the summer is hot and they are in full sun.

	spring			summer			fall			winter		
	E	M	L	E	M	L	E	M	L	E	M	L
sow under cover		■	■				■					
plant out				■	■	■						
harvest						■	■					

Black-eyed peas

Black-eyed peas have numerous aliases: black-eyed beans, southern peas, crowder peas, cowpeas, field peas, and more. They originated in Africa but are now grown widely throughout the world—particularly in other warm climates such as the southern United States and Asia. Seeds won't germinate until the temperature reaches 70°F (21°C), and conditions must remain at least that warm throughout their two- to three-month growing season. Black-eyed peas can be harvested young and the beans shelled, cooked, and eaten fresh. Or the pods can be left on the plant to dry out, and the peas then stored.

	spring			summer			fall			winter		
	E	M	L	E	M	L	E	M	L	E	M	L
sow under cover		■	■				■					
plant out				■	■	■						
harvest				■	■	■	■					

Yardlong beans

As their name suggests, yardlong beans can grow to a yard (or meter) in length—though it's better to pick them when they're about half that long, before they become tough and stringy. They can then be eaten fresh or cooked, like green beans. Also known as asparagus beans or Chinese long beans, they're tropical plants and may be hard to grow outdoors in temperate climates. However, in mild areas they can be grown under fabric, under glass, or in a polytunnel—though they are climbers and do grow very tall.

	spring			summer			fall			winter		
	E	M	L	E	M	L	E	M	L	E	M	L
sow under cover		■	■				■					
plant out			■	■	■	■	■					
harvest					■	■	■	■	■	■		

Soybeans

Soybeans originated in Southeast Asia but are now grown as an important source of protein and oil all over the world. They usually need a warm climate, with hot summers and temperatures consistently between 68 and 86°F (20 and 30°C), but some modern cultivars will tolerate cool climates, under cover if necessary. They are grown like green beans, and produce short green pods covered with downy hairs. Once dry, the beans can be used in the same way as any other dried beans, but fresh pods can also be boiled or steamed whole, then the cooked beans shelled and eaten with salt as a snack—called "edamame" in Japan.

	spring			summer			fall			winter		
	E	M	L	E	M	L	E	M	L	E	M	L
sow under cover		■	■				■					
plant out				■	■	■						
harvest					■	■	■	■				

(top) **Yardlong beans**
(bottom) **Soybeans**

Salads

In truth, you can throw pretty much anything into a salad—as long as it's not too tough or too strong-tasting. But there are certain staples that it's hard to imagine doing without. Lettuces—in all their countless varieties—are one. Arugula is another. And, provided you like their distinctive bitter taste, endive and chicory as well. Then there are the less well-known leaves such as corn salad, purslane, and land cress, all of which can be harvested almost year-round in mild climates, and the numerous Asian salads such as mizuna, mibuna, komatsuna, and mustard greens, many of which have become readily available only in recent years.

Finally, for those cold, dark winter days when you'd rather stay indoors, there are sprouting seeds such as mustard and cress, mung beans, and alfalfa, which can be grown on a kitchen windowsill.

Baby leaf salad mixes provide a cut-and-come-again crop that will keep replenishing itself for several weeks.

1 **Lettuces** are easy to grow, as long as you can get seeds to germinate and prevent plants from bolting.

2 **Arugula** is a peppery, mustard-tasting salad leaf sometimes known as rocket, rucola, or roquette.

3 **Corn salad** is hardier than most lettuces and will last well into the winter.

4 **Purslane** can be eaten either raw as a salad or lightly cooked, like spinach.

5 **Mibuna** is just one of a range of Asian leaves that can be harvested when young for use in salads.

6 **Land cress** looks and tastes like watercress but can be grown on dry land rather than in or under water.

7 **Chicory**, whether blanched or not, tastes bitter. Even its most devoted fans accept it is an acquired taste.

8 **Endive** comes in two forms: a curly type ("frisée") and a broad-leaf one ("escarole" or "Batavian").

9 **Radishes** for salads are easy to grow and mature quickly. Winter radishes for cooking take longer but can be stored after harvesting.

10 **Sprouting seeds** like these alfalfa shoots can be grown indoors and need no more than water, warmth, air, and light.

Lettuce

There are four main types of lettuce, three of which form hearts (or heads) at their center. *Butter* lettuce is soft and round with either flat or frilly leaves. *Romaine* and semicos lettuces are upright and more oval in shape, with longer, crisper leaves; they are sometimes called cos lettuces. *Head* lettuce has round, dense heads and very crunchy leaves; at their most extreme, when their outer green leaves are removed, they are known as iceberg. And the fourth type, the *loose-leaf* lettuces, don't form a heart at all. Loose-leaf varieties can be grown as cut-and-come-again crops.

Lettuces are not hard to grow. The trickiest aspects are getting the seeds to germinate in the first place (they must not be too cold or too hot), preventing them from bolting (give them lots of water in hot weather), and avoiding a situation in which they're all ready to pick at once (sow seeds gradually, just a few at a time).

	spring			summer			fall			winter		
	E	M	L	E	M	L	E	M	L	E	M	L
sow indoors	■											■
sow under cover	■	■					■					
sow outdoors		■	■	■	■	■	■					
plant out		■	■									
harvest	■	■	■	■	■	■	■	■	■			

Where to plant

Lettuces are not too picky about soil, provided it retains moisture to prevent them from drying out. They don't like hot weather, so in summer they are happy to be in partial shade.

Crop rotation is an important consideration, too: don't plant lettuces where you've grown them in the last two years. It's also worth remembering that lettuce isn't part of any of the major crop rotation groups, so it comes in handy when filling in gaps.

(left) **Close planting** produces a dense leaf canopy that helps to suppress weeds by denying them any light.

(right) **Cut-and-come-again lettuces** can be harvested a handful of baby leaves at a time. Leave the stems in place and new leaves will regrow.

(top) **When transplanting lettuce seedlings**, plant them so the base of the leaves is just above the soil level. They may rot if planted too deeply.

(bottom) **A floating mulch** is a loose covering of fabric. It protects against frost and keeps out both insects and birds.

When to plant

Lettuces are easiest to grow if you sow seeds directly into the ground as soon as the soil has warmed up in the spring. However, don't sow them all at once. If you sow a handful every couple of weeks, you should have a continuous crop that will last you throughout the whole summer.

To achieve an early summer crop, sow under cover from winter to early spring, and then transplant. And for even earlier lettuces, choose hardy varieties that you can plant the preceding fall, protecting them with cloches or cold frames during the winter.

How to sow seeds

Outdoors, make a shallow furrow in the soil, sow seeds at a depth of about $\frac{1}{2}$ in (1 cm), then water them in. Avoid sowing when the weather is very hot; germination is more likely to be successful if you wait until late afternoon when the temperature has dropped. If you are sowing early or late in the year, use fabric, cloches, or cold frames to protect against the cold. As seedlings appear, gradually thin them out, leaving the strongest and healthiest to develop fully.

Either indoors or under cover, sow seeds in modules or biodegradable pots and then transplant them to their final location once they're established.

How to plant out seedlings

Seedlings are ready to transplant when they have four or five leaves. To prevent them from wilting, keep them moist, shade them from hot sun, and disturb the roots as little as possible.

Lettuces grow quickly—much faster than, say, Brussels sprouts, cabbages, or sweet corn—and you can sow and harvest them long before the slower-growing vegetables reach maturity. This is called "intercropping," and the vegetable that is harvested first (in this case the lettuce) is known as the "catch crop."

Routine care

Keep lettuces well weeded and well watered, especially in the period about a week or two before harvesting. Very hot weather and lack of water put plants under stress. They react by panicking—they desperately try to flower and produce seeds in order to propagate themselves before dying, an act known as "bolting." Lettuces that have bolted are too bitter to eat.

Harvesting

Butter, Romaine, and head lettuces all take longer from sowing to harvesting than loose-leaf lettuces—simply because they need additional time to develop hearts. Once the hearts are mature, pick them before they have a chance to bolt (if the weather is hot and dry) or to rot (if it is wet).

Loose-leaf lettuces can be harvested whole, or as a cut-and-come-again crop to give a steady supply of either fully grown or baby leaves throughout the growing season.

These lettuces are ideal catch crops because they can be grown and harvested long before the sweet corn reaches full size.

HARVESTING LOOSE-LEAF LETTUCES

1 Cut off the whole young lettuce about 1 in (2.5 cm) above the surface of the soil.

2 Within a few weeks, new leaves will have resprouted from the stump left behind in the ground; you may be able to get a second or even a third harvest.

What can go wrong

Pests

Slugs and snails (*see pp.324–325*) may eat young leaves and burrow into lettuce hearts. Leaves should be washed carefully before eating. Aphids (either blackfly or greenfly) can be a problem (*see p.326*). Roots are sometimes attacked by cutworms (*see p.328*), wireworms (*see p.333*), and leatherjackets (*see p.329*).

Lettuce root aphids are more serious. They feed on roots and cause any affected lettuces to wilt. A waxy white powder in the soil is one of the telltale signs. There are no permitted insecticides available, so it's best to grow resistant varieties.

Diseases

In wet weather, downy mildew (*see p.321*) might be a problem. ***Botrytis*** (gray mold) is a fungal rot that can damage leaves or even destroy whole plants; infections are at their worst in wet summers. Fluffy gray, off-white, or gray-brown mold appears on leaves. Spores are spread in the air or by rain or water splash, and usually enter the plant through damaged areas. Remove and destroy affected parts of the plant, and ensure the remaining plants have space for air to circulate freely.

Recommended lettuces

Loose-leaf lettuces for growing as cut-and-come-again crops are often sold in packets of mixed seeds. Mesclun is a type of salad mixture that may consist of lettuce, spinach, arugula, chard, mustard greens, or other leafy vegetables or herbs. Mixes include Mild Mesclun Mix, Spicy Mesclun Mix, and Mesclun Salad Mix.

BUTTER **All The Year Round, Clarion, Marvel Of Four Seasons, Sangria, Tom Thumb (mini)**

ROMAINE **Amaze, Little Gem (mini), Lobjoit's Green Cos, Maureen, Winter Density, Winter Gem**

HEAD **Black-Seeded Simpson, Lakeland, Match, Webb's Wonderful (Iceberg)**

LOOSE-LEAF **Green Salad Bowl, Red Salad Bowl, Lollo Bionda, Lollo Rossa**

(clockwise from top left)
**Lollo Rossa, Iceberg,
All The Year Round, Little Gem**

(top) **Bolting can occur** when plants are put under stress, often due to very hot weather and lack of water.

(bottom) **Winter lettuces** can be grown in cold frames for harvesting in spring.

Arugula

Arugula is a peppery, mustard-tasting salad leaf also known as rucola, rocket, and (pretentiously, unless you are French) roquette. There are two types: salad arugula and wild arugula. Both can be grown as cut-and-come-again crops, and are best eaten while the leaves are still young; the older they get, the more bitter they become.

Wild arugula has narrow leaves and a strong taste. It is slow-growing (and therefore slow to bolt in summer) and, because it's a perennial, it produces leaves throughout winter, provided it is protected from very low temperatures. Salad arugula has broader leaves and a slightly milder taste. It goes to flower very easily in summer, especially if it isn't well watered. The flowers can be eaten in salads, but they tend to be quite peppery.

	spring			summer			fall			winter		
	E	M	L	E	M	L	E	M	L	E	M	L
sow under cover	■	■					■					
sow outdoors			■	■	■	■						
harvest		■	■	■	■	■	■	■	■	■		

Salad arugula

Where to plant

Arugula is not fussy. It should grow in any fertile soil that retains moisture. However, it doesn't like hot sun and will be happy in partial shade.

When to plant

Sow seeds directly into the ground as soon as the soil has warmed up in the spring. Sow only a few seeds at a time. Repeated sowings every two or three weeks should provide you with a continuous crop.

How to sow seeds

Sow thinly in rows or blocks at a depth of about $1/2$ in (1 cm). If you are sowing early or late in the year, use fabric, cloches, or cold frames to protect against the cold. Arugula is a good candidate for growing in pots and containers, too.

Routine care

Keep arugula well watered—especially in hot, dry weather—to keep it from bolting for as long as possible.

Harvesting

Start picking young leaves as soon as they are as long as your thumb. The more you pick, the more will grow, so either cut a few leaves at a time or slice off the whole plant about $1\frac{1}{2}$ in (4 cm) above the surface of the soil and wait for another crop to sprout from the stump.

What can go wrong

Arugula is fairly indestructible. The biggest problems are likely to be caused by slugs and snails (*see pp.324–325*) when the seedlings are still young, and flea beetles (*see p.329*) as the plants grow larger. Flea beetles eat tiny round holes, like perforations, in the leaves. In the early stages, affected leaves are still edible, but they don't look very appetizing.

(top) **Wild arugula**

(bottom) **When arugula bolts**, it produces a mass of small, creamy white flowers. They are edible, but they taste very spicy.

Corn salad

Also known as lamb's lettuce or mache, corn salad is available in two forms: a large-leaf light-green variety that grows in the shape of a floppy rosette, and a more upright variety with smaller, darker-green leaves. Both types are mild-tasting and can be added to mixed salads throughout the summer. However, their real advantage is that they will last well into the winter and provide you with fresh salads when all your other lettuces are finished.

	spring			summer			fall			winter		
	E	M	L	E	M	L	E	M	L	E	M	L
sow under cover		■	■				■					
sow outdoors			■	■	■							
harvest	■	■	■	■	■	■	■	■	■	■	■	■

Where, when, and how to plant

Corn salad will grow pretty much anywhere. Sow seeds thinly, a few at a time, in rows or blocks at a depth of about ½ in (1 cm). Sow in late spring for harvesting in summer, or in late summer for harvesting during winter.

Routine care

Weed and water regularly, and thin out seedlings to 4–6 in (10–15 cm) if they are overcrowded.

Harvesting

In summer, pick the young leaves once they are large enough to handle—and continue picking them regularly to deter the plants from bolting. In winter, protect plants with cloches or cold frames, and allow them to grow a little larger.

What can go wrong

Corn salad is resistant to most pests and diseases. Any problems are likely to be caused by slugs and snails (*see pp.324–325*), aphids (*see p.326*), and rot or mildew in wet weather.

Recommended corn salad

Favor, Trophy, Valentin, Verte de Cambrai, Vit

Vit

Purslane

There are two separate kinds of purslane. *Summer purslane*, considered a weed in some areas, has thick, fleshy stalks and crunchy, lobelike leaves that are green or bright yellow-gold. *Winter purslane*—known as miner's lettuce or claytonia—has fleshy, heart-shaped leaves. Both make excellent cut-and-come-again salad-leaf vegetables, though they can also be lightly cooked and eaten like spinach. And both types are refreshingly easy to grow.

	spring			summer			fall			winter		
	F	M	L	E	M	L	E	M	L	E	M	L
sow outdoors		■	■	■	■	■						
harvest				■	■	■	■	■	■	■	■	■

Where, when, and how to plant

Purslanes like a well-drained site; they need water but may rot if they get waterlogged. They like sun but will tolerate partial shade.

Sow summer purslane outdoors between late spring and midsummer. Sow winter purslane in late summer for harvesting in fall and early winter. Scatter seeds thinly and cover with soil to a depth of about ½ in (1 cm).

Routine care

Weed and water regularly, and thin out the seedlings. Pick any flowers as soon as they appear to prevent the plants from bolting.

Harvesting

Both summer and winter purslanes can be harvested as cut-and-come-again crops. The more leaves you pick, the more will grow, as long as you leave a couple at the base of the plant. Winter purslane may self-seed to give you another crop the following year.

What can go wrong

Purslanes are usually problem-free. The most likely causes of trouble are slugs and snails (*see pp.324–325*), aphids (*see p.326*), and rot or mildew in wet weather.

(top) **Summer purslane** (bottom) **Winter purslane**

Asian salad leaves

These are all members of the Oriental brassica family (*see pp.76–77*). Like bok choy, choy sum, and their numerous other relatives, they can be allowed to grow until the leaves are quite large, then harvested, cooked, and eaten steamed, boiled, or stir-fried like spinach. However, when the leaves are still young—before they become tough and too peppery—they all make wonderful cut-and-come-again salad crops.

Asian salad leaves are easy to grow, are less prone to bolting than lettuces, and many are sufficiently hardy to withstand low fall and winter temperatures. They are therefore a valuable source of fresh, homegrown leaves for end-of-year salads and stir-fries.

Mizuna

Mizuna

Mizuna looks like a cross between arugula and a curly endive. Its feathery leaves are deeply serrated and grow in a loose, floppy rosette that reaches about 18 in (45 cm) across. They taste slightly mustardy or peppery and are at their best when fresh and young.

It's hard to fail with mizuna. It will survive both hot summers and cold winters, and is almost indestructible. Sow seeds outdoors a few at a time from late spring to early fall, or sow earlier in the spring under cover in modules and plant out later. Thin seedlings to 4 in (10 cm) for cut-and-come-again salad crops and to 18 in (45 cm) apart for larger plants intended for cooking. If necessary, protect against slugs (*see pp.324–325*) and flea beetles (*see p.329*).

	spring			summer			fall			winter		
	E	M	L	E	M	L	E	M	L	E	M	L
sow			■	■	■	■	■					
plant out			■	■								
harvest				■	■	■	■	■	■	■	■	■

Mibuna

Mibuna is closely related to mizuna but has wider, more rounded leaves without serrations that grow to about 6 in (15 cm) in length. Mibuna has a mild peppery taste not unlike arugula—but not as strong when mature. It is as easy to grow as mizuna and is very nearly as hardy. It's not prone to bolting in summer (as long as you keep it watered) and will withstand cold in all but the most severe winters. Grow and harvest in the same way as mizuna.

	spring			summer			fall			winter		
	E	M	L	E	M	L	E	M	L	E	M	L
sow		■	■	■	■	■	■					
plant out			■	■								
harvest				■	■	■	■	■	■	■	■	■

Komatsuna

Komatsuna

Also known as mustard spinach or spinach mustard, komatsuna is a generic term for a number of leafy vegetables that all share the same characteristics: they produce clumps of upright dark green or red leaves that taste midway between spinach and cabbage, with a mild mustardy tang.

Komatsuna is not hard to grow. Sow outdoors in spring and summer, or under cover in fall and winter, at a depth of $1/2$ in (1 cm). Thin seedlings to 4 in (10 cm) for cut-and-come-again salad crops or 18 in (45 cm) for larger plants. Some varieties survive temperatures as low as 10°F (−12°C) and can be harvested throughout winter; others need protection with cloches or frames.

	spring			summer			fall			winter		
	E	M	L	E	M	L	E	M	L	E	M	L
sow under cover									■	■	■	■
sow outdoors			■	■	■	■	■					
plant out			■									
harvest	■	■	■	■	■	■	■	■	■	■	■	■

Mustard greens

Also known as Asian or leaf mustards, these vegetables have large green, red, or purple leaves that may be smooth, crinkled, or curly. The young leaves give salads a welcome mustardy kick, but as they age, the taste becomes stronger and they're better when cooked.

Sow seeds under cover in modules in late spring or outdoors directly into the ground from early summer onward. Keep plants warm and well watered to discourage them from bolting. Start harvesting young leaves within a couple of months; more will grow to replace them. Some varieties will survive well into the fall and winter.

	spring			summer			fall			winter		
	E	M	L	E	M	L	E	M	L	E	M	L
sow under cover		■	■		■							
sow outdoors				■	■	■						
plant out				■	■	■						
harvest						■	■	■	■	■	■	■

Land cress

Also known as American or upland cress, land cress looks and tastes like watercress. Its big advantage, however, is that unlike watercress, it can be grown on dry land rather than in water. It is easy to grow, provided you water it generously and don't let it bake in hot sun, and once established it should self-seed to provide you with new plants year on year. It can be eaten raw or cooked.

	spring			summer			fall			winter		
	E	M	L	E	M	L	E	M	L	E	M	L
sow outdoors				■	■	■						
harvest	■	■	■	■	■	■	■	■	■	■	■	■

Where, when, and how to plant

Land cress needs a soil that stays moist and does not dry out, so dig in plenty of well-rotted organic material well in advance. It prefers to be out of full sun, in a sheltered, shady spot. Sow seeds outdoors in spring for picking in early summer, and again in late summer for harvesting in fall and winter. Scatter seeds thinly and cover with soil to a depth of about ½ in (1 cm).

Routine care

Thin out seedlings, and water regularly and generously to prevent leaves from becoming tough and too peppery to eat. In fall and winter, protect plants with cloches or cold frames.

Harvesting

Harvest land cress as a cut-and-come-again crop. The first leaves should be ready to pick within two months of sowing.

What can go wrong

Slugs and snails (*see pp.324–325*) may attack new seedlings, and flea beetles (*see p.329*) can pepper the leaves with their trademark tiny round holes.

Land cress is one of the few vegetables that positively prefers to be grown in shade.

Chicory

There are three types of chicory. *Belgian* or *Witloof* takes the form of elongated, fat "chicons" of crisp white leaf shoots that have been forced and blanched in order to make them less bitter. *Red chicory* or *radicchio* usually forms tight, dense hearts, rather like small head lettuces. And *sugarloaf* chicory has green leaves and forms larger, looser heads, more like Romaine lettuces. Neither of the latter needs forcing, since their inner leaves are naturally blanched.

All chicory, blanched or not, is bitter and even its most devoted fans would accept that it is an acquired taste. It tends to be something that either you like or you don't. It's worth pointing out, however, that chicory you grow and force yourself is usually less bitter than the packaged chicory you buy at the store. By the time you get them home, they have already been exposed to so much light that the benefits of blanching will have begun to wear off.

	spring			summer			fall			winter		
	E	M	L	E	M	L	E	M	L	E	M	L
Witloof/Belgian chicory												
sow outdoors		■	■									
lift roots							■	■	■			
harvest forced	■										■	■
Sugarloaf chicory and Radicchio												
sow indoors		■	■									
sow outdoors				■	■	■						
plant out				■								
harvest						■	■	■	■			

"Blanching helps to reduce chicory's bitter taste."

Sugarloaf chicory has a loose head, so its outer leaves will be more bitter than the tightly compacted inner ones.

FORCING AND BLANCHING CHICORY

Belgian chicory needs to be forced to reduce its bitter taste and produce its characteristic white, blanched shoots or chicons. This can be done while the plants are still in the ground, by cutting off the leaves and earthing up around the stumps, but it's more successfully done by lifting them, replanting in containers, bringing them indoors, and covering them up.

1 Dig up the mature plants after the first frost, in late fall or early winter.

2 Cut off all the leaves about 1 in (2.5 cm) above the crown. Chop off the bottom of the root to leave an 8–9-in (20–22-cm) length.

3 Plant three trimmed roots upright in a 10-in (25-cm) pot full of moist potting mix so that the crowns are showing just above the surface. Place a second pot over the top, and cover any drainage holes with paper or burlap so light cannot enter.

4 Keep the pot in a warm, dark place until the blanched chicons are ready to harvest in three or four weeks.

Where to plant

Chicory is extremely accommodating. It grows happily in almost any kind of soil, even in poor, relatively infertile ground. And although it likes sun, it will tolerate partial shade.

When to plant

Chicory is best grown by sowing seeds directly into the ground between late spring and midsummer. Don't sow any earlier or your plants may bolt.

Belgian chicory is usually lifted in the fall, so that it can be forced and blanched. Red and sugarloaf chicory, which do not need forcing, are left in the ground for harvesting from late summer right through to early winter.

How to sow seeds

Sow seeds thinly at a depth of about ½ in (1 cm) in blocks or rows at least 12 in (30 cm) apart. Thin out the seedlings, to about 9 in (23 cm) for Belgian chicory, and about 12 in (30 cm) for red and sugarloaf varieties.

Routine care

Weed and water regularly, ensuring that the soil doesn't dry out.

Before it is forced, Belgian chicory looks alarmingly like a giant dandelion. Red and sugarloaf chicory look much more promising— more like Romaine or head lettuces.

Harvesting

Cut chicons of forced Belgian chicory when they are about 6 in (15 cm) high. If you leave the stumps in place and cover the pot again, you may get a second harvest.

Red and sugarloaf chicory are quite hardy, and although they may be ready to harvest in late summer, they can be left in the ground for longer—they may even survive a light frost. They keep well, too, and can be stored for several weeks after cutting if kept somewhere cool and dry.

What can go wrong

Slugs and snails (*see pp.324–325*) may eat young leaves and find their way into the hearts of red and sugarloaf chicory. Leaves should be washed carefully before eating. Aphids (either blackfly or greenfly) can be a problem, too (*see p.326*). Attacks by lettuce root aphids (*see p.172*) are less common but can be more serious.

Recommended chicory

BELGIAN/WITLOOF **Apollo, Zoom**

RED/RADICCHIO **Firestorm, Palla Rossa, Rossa di Treviso**

SUGARLOAF **Grumolo Verde, Variegato di Castelfranco**

(top) **Witloof** will grow a tight, cigar-shaped head of blanched white leaves if the root is lifted, trimmed, replanted, and kept under cover in the dark.

(bottom) **Palla Rossa**

Endive

To put it bluntly, endive tastes like an extremely bitter lettuce. Yet not everyone finds it unpleasant. To some, the bitterness is an attractive component in a mixed salad—and if it is too overpowering, it can be reduced by artificially blanching or whitening the leaves.

Technically, endive is a form of leaf chicory—one that grows in a flat, spreading rosette shape. It comes in two forms. The curly type has thin, frilly leaves and is often called "frisée" (or, confusingly, "chicory."). The broad-leaf type has larger, flatter leaves and may be called "escarole" or "Batavian."

	spring			summer			fall			winter		
	E	M	L	E	M	L	E	M	L	E	M	L
sow indoors		■	■									
sow outdoors				■	■							
plant out				■	■							
harvest	■						■	■	■	■	■	■

BLANCHING CURLY ENDIVES

Covering endive plants in order to exclude light blanches or whitens the leaves and makes them less bitter.

1 Shortly before the plant is ready to harvest, cover it with a plate. It must be completely dry or it may rot. Protect against slugs at the same time.

2 After about ten days, the center should have turned white or pale yellow.

Where to plant
Endives are not too picky about the soil in which they grow, as long as it retains moisture and doesn't dry out. They like sun but will tolerate partial shade, too.

When to plant
Either sow seeds outdoors directly into the ground in early summer, or sow under cover in spring and plant out seedlings in early or midsummer. Don't plant too early or the cold weather may encourage your plants to bolt.

How to sow seeds
Sow seeds thinly at a depth of about $1/2$ in (1 cm) either in blocks or in rows 10–15 in (25–38 cm) apart. Thin out seedlings—to about 9 in (23 cm) for compact varieties and about 15 in (38 cm) for larger, spreading varieties.

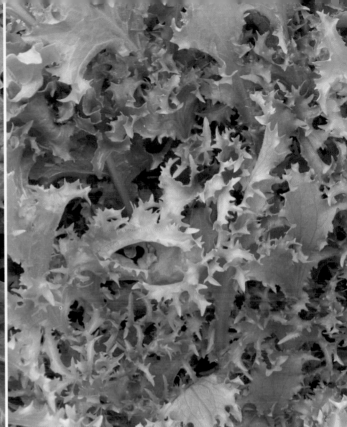

(left) **Cornet de Bordeaux** (right) **Pancalieri**

Routine care

Weed and water regularly, ensuring that the soil doesn't dry out. Blanch curly endives by covering them, and broad-leaf ones by bunching up the leaves and tying them with string.

Harvesting

Either pick a few leaves at a time or cut off the whole head just above the surface of the soil. If you leave the stumps in place, they may resprout. As the temperature drops at the end of the year, cover with frames or cloches to extend the harvest into fall and winter.

What can go wrong

Slugs (*see pp.324–325*) are likely to be the biggest enemy. They seem irresistibly drawn to endives.

Aphids (*see p.326*), caterpillars (*see p.328*), and lettuce root aphids (*see p.172*) may be a problem, too.

Recommended endives

CURLY/FRISEE **Frenzy, Pancalieri, Wallonne**

BROAD-LEAVED/BATAVIAN **Cornet de Bordeaux, Natacha**

Radishes

It's easy to take radishes for granted. We're all more than familiar with the small, crunchy pink- or scarlet-colored roots that are a standard ingredient of so many summer salads. Yet they are only a tiny part of the story. In fact, there are hundreds of different varieties: white, yellow, purple, and black versions of regular salad radishes; white Asian mooli (or daikon) radishes that can grow as long as 24 in (60 cm) and weigh up to 4½ lb (2 kg); and large turnip-sized winter radishes, which are often cooked or pickled. Summer radishes are easy to grow, mature quickly, and are best eaten raw when crisp and young. Winter radishes take longer, and can be stored after harvesting.

	spring			summer			fall			winter		
	E	M	L	E	M	L	E	M	L	E	M	L
Summer radishes												
sow indoors										■	■	
sow under cover	■											
sow outdoors		■	■	■	■	■						
plant out		■										
harvest			■	■	■	■	■	■				
Winter radishes												
sow outdoors					■	■						
harvest								■	■	■	■	

Fast-growing radishes can be intersown with another, slower-growing crop. Harvest them carefully, without disturbing the seedlings that remain.

Where to plant

Radishes will grow in any moist and reasonably fertile soil, although not on sites that have been freshly manured. In summer, they are happy in partial shade and have no objection to being planted between or around other crops.

When to plant

Sow seeds of summer radishes directly into the ground from early spring onward, as soon as the soil has warmed up.

Sow winter radish seeds in mid- to late summer—not too early or they will bolt.

How to sow seeds

Sow a few seeds at a time, every couple of weeks. Sow thinly in rows or blocks at a depth of about ½ in (1 cm). Thin seedlings before they get too lanky; summer radishes should be thinned to about 1 in (2.5 cm) apart, and winter radishes to at least 6 in (15 cm) apart.

Routine care

Water regularly—especially in hot, dry weather—but don't overdo it or you will just encourage too much leaf growth.

Harvesting

Summer radishes should be ready to pick within a month or so of sowing. Don't let them get too big or they will become woody and taste too strong. Winter radishes grow much larger and take longer to mature; they can be left in the ground well into the fall and even throughout winter if the soil isn't too heavy, although they will need protection from hard frost.

What can go wrong

Flea beetles (*see p.329*) can riddle the leaves with tiny round holes, though they very rarely damage the radishes themselves. Slugs and snails (*see pp.324–325*) may nibble at the roots, which may still be edible even if they don't look very appetizing.

Winter radishes can be affected by cabbage root flies (*see p.61*) and by clubroot (*see p.62*). To reduce the risk, crop rotate them in the same cycle as cabbages and other brassicas.

Recommended radishes

SUMMER RADISHES **Amethyst, Cherry Belle, French Breakfast, Munchen Bier (edible pods), Purple Plum, Scarlet Globe, Sparkler, Ziata**

WINTER RADISHES **April Cross, Black Spanish Long, Black Spanish Round, China Rose, Mantanghong, Neptune**

(top) **Mantanghong** (bottom) **French Breakfast**

Sprouting seeds

Here's a way to grow vegetables that's as easy as it gets: no garden, no soil, no rain, no sun, and no digging or weeding! The seeds of beans, legumes, and leaf vegetables are like miniature superfood capsules, packed with nutrients such as vitamins, enzymes, and proteins. Sprouting these releases all this healthy goodness and produces some of the freshest, tastiest salad ingredients you'll ever eat.

SPROUTING IN JARS

1 **Wash the seeds** in cold water, let them soak overnight, then rinse and drain them again.

2 **Rinse and drain** twice a day until the sprouts are ready to eat. Once dry, they can be stored in the refrigerator for up to five days.

Most seeds need nothing more than water, warmth, air, and some light to break their dormancy and encourage them to sprout. There are three ways of doing this: spreading them out in trays lined with damp paper, storing them in jars with perforated lids, or suspending them in water-permeable bags. In addition, it is possible to buy specially designed sprouters, some with built-in automatic water sprays.

Beans and peas usually take two to three days, while seeds like alfalfa and fenugreek take three to five days. Most seeds germinate more quickly if they are first soaked in water overnight. Thereafter, they need to be kept warm and moist, and with enough air around them to prevent them from rotting.

Sprouting in trays

Put a few layers of newspaper or paper towels in the bottom of a flat tray. Soak with water and pour off any excess. Scatter seed thinly over the surface. Put the tray somewhere warm, and keep it moist.

Sprouting in jars

Put a small handful of seeds in a clean jar—not too many, since they will expand. Fill with water to wash them, add a perforated lid, then pour out the water. Store the jar somewhere warm, set at an angle so the seeds don't get waterlogged. Refill and drain it twice a day.

Sprout bags

Place a handful of seeds in a porous bag made of hemp, flax, or linen. Dip the bag in water, let it drain, and then hang it up somewhere warm. Dip and drain again twice a day.

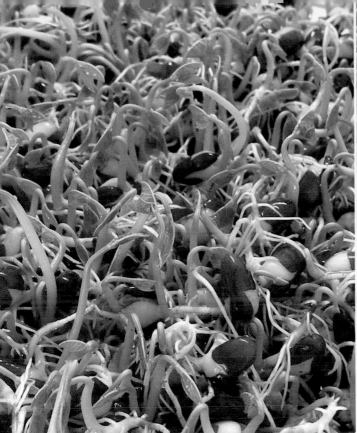 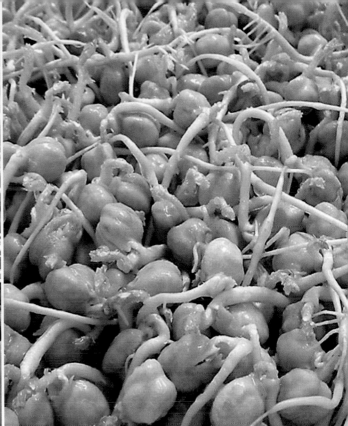

(left) **Mung beans** (right) **Garbanzos**

Mustard and cress Cress is available in plain- or curled-leaf forms. Both have a peppery taste. In commercially sold packets of mixed seed, mustard may be replaced by salad rape. Grow mustard and cress in trays: it's too sticky and gooey for jars or bags.

Mung beans Green mung beans produce the familiar Chinese bean sprouts for use in salads and stir-fries. They will grow to about 2 in (5 cm) long.

Adzuki beans Also known as aduki, these red-brown beans are related to mung beans but produce slightly nuttier, shorter sprouts.

Alfalfa Very fine, wispy, white sprouts with a mild, slightly nutty taste and a very high protein content.

Broccoli Thin white sprouts with green leaves that are similar in both taste and appearance to alfalfa. Reputed to have powerful health-giving properties.

Garbanzos (chick peas) Sweet, nutty sprouts best eaten when small and crunchy.

Fenugreek Long white shoots with green leaves and a distinctive curry flavor that is most spicy when the seeds first sprout.

Fruiting Vegetables

These vegetables are all grown for their fruits rather than for their leaves, stems, or roots. Many originate in tropical or subtropical climates and need warm, humid growing conditions. They take a relatively long time to mature, too; without a long, hot summer, it may be a battle to ensure that they ripen fully. For this reason, in temperate zones where summers are likely to be cool and short, they are often grown in greenhouses or polytunnels. Even those grown outdoors are usually started off under cover so that seeds germinate and seedlings begin to develop as early in the year as possible. Alternatively, ready-grown plants can be bought from most garden centers and planted out in late spring or early summer, once all danger of frost has passed.

Homegrown tomatoes ripened on the vine and warmed by the sun have a flavor that is very hard to beat.

1 **Eggplant** are best picked when they are at their shiniest. They can turn bitter once they lose their shine.

2 **Chili peppers** gradually change color and becoming increasingly hot as they ripen.

3 **Sweet corn** is available in modern "supersweet" varieties that taste sweeter than traditional cultivars.

4 **Tomatoes** taste best if you are able to leave them on the vine until they are fully ripe and ready to eat.

5 **Tomatillos** are relatives of the Cape gooseberry and are grown in the same way as tomatoes.

6 **Okra** forms slender, pod-shaped fruits—often referred to as ladies' fingers—full of round, white seeds.

3

5

4

6

Eggplant

The eggplant with which we are most familiar is smooth, shiny, and a deep purple, almost black, color. It may be long and slender, pear-shaped, or almost circular. But other varieties are creamy white (which probably explains where the name "eggplant" comes from), pale lilac, streaky violet, even yellow or red. All of them originally come from the warm, humid conditions of the tropics or subtropics, so they are hard to grow outdoors in cool temperate climates. However, choose the right variety and you might be fortunate—if you're blessed with a long, hot summer. Otherwise, grow them in containers or growing bags on a sheltered patio, preferably against a warm, south-facing wall, or in a greenhouse or polytunnel.

	spring			summer			fall			winter		
	E	M	L	E	M	L	E	M	L	E	M	L
sow indoors	■	■										
plant out			■	■								
harvest					■	■	■	■				

Bonica

Where to plant

The most important requirement is a sunny, sheltered site. Eggplant need warmth, and without it they won't produce good-sized fruit. They also need deep, fertile, well-drained soil.

When to plant

Eggplant have a long growing season—at least five months between sowing and harvest—so get ahead as early in the year as you can. Seeds may not germinate if the temperature is below 70°F (21°C), so in early or mid-spring, start them off indoors or under cover. They can be planted out in late spring or early summer, depending on the climate.

How to sow seeds

Before sowing, soak seeds in warm water for a day to encourage germination. Sow thinly in seed flats and keep in a propagator at 70–86°F (21–30°C) until they germinate. Thereafter, keep the flats somewhere humid and don't let

(left) **Eggplant flowers**, if successfully fertilized, should each produce a tiny fruit that will grow into a full-size eggplant.

(right) **Harvest eggplants** so that at least 1 in (2.5 cm) of the stem is left on the fruit.

Pinstripe

them get any colder than 64°F (18°C) in the day and 60°F (16°C) at night. When the seedlings are 2 in (5 cm) tall, prick out into individual pots, modules, or biodegradable tube pots.

How to plant out seedlings

Once the first flowers appear, by which time the seedlings should be 3–4 in (8–10 cm) tall, harden them off by moving them outside during the day. Once the risk of frost has passed, plant them out about 24–30 in (60–75 cm) apart.

Routine care

Keep the plants well-weeded and well-watered. Eggplants need high humidity, so don't let them dry out. A layer of mulch will help. Pinch out the growing tip to encourage bushy growth. Once the fruit begins to set, water with a general fertilizer or liquid tomato fertilizer every two weeks. Stake the plants if necessary.

Harvesting

Pick eggplant when they're at their most shiny. As they lose their shine and start to show signs of wrinkling, the fruits tend to turn bitter.

What can go wrong

Eggplant grown outdoors are generally healthy, provided conditions are warm and humid enough. Aphids (*see p.326*) are probably the most troublesome pest. Under cover, plants might suffer from infestations of spider mites, whiteflies, mealybugs, and caterpillars (*see pp.328–333*).

Recommended eggplant

For growing outdoors, choose varieties suited to cooler conditions. Grafted plants may be stronger and less prone to disease.

Black Beauty, Bonica, Clara, Long Purple, Moneymaker, Ophelia, Pinstripe

Peppers and chilies

All peppers are members of the capsicum family. Sweet or bell peppers are the large variety. They can grow up to 9 in (23 cm) in length and are green when young, ripening to yellow, orange, and red or even dark purple when fully ripe. The riper they are, the sweeter they taste. Chili peppers are much smaller, but what they lack in size they make up for in heat: they can be eye-wateringly hot. Peppers are tropical and subtropical plants. They need heat and humidity in order to grow well; if you're raising them from seed, you'll certainly need to start them off indoors or under cover. In a bad summer you may find that only a few fruit ripen fully before the onset of fall.

They can be grown in the ground, but they make perfect container plants, especially if you can place them in a warm, sunny, sheltered spot.

	spring			summer			fall			winter		
	E	M	L	E	M	L	E	M	L	E	M	L
sow indoors	■	■										
plant out				■	■							
harvest						■	■	■	■			

Where to plant

Peppers need heat and humidity, so choose a sheltered and sunny area, whether you're growing them in the ground or in containers, and be prepared to cover them if the weather turns cold. They like light, fertile soil that retains moisture.

When to plant

The earlier in the season you can start, the better your chances that the fruit will ripen fully later on in the year. Peppers need warmth to germinate reliably, so sow indoors or in a heated greenhouse in early spring, and outdoors under cover a few weeks later, in mid-spring. Plant them out into large pots or into the ground either in late spring or in early summer—make sure that there is no risk of frost when you do so.

Chili peppers range from mild to scorching hot. Of course, aficionados will tell you that it's not just about heat. It's about taste, too...

"The ideal specimen is **firm** and **waxy** to the touch."

How to sow seeds

Sow seeds thinly in seed flats or modules and maintain them at a temperature of 64–70°F (18–21°C) until they germinate. Thereafter, ensure that the soil does not dry out and don't let them get any colder than 64°F (18°C) during the day and 61°F (16°C) at night.

When your seedlings develop leaves that are large enough to handle, carefully prick them out—first into individual 3–3½-in (6–9-cm) pots, and then a few weeks later, when the plants are about 3½–4 in (8–10 cm) tall, into larger 8–9-in (21–23-cm) pots.

How to plant out seedlings

Once any danger of frost has passed, and you have hardened off the seedlings by moving them outside during the day, transplant them into growing bags, large containers, or directly into the ground. Space sweet peppers at least 20 in (50 cm) apart; chili pepper plants, which don't grow as large, can be a little closer.

Grafted chili and sweet pepper plants are now available. These are young seedlings of selected varieties grafted onto vigorous, disease-resistant rootstocks. The plants are claimed to grow more strongly and produce better crops.

(left) **Chilies form and ripen** at different rates on the same plant, so at any one time, each should carry both green and red fruit.

(right) **Sweet peppers change color** as they ripen—usually from green to red. Fully ripe red peppers taste sweeter than immature green ones.

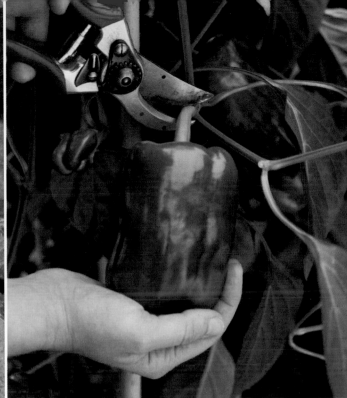

(left) **Chilies become hotter** the riper they get. Indeed, some varieties may become so hot that you need gloves to handle them. Green and yellow ones such as these are probably safe.

(right) **Cut sweet peppers** so that 1 in (2.5 cm) of the stalk remains on the fruit. Eat them promptly; as with peas and sweet corn, the sugar they contain begins to turn to starch after harvesting.

Routine care

Weed and water on a regular basis. If you allow your plants to dry out, the flower buds and leaves may drop off. A layer of mulch will help prevent moisture in the soil from evaporating. As soon as the fruit begins to set, water with a general fertilizer or liquid tomato fertilizer every two weeks.

Stake up the plants to give them a degree of support if they need it and to keep the peppers from trailing on the ground. Place three or four poles around each plant in a sort of upside-down tepee shape, and loosely tie in the stems with string.

Harvesting

Deciding when to harvest is a bit of a balancing act. If you pick the peppers when they're green, the plant will go on producing lots more fruit so you'll get a bigger harvest. If you resist picking them until they've ripened to red, the fruits will be sweeter and better-tasting—but you'll have fewer of them.

What can go wrong

Aphids (*see p.326*) are a common problem, and you may need to spray with pyrethrum or insecticidal soap if you get a bad attack. Under cover, peppers can suffer from infestations of spider mites (*see p.331*) and whiteflies (*see p.333*).

Recommended sweet peppers

For growing outdoors in temperate climates, look for varieties that are suited to cooler conditions. Grafted plants may be stronger and less prone to disease.

California Wonder, Gourmet, Gypsy, King of the North, Lany, Marconi Rosso, Mohawk, Redskin, Snackbite, Thor

Recommended chili peppers

Apache, Basket of Fire, Cayenne, Cheyenne, Demon Red, Fuego, Gusto, Habanero, Hungarian Hot Wax, Jalapeno, Joe's Long, Loco, Padron, Paper Lantern, Pot Black, Prairie Fire, Ring o' Fire, Super Chili, Tabasco

(clockwise from top left)
sweet peppers: **Gypsy, Mohawk**
chilies: **Jalapeño, Habanero**

HOW HOT IS HOT?

All chilies are hot, but they range from the mildly warm to the frankly volcanic. The heat comes from the chemical capsaicin, most concentrated in the seeds and the white pith. It stimulates nerve endings in the mucus membranes in your mouth and throat, and in your skin, too. It's this that produces the burning sensation and causes eyes to water, noses to run, and saliva to flow.

Wilbur Scoville, an American chemist, invented a method of measuring chili heat, now known as the Scoville rating. A sweet pepper has a score of zero, as it has no heat at all. A relatively mild chili such as a jalapeño ranks at 2,500–8,000 Scoville units. The chili claimed to be the world's hottest—the Carolina Reaper—has been measured at 2,000,000 Scoville units; it can only be handled wearing gloves.

	MILD	MEDIUM	HOT
Pimento	■		
Jalapeño		■	
Cayenne		■	
Bird's Eye		■	
Scotch Bonnet			■
Habanero			■
Ghost			■
Naga			■
Scorpion			■
Carolina Reaper			■

Sweet corn

Sweet corn is actually a grass, and is pollinated by wind—which is why it is best to grow it close together in a block rather than singly or spaced out in long rows. Many sweet corn varieties grow tall, as high as 6 ft (2 m), and are dramatic plants ideal for an ornamental kitchen garden. Miniature cultivars are also available, as are varieties ideal for popping and some that are purely decorative.

All sweet corn should be eaten as soon as possible after harvesting. Once it has been picked, its sugar starts converting to starch and it begins to lose its sweetness. Modern varieties tend to be sweeter and tastier than old ones. Referred to as "supersweet" or "extra tendersweet," they are bred to have a higher concentration of sugar and to turn more slowly from sugar to starch after picking.

	spring			summer			fall			winter		
	E	M	L	E	M	L	E	M	L	E	M	L
sow indoors		■										
sow outdoors				■								
plant out				■	■							
harvest							■	■				

Where to plant

Sweet corn needs warmth and sunshine if the cobs are to ripen fully. Because it grows tall, it also needs shelter from the wind. It will grow in most soils, though it tends to prefer a light, well-drained, fertile site.

When to plant

Timing can be tricky. On one hand, sweet corn has a long growing season, so it should be planted as early as possible; on the other hand, seeds won't germinate if planted too early when the soil is cold and wet. To get ahead, sow seeds in a greenhouse or under cover in early or mid-spring, and transplant them later. Alternatively, if you are sowing seeds outdoors or buying ready-to-plant seedlings, wait until the temperature of the soil reaches 50°F (10°C).

You can eat ripe corn raw, straight from the plant.

PLANTING SWEET CORN IN BLOCKS

1 Sweet corn plants are pollinated by the wind instead of by insects or birds, so sow or plant out in square or rectangular blocks rather than in long rows.

2 The pollen is blown from the male to the female flowers by the wind. Male flowers grow at the top of the plant and form long "tassels" from which the pollen is produced. Female flowers are called "silks." They grow from the top of each cob and form silky strands to which pollen attaches.

HARVESTING SWEET CORN

1 To test for ripeness, peel back a few leaves around the tip of the cob and prick one of the kernels with your fingernail. If the juice is milky, the cob is ripe.

2 Harvest the cobs by breaking them off—pull them downward with one hand while steadying the main stem with the other.

How to sow seeds

Indoors, sow seeds in modules or biodegradable pots at a depth of 1–1½ in (2.5–4 cm) and do not let the temperature fall below 68–80°F (20–27°C).

Outdoors, it may be necessary to prewarm the ground using cloches and frames or by covering it with plastic sheeting—you can plant through this if you wish. Sow seeds directly into the ground 1–1½ in (2.5–4 cm) deep and 14–18 in (35–45 cm) apart. It's a good idea to sow two or three seeds in each location and, if they all germinate, thin out the weaker ones.

Sow sweet corn in blocks rather than long rows: the plants are pollinated by wind, so this will increase your chances of successful pollination.

How to plant out seedlings

When they are about 3 in (8 cm) tall, seedlings are ready to plant out—provided that the soil is warm enough. Move them outside or uncover them during the day in order to harden them off, and once there is no longer a risk of frost, plant them out about 14–18 in (35–45 cm) apart.

Routine care

Weed carefully around the growing plants; roots near the surface can easily be damaged. Unless there's a drought, you should have to water only when the plants start flowering and again when the cobs are starting to fatten up. Earth up around the stems or stake the plants to give them a bit of support.

Harvesting

Sweet corn should be ready to pick when the silks turn brown or black, but to get the optimal moment, when they're at their tastiest, you need to test them by pricking one of the kernels with a fingernail. A ripe cob should produce a milky juice. If the juice is clear and watery, leave it to ripen a little longer. If it's starchy, you're too late: it's overripe. Cook and eat sweet corn as soon as possible after picking.

(left) **Swift** (right) **Sundance**

What can go wrong

Wildlife is likely to be your biggest problem. Mice adore sweet corn, and they may eat all your seeds before they get a chance to germinate. They love the cobs, too, and—along with birds, squirrels, and raccoons—may systematically nibble or peck them all off your plants. Encasing each cob in a large plastic soft-drink bottle from which you've sliced off the end may protect them. Otherwise, you may have to net your entire crop. Fruit flies and aphids (*see p.326*) can be troublesome, too.

Recommended sweet corn

Modern "supersweet" or "extra tendersweet" varieties produce a heavier crop and taste sweeter than traditional cultivars.

Ambrosia, Incredible, Lark, Minipop, Mirai Picnic, Sundance, Sweet Nugget, Swift

Tomatoes

There are two major types of tomatoes, classified according to the way in which they grow: vine and bush. Vine (or cordon or indeterminate) tomatoes have a tall central stem that, in a perfect never-ending summer, would go on growing up and up indefinitely, much like Jack's beanstalk. The tomatoes form on trusses that grow from the main stem (as do unwanted sideshoots, which are removed). Vine tomatoes produce larger fruit and tend to be more successfully grown in greenhouses or polytunnels.

Bush (or determinate) tomatoes are more compact, with lots of spreading or trailing side branches. They are quicker to ripen than vine tomatoes and generally grow well outdoors. In addition, a third category of semideterminate varieties lies somewhere between vine and bush. They can grow tall enough to need supporting but their sideshoots are not removed.

Growing traditional vine tomatoes may at first appear daunting—there's a certain mystique about them. They do need tender loving care—watering, fertilizing, staking up, tying in, pinching out, and so on—but it all looks more complicated than it really is, and they do repay the effort.

	spring			summer			fall			winter		
	E	M	L	E	M	L	E	M	L	E	M	L
sow indoors	■	■										■
plant out			■	■								
harvest					■	■	■	■				

(left) **Vine tomatoes** tend to taste better than bush ones, and ripen gradually so you don't get a sudden glut.

(right) **Bush tomatoes** can be grown in hanging baskets if you are tight for space.

TRAINING VINE TOMATOES

Vine tomatoes can grow very tall. As the flower trusses transform into growing tomatoes, they get heavy and need support. They also need to have their growing tips and sideshoots pinched out to concentrate their energy on producing tomatoes rather than foliage. It's worth removing any leaves below the lowest fruiting truss, to aid ventilation and prevent disease.

1 Push a stake or strong pole into the ground alongside each of the seedlings, and tie in the main stem with garden twine or string as it grows.

2 Regularly pinch out sideshoots that appear in the "V" between the leaf stems and the main stem. If you let them grow, they simply waste the plant's energy.

3 In late summer, nip off the tip of the main stem two leaves above the top of the highest flower truss. Outdoors, you will probably have four or five trusses that have set fruit. The plant's task now is to concentrate solely on ripening those.

Where to plant

Whether grown in a greenhouse or outdoors, tomatoes are not particularly fussy about the soil, as long as it is rich and fertile. Either dig in well-rotted compost or manure to a depth of at least 12 in (30 cm) before planting or apply general high-phosphorous fertilizer or pellets of poultry manure. Lime acidic soils only if the pH is below 5.5 (see p.21).

Tomatoes need lots of light, so choose a site that is in full sun. If you're using growing bags, a south-facing wall is ideal.

Crop rotation is important to help prevent the buildup of diseases in the soil, so don't plant tomatoes where you've grown them in the previous two years.

When to plant

Tomatoes need warmth to germinate so, although they can be sown from early spring onward, they must be kept indoors or in a heated greenhouse. Outdoor varieties should be ready to plant out after about eight weeks, in late spring and early summer, depending on the weather.

How to sow seeds

Sow seeds thinly in seed flats or in modules full of multipurpose potting mix. Cover them with a thin layer of more potting mix, and water carefully, from underneath if possible. They are unlikely to germinate at temperatures lower than 59°F (15°C), so you may want to put them in a heated propagator. When seedlings appear, move the flats or modules somewhere with bright light and a constant temperature of 70–81°F (21–27°C).

When your seedlings develop two or three true leaves and are large enough to handle, carefully prick them out into individual 2–3-in (5–8-cm) pots or biodegradable tubes. Keep them in a warm, bright, well-ventilated place.

(right) **Growing bags** can be sited almost anywhere—patios, roof terraces, or balconies—and the soil is guaranteed disease-free. However, the plants may be difficult to support. Keep the soil well-watered, and fertilize the plants regularly.

(far right) **Cover bush tomatoes** with fabric or a cloche in fall to encourage ripening. To do the same with vine tomatoes, untie them from their poles, carefully bend them over, and lay them flat on a layer of straw.

How to plant out seedlings

It is now possible to buy grafted tomato plants. Young seedlings of particular varieties are grafted onto vigorous, disease-resistant rootstocks to produce plants that are claimed to grow more strongly and crop more heavily.

If you have grown tomatoes from seed, they should be ready to plant out when you see the first flowers forming. Harden them off first, but still be prepared to cover them with fabric or cloches if there is any risk of a late frost.

Plant vine tomatoes quite deeply, 15–18 in (38–45 cm) apart in single or staggered double rows at least 36 in (90 cm) apart. Bush tomatoes may need more room: plant them up to 36 in (90 cm) apart—though perhaps as close as 12 in (30 cm) if they are dwarf varieties.

If you are planting in growing bags or large containers, place them in a warm spot, ideally protected by a sunny, south-facing wall.

Routine care

Regular fertilizing and watering is essential. But don't flood the plants; it's better to water little and often, ensuring that the soil and the roots never dry out—especially in the case of containers and growing bags. An organic or plastic mulch around the plants will stop water from evaporating and help retain moisture.

Begin feeding with a high-potassium fertilizer (liquid tomato fertilizer, for example) once the flowers have formed fruit. It will stimulate both flowering and fruiting, and should help to reinvigorate any plants whose leaves begin to lose their color and drop.

Bush tomatoes shouldn't need much attention, though a mulch of straw or plastic will keep fruit from trailing on the soil and being eaten by slugs. Vine tomatoes, whether grown under glass or outdoors, need supporting and pruning.

Harvesting

Tomatoes taste best if you are able to leave them on the vine until they are fully ripe and ready to eat. However, as summer turns to fall, and the weather begins to cool, you'll probably have some that remain stubbornly green. Either pick them and bring them indoors to ripen, or pull up the whole plant and hang it upside down somewhere warm. Alternatively, leave the plants in place and ripen them off under cover.

What can go wrong
Pests

Plants outdoors can be attacked by leafhoppers (see *p.329*) and potato cyst eelworms (*see p.93*). Plants grown under cover, in greenhouses or polytunnels, are most likely to suffer from whiteflies (*see p.333*), and sometimes from aphids (*see p.326*) and spider mites (*see p.331*).

Diseases

Tomato blight is the same as potato blight (*see p.93*). It is a virus that causes leaves to curl and blacken, and the tomatoes themselves to turn brown, then shrink, and rot. Copper-based fungicides such as traditional Bordeaux mixture are no longer available to amateur gardeners, so try tomato varieties such as 'Ferline' and 'Losetto', which may have some resistance.

Tomato ghost spot is a *Botrytis* fungus. Unripe green tomatoes develop pale rings on their skin that may turn yellow or orange. It's not fatal, and unaffected parts of the fruit are fine to eat.

Blossom end rot causes the skin at the tomato base to turn leathery and go brown or black. It is caused by the roots of the plant drying out and being unable to absorb enough calcium. Remove any affected tomatoes, and water plants regularly.

Damp growing conditions and poor air circulation can cause a variety of other fungal growths, leaf molds, and foot and root rots (*see pp.320–323*). The best preventative is good hygiene. Remove and destroy infected leaves or stems when you spot them.

Recommended tomatoes

VINE TOMATOES **Ailsa Craig, Alicante, Black Russian, Ferline, Golden Sunrise, Green Zebra, Moneymaker, Shirley, Tigerella, Tomatoberry**

CHERRY TOMATOES **Chocolate Cherry, Gardener's Delight, Ildi, Losetto, Sun Cherry, Sungold, Sungrape, Sweet Aperitif, Sweet Million, Tumbler, Tumbling Tom**

PLUM TOMATOES **Principe Borghese, Roma, San Marzano**

BEEFSTEAK TOMATOES **Black Krim, Brandywine, Costoluto Fiorentino, Country Taste, Marmande**

(clockwise from top left)
Black Russian, Golden Sunrise, Sungold, Tumbler, Roma, Tigerella

Tomatillos

Also known as the Mexican husk tomato or jamberry, the tomatillo originated in Mexico and Central America, although is now grown worldwide. It looks like a small green tomato, but grows inside a papery shell or husk like a hanging Chinese lantern. The husk starts off green and purple, then dries to brown as the fruit swells until it splits it open. Ripe fruit may be green, yellow, or even purple. It tastes tart, with a distinctive sweet-and-sour flavor, and is used in Mexican salsas and sauces.

	spring			summer			fall			winter		
	E	M	L	E	M	L	E	M	L	E	M	L
sow under cover	■	■										
plant out			■	■								
harvest					■	■	■					

When fully ripe, tomatillos can be eaten raw, straight from the bush—wait until they emerge from their dried brown or yellow husks.

Where, when, and how to plant

Sow seeds indoors in flats or modules and use a propagator to maintain a temperature of at least 60°F (16°C)—warmer once germination has taken place. Prick out seedlings into 2–3-in (5–8-cm) pots once they are large enough to handle, then harden off and plant out in a warm, sunny, sheltered site with fertile soil in late spring or early summer after the last frost.

Routine care

Tomatillos can grow to 3 ft (1 m) tall or more, so they may need support. Tie in each plant to three or four poles in an upside-down tepee. Water only if conditions are extremely dry.

Harvesting

Fruit are ripe when they are fully colored and have pushed their way out of their husks. The riper they are, the sweeter they taste.

What can go wrong

Attacks from pests and diseases are rare, and are likely to be those that affect tomatoes (see p.210). In temperate climates, the most likely problem is a cool summer in which few fruit ripen.

Okra

Sometimes referred to as ladies' fingers, okra forms slender, pod-shaped fruit full of round, white seeds. Pods are usually green, but may be white or red. When picked young, before they become stringy, the pods are cooked and eaten as a vegetable. They are particularly popular in the southern United States, in Africa and the Middle East, in India, and in Japan.

	spring			summer			fall			winter		
	E	M	L	E	M	L	E	M	L	E	M	L
sow indoors	■	■										
plant out			■	■								
harvest					■	■	■					

For a good crop, okra needs the warmth and humidity of a hot summer—it is difficult to grow outdoors in cool climates, and may require a greenhouse.

Where, when, and how to plant

Soak seeds in water overnight to soften them, then sow them thinly in flats or modules. Keep them indoors or in a heated propagator at a minimum temperature of 60°F (16°C). When they germinate, move them somewhere bright and warm. Prick out seedlings as soon as they are large enough to handle. In late spring or early summer, when they are about 3–4 in (8–10 cm) high, harden them off and plant them out in a sunny, sheltered site. Protect them from late frost.

Routine care

Weed and water regularly. Use poles to support tall plants, and when they are about 24 in (60 cm) tall, pinch out growing tips to encourage bushiness.

Harvesting

Start picking the pods when they are 2–4 in (5–10 cm) long. Any longer and they become tough and woody. Their stems are thick, and need to be cut with a sharp knife or pruners.

What can go wrong

Okra is generally problem-free, although plants can be affected by aphids (*see p.326*), by mildew and rot in cool, wet weather, and by whiteflies (*see p.333*) and spider mites (*see p.331*) if grown under cover.

Recommended okra

Cajun Delight, Clemson's Spineless, Pure Luck

When cooked, okra develops a slimy, gelatinous texture that makes it good for thickening soups and stews.

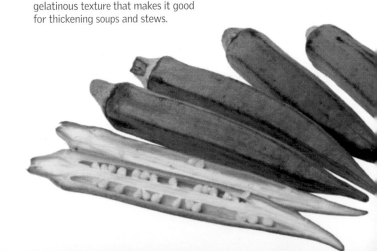

Cucumbers & Squashes

Here is a group of vegetables that ranges from some of the tiniest to some of the very largest. Gherkins—which are, in truth, no more than miniature cucumbers—may measure just 1 in (2.5 cm) in length when picked, while gigantic, record-breaking pumpkins can grow to as much as 13 ft (4.5 m) in circumference and weigh over 1,000 lb (450 kg). They all have one thing in common: they are extremely hungry and thirsty, and to grow them successfully you must plant them in rich, fertile soil and give them plenty of water. Giant pumpkins may need as much as 2$\frac{1}{2}$ gallons (10 liters) per week.

Cucumbers, zucchini, and summer squash are best eaten as soon as possible after picking, but vegetable marrows, pumpkins, and winter squash can be stored and used during winter when other fresh foods may be scarce.

Many squashes are natural climbers and will readily clamber over whatever supports you can provide them with.

1 **Cucumbers** you grow yourself can be harvested young and eaten while still fresh and tasty.

2 **Gherkins** grow very, very fast. At the height of their growing season, pick a few every day.

3 **Vegetable marrows** are an instance where size matters: the bigger the better, it seems.

4 **Zucchini** are delicious if you pick them when they're no larger than your little finger.

5 **Summer squash** can be allowed to grow quite large but taste best when still young.

6 **Pumpkins** are the focus of fiercely competitive contests. Giants may weigh over 1,000 lb (450 kg).

7 **Winter squash** will keep for six months or more if cured and stored carefully.

Cucumbers

Traditionally, there are two main types of cucumbers: greenhouse cucumbers and outdoor ones. Greenhouse cucumbers, which are not commonly grown by home gardeners, need to be raised under cover, as the name suggests. They are smooth-skinned, grow to over 12 in (30 cm) long, and don't need pollinating. Outdoor (or "ridge") cucumbers are hardier. They tend to be rough-skinned, perhaps even spiny, somewhat shorter, and require pollinating. Modern Japanese outdoor varieties offer the best of both worlds: they are as long and tasty as greenhouse cucumbers, but will grow outdoors. In addition to these, there are unusual round, yellow varieties such as 'Crystal Apple'. Most cucumbers are climbing plants.

	spring			summer			fall			winter		
	E	M	L	E	M	L	E	M	L	E	M	L
sow indoors	■	■										
sow under cover	■	■	■									
sow outdoors				■								
plant out			■	■								
harvest						■	■	■				

Where to plant

Cucumbers need a warm, sheltered, sunny site. Traditionally, they were grown in specially prepared super-rich mounds, ridges, or raised beds, but any rich soil that has had plenty of well-rotted manure or compost dug into it should produce a good crop, provided it is well drained.

Cucumbers can do well in growing bags or large containers in a sunny part of the garden.

When to plant

You can start sowing in early spring provided you do so in a propagator or a heated greenhouse. In mid-spring, seeds can be sown outdoors in pots if kept under cover. And by early summer, it should be possible to sow seeds directly into the ground or to plant out seedlings.

Modern cultivars such as 'Zeina' are bred to produce high yields of small, smooth-skinned fruit.

SOWING AND PLANTING OUT

Cucumbers need heat and humidity to germinate, so they must be sown in pots or modules and kept indoors or under cover until the ground warms up.

1 To reduce the risk of rotting, place seeds on their edge. Sow two or three seeds per pot.

2 Dig a generously sized hole 12 in (30 cm) wide and 12 in (30 cm) deep. Fill it with well-rotted compost and draw the soil back over it in order to make a mound. Plant your seedling in the top of the mound.

(top) **Erect a cane tepee** to act as a support for cucumber plants. Tie them in securely to keep them from collapsing under the weight of the fruit.

(bottom) **Greenhouse cucumbers** can be supported on a network of strings or wires strung between the roof and ground.

How to sow seeds

Indoors or under cover, sow seeds in modules or 2–3-in (5–8-cm) pots full of soilless potting mix at a depth of ¾ in (2 cm). Set the seeds on edge to minimize the risk that they will rot, and sow two or three per pot so you can later thin them out to leave the strongest seedling. The temperature needs to be 68°F (20°C) or higher to ensure that they germinate, so in early spring use a propagator and in mid- or even late spring keep them covered with cloches or in a cold frame.

If you are sowing seeds outdoors directly into the ground, it may help to prewarm the soil using cloches or a covering of plastic sheeting. Sow two or three seeds together in stations, each at least 18 in (45 cm) apart. If all the seeds in a station germinate, thin out the weaker ones.

How to plant out seedlings

Seedlings should be ready to plant out about four weeks after sowing—provided that the soil is warm enough. Harden them off, and once there is no longer a risk of frost, plant them out about 18 in (45 cm) apart, or more if you're going to let them trail instead of climb. Handle seedlings carefully, as their roots are easily damaged. After planting, protect them with cloches or fabric if nights are still cold.

Routine care

Construct a cane tepee, trellis, or framework of strings and wires as a support for climbing plants, and train the plants up it as they grow. Pinch out the growing tips when the plants reach the top of their supports.

Water regularly; it's very important never to let cucumbers dry out. An organic surface mulch will help retain moisture in the soil. Once the fruit start to form, feed every two weeks with a general liquid fertilizer—especially if you are using growing bags.

Harvesting

Harvest cucumbers while they are still quite young, before they reach the size of those you'd buy in the supermarket. If they start to turn yellow, it's too late, and if you still fail to remove them, they will weaken the rest of the crop. Regular harvesting encourages the plants to go on producing new fruit.

What can go wrong
Pests
Slugs and snails are attracted to young seedlings. Cucumbers grown under cover, in greenhouses or polytunnels, may be attacked by whiteflies (*see p.333*) and spider mites (*see p.331*).

Diseases
Powdery mildew (*see p.322*) is often a problem as summer goes on, although regular watering, fertilizing, and good air circulation should prevent it. Foot and root rots (*see p.321*) might occur if the summer is very rainy or if you overwater the plants.

Cucumber mosaic virus is deadly. Leaves are mottled with a yellow mosaic patterning, fruits are small, hard and inedible, and plants become stunted and may die. There is no cure other than to destroy all affected plants, and try resistant cultivars in future.

Recommended cucumbers
It is now possible to buy grafted cucumber plants. Young seedlings of particular varieties are grafted onto vigorous, disease-resistant rootstocks to produce plants that are claimed to grow more strongly and crop more heavily.

GREENHOUSE CUCUMBERS **Bella, Carmen, Corinto, Mini Munch, Passandra, Telegraph Improved**

OUTDOOR CUCUMBERS **Burpless Tasty Green, Crystal Apple, Cucino, La Diva, Marketmore, Masterpiece, Zeina**

(top) **La Diva** (bottom) **Crystal Apple**

Gherkins

Gherkins (or "cornichons") are essentially immature cucumbers, harvested when about 1–3 in (2.5–7.5 cm) long. They are preserved by being pickled in vinegar or brine, often flavored with herbs such as dill and spices such as peppercorns or mustard seeds. A number of special cucumber cultivars have been developed specifically for growing as gherkins.

There is also an oval-shaped, warty, spiny variety—the West Indian or Burr Gherkin—that is in fact a different (though related) species.

	spring			summer			fall			winter		
	E	M	L	E	M	L	E	M	L	E	M	L
sow under cover	■	■	■									
sow outdoors					■							
plant out				■	■							
harvest						■	■	■				

Vert Petit de Paris

Where, when, and how to plant

Gherkins should be grown in the same way as outdoor cucumbers (see *pp.218–221*). In cool climates, sow them under cover and transplant seedlings in late spring or early summer, when the soil has warmed up and there is no longer any chance of frost.

Routine care

Weed and water regularly, ensuring that the soil never dries out. Use poles to support tall plants. Apply liquid fertilizer every couple of weeks, especially if growth is slow or leaves lose their color.

Harvesting

Either pick gherkins when they reach about 1 in (2.5 cm) in length, or leave them to grow larger—if you are using them for sliced dill pickles, perhaps. The important thing is to pick them regularly. They grow very quickly, and if they get too large they will turn yellow, become bitter, and inhibit the growth of new fruit.

What can go wrong

Gherkins suffer from the same pests and diseases as outdoor cucumbers (*see p.221*).

Recommended gherkins

Diamant, Partner, Vert Petit de Paris

Vegetable marrows

In a sense, a marrow is simply an overgrown zucchini. However, true marrows are usually grown from specialty varieties, and while they are uncommon in North America, there is fierce competition at UK horticultural shows for the heaviest marrow: the winner is likely to have been raised on a bed of a super-rich compost and manure, cosseted to gigantic perfection. It's hard not to feel that marrows are grown more for their epic proportions than for their rather bland, watery taste.

	spring			summer			fall			winter		
	E	M	L	E	M	L	E	M	L	E	M	L
sow indoors	■	■										
sow outdoors				■								
plant out			■	■								
harvest					■	■	■	■				

Where, when, and how to plant
Grow marrows in the same way as zucchini (*see p.224*). In cool climates, sow under cover and transplant seedlings in late spring or early summer. Alternatively, sow seeds directly into the ground when the soil has warmed up and there is no chance of frost.

Routine care
Weed and water regularly, especially during flowering—don't let the soil dry out. Apply liquid fertilizer every two weeks if growth is slow.

Harvesting
Marrows can be picked as small as 6 in (15 cm) in length, but are usually left to grow larger. As they ripen, lift them up off the soil onto a brick, and turn from time to time so their skins harden in the sun. Store in a dry, cool place for use during winter.

What can go wrong
Marrows suffer from the same pests and diseases as zucchini (*see p.226*).

Recommended vegetable marrows

Badger Cross, Bush Baby, Honeygold, Long Green Bush, Long Green Trailing, Sunbeam, Table Dainty, Tiger Cross

(top) **Long Green Trailing**

(bottom) **Place a brick** under a ripening marrow to stop it from rotting on the soil.

Zucchini and summer squash

Zucchini may be either green or yellow, and as well as being cigar-shaped, they can also be elongated, curved, or even round. They are best harvested when still young: if they are allowed to keep growing, they have a tendency to lose their taste and texture, start to develop seeds, and eventually turn into vegetable marrows. It is possible to leave summer squash to ripen for longer and use them for ravioli, risotto, or soup, but they also taste at their best when young.

Zucchini and squash take up a lot of space and produce a large harvest, so don't be tempted to grow too many. Two or three green zucchini plants, two or three yellow ones, and a couple of unusual varieties of summer squash should feed an average family. At the height of summer, they grow alarmingly fast. You would almost swear you can actually see them grow before your eyes. Pick a few every day, before they swell so much that the compost pile is the best place for them.

	spring			summer			fall			winter		
	E	M	L	E	M	L	E	M	L	E	M	L
sow indoors		■	■									
sow outdoors				■								
plant out			■	■								
harvest					■	■	■	■				

Harvest the flowers along with the zucchini; they can also be eaten, deep-fried or stuffed.

Where to plant

Zucchini like a warm, sunny, sheltered site. They are hungry and thirsty plants, so they grow best in rich soil that has had plenty of well-rotted manure or compost dug into it. A layer of mulch on the surface will help retain moisture in the soil.

When to plant

You can begin to sow seeds in mid-spring if you start them in a propagator or in a heated greenhouse. In late spring they can be sown outdoors in pots if you protect them from the cold with cloches or cold frames. By early summer, when the ground has warmed up, it should be possible to sow seeds directly into the soil or to plant out seedlings.

How to sow seeds

Indoors or under cover, sow seeds in modules or 2–3-in (5–8-cm) pots full of soilless mix at a depth of ¾ in (2 cm). To ensure that they germinate, maintain a temperature of 68°F (20°C) or higher either by using a propagator or by keeping them covered with cloches or in a cold frame.

When the weather is warm enough, sow seeds outdoors directly into the ground. It may help to prewarm the soil using cloches or a covering of plastic sheeting. Sow at a depth of about 1 in (2.5 cm), planting two or three seeds together in stations at least 18 in (45 cm) apart. If all the seeds in a station germinate, thin out the weaker seedlings.

Routine care

Water regularly, especially when the plants are starting to flower and when the fruit are swelling and ripening. It's very important not to let them dry out.

If your soil is rich and fertile, plants shouldn't need additional fertilize, but if growth is slow you can water with a general liquid fertilizer.

Plants grown under cover may not be pollinated if insects are denied access to them. If that is the case, you may have to pollinate them yourself (*see p.226*).

SEEDLINGS IN BIODEGRADABLE POTS

Seedlings that have been grown in biodegradable pots can be planted out whole—pot and all—to avoid disturbing fragile root systems. They should be ready to plant out two to four weeks after sowing, provided the soil is warm enough. Harden them off, and once there is no longer a risk of frost, plant them out 3 ft (90 cm) apart—more if you are growing trailing varieties.

1 Top off pots right to the brim with additional potting mix. It will earth up the growing stems and strengthen roots.

2 Once the seedling has developed three or four true leaves, look for roots starting to push through the sides and bottom of the pots.

3 Make a shallow circular hollow about 12 in (30 cm) wide and dig a planting hole in the center. Plant the seedling in its pot so that its leaves are just above the surface, then mound up a little soil around the stem. When you water, the hollow will fill up but the stem won't be waterlogged. Finally, spread a little mulch to retain moisture.

HAND POLLINATION

Zucchini and squash develop male and female flowers on the same plant. Insects carry pollen from the male flower to the female one, which then sets fruit—a young zucchini starts to develop. Plants grown under glass or covered with fabric don't often get visited by insects, so pollination may not take place. Therefore, you may have to lend a helping hand.

1 You can identify male flowers by the fact that they do not have a swelling at the top of the stem where the fruit will develop. Gently pull off the petals to expose the stamens.

2 A thicker or swollen stem indicates the embryonic fruit and identifies female flowers. Insert the male flower carefully into the female flower so that some of the yellow pollen is transferred from the male stamen to the female stigma.

3 To ensure that insects do not introduce any foreign pollen, or to retain any seeds you wish to save, tie up the petals with some twine, then leave until the petals fall off naturally.

Harvesting

Harvest zucchini young and often. Pick them when they're still tiny—no larger than your little finger—or leave until they are about 4 in (10 cm) in length. Any larger, and they become watery and tasteless. Regular harvesting encourages the plants to go on producing new fruit.

Summer squash can be allowed to grow a little larger, but they, too, taste at their best when still young.

What can go wrong
Pests

Slugs and snails can strip the young seedling leaves overnight, so watch out for them, particularly in damp weather (*see pp.324–325*). Zucchini grown under cover, in greenhouses or cold frames, may be attacked by whiteflies (*see p.333*) and spider mites (*see p.331*).

Diseases

Powdery mildew (*see p.322*) is the most common problem, particularly later in the summer. Regular watering, fertilizing, and good air circulation can help prevent it. Foot and root rots (*see p.321*) can occur if the summer is very damp or if you overwater. And, if you are really unlucky, you may sustain an attack of the deadly cucumber mosaic virus (*see p.221*).

Recommended zucchini and summer squash

ZUCCHINI **Alfresco, Black Forest, Defender, Eight Ball, Floridor, Midnight, Parthenon, Romanesco, Soleil, Sunstripe**

SUMMER SQUASH **Custard White, Patty Pan, Sunburst, Tromboncino**

(clockwise from top left)
summer squash—**Custard White, Sunburst, Tromboncino**
zucchini—**Defender**

Pumpkins and winter squash

Pumpkins and winter squash are available in an extraordinary variety of sizes, shapes, textures, and colors. Some form bushy plants, but most are trailing and will spread widely over the ground unless kept in check. Fruit that do not grow too large and heavy can be trained to climb up trellises, arches, and tepees.

The majority of winter squash can be harvested and eaten when they are young, but what generally differentiates them from summer squash is that they are allowed to grow a bit bigger and to ripen more fully so that their skins harden. After this they can, if necessary, be stored for the winter. Of course, in the world of competitive pumpkin growing, size is what matters more than anything else. Mammoth pumpkins weighing in at more than 2,200 lb (1,000 kg) are not unheard of. You wouldn't want to eat them—but that's not the point...

	spring			summer			fall			winter		
	E	M	L	E	M	L	E	M	L	E	M	L
sow indoors		■	■									
sow outdoors				■								
plant out			■	■								
harvest							■	■				

Where to plant

Pumpkins like a warm, sunny, sheltered site with plenty of space to spread out. They are both hungry and thirsty, and benefit from a fertile, well-drained soil that has had plenty of well-rotted manure or compost dug into it. Spreading a layer of mulch will help retain moisture in the soil.

When to plant

Pumpkins have a long growing season so it's good to start them off as early as you can. Sow seeds in mid-spring in a propagator or a heated greenhouse, or in late spring outdoors in pots that are protected from the cold with cloches or cold frames. By early summer, it should be possible to sow seeds directly into the soil or to plant out seedlings, especially if you have warmed up the soil in advance.

Squash are ready to harvest when they sound hollow if you tap them and when, like these 'Uchiki Kuri', they are fully colored.

"The **tougher** their skin, the **longer** they will last."

Seedlings can be planted out when they have three or four true leaves. Dig some organic matter into the soil, then create holes for the plants using a bulb planter or trowel. Once they are in place, firm and water in.

How to sow seeds

Indoors or under cover, sow seeds in 3-in (8-cm) pots full of soilless potting mix at a depth of 1 in (2.5 cm). Sow seeds vertically, not flat, so that they are less likely to rot, and sow two per pot so you can later thin out the weaker of the two seedlings. Cover them and keep them at a temperature of 59–64°F (15–18°C). They should germinate within a week.

Alternatively, sow seeds outdoors directly into the ground, once all danger of frost is past. It may help to prewarm the soil using cloches or a covering of plastic sheeting. Sow at a depth of about 1 in (2.5 cm), two or three seeds together between 3 ft (1 m) and 5 ft (1.5 m) apart, depending on the extent to which the plants will spread. If all the seeds germinate, simply thin out the weaker seedlings.

(left) **A fan trellis** made from sturdy poles and strong twine supports a few small climbing squash.

(middle) **A tepee** constructed from sturdy poles should be strong enough to support medium-sized pumpkins.

(right) **A bamboo tripod** will keep pumpkins off damp ground and help to ensure that the sun reaches them.

Routine care

Weeds won't stand much of a chance once the pumpkins' huge leaves begin to grow, but you must water regularly. Giant pumpkins may need as much as 2–3 gallons (10 liters) per week. Adding a general liquid fertilizer will help stimulate growth, too.

Sideshoots of some trailing varieties can grow surprisingly long. They're often trained around short poles into circles to keep them neat. If you're attempting to grow very large specimens, remove all except one or two fruits per plant while they're still young. Cut away leaves to allow the sun to get to the pumpkins. Smaller varieties can be trained up over fences, trellises, and other support frameworks, but make sure you tie them in securely as the heavy fruit develop.

Plants grown under cover while in flower may not be pollinated unless insects are allowed to get to them. You may have to pollinate them by hand (*see p.226*).

Harvesting

Pumpkins and squash that you plan to store rather than eat right away are best left to grow for as long as possible. When the stems begin to crack and the skins harden, cut them off with a sharp knife, leaving a good length of stalk on each fruit. Leave them outdoors in the sun to cure, or harden further, for another ten days or so. The tougher the skin, the more water they will retain and the longer they will last.

What can go wrong

In the early days, seedlings are vulnerable to slugs and snails, so watch out for these. You might also find that no female flowers form in cold climates.

The only other problems you might encounter are powdery mildew (*see p.322*) and cucumber mosaic virus (*see p.221*).

Recommended pumpkins and winter squash

PUMPKINS **Atlantic Giant, Jack Be Little, Jack O' Lantern, Racer, Rouge Vif d'Etampes**

WINTER SQUASH **Autumn Crown, Butterbush, Crown Prince, Festival, Golden Hubbard, Harrier, Honey Bear, Hunter, Potimarron, Queensland Blue, Sweet Dumpling, Turk's Turban, Uchiki Kuri (also known as Red Kuri or Onion Squash), Vegetable Spaghetti, Waltham Butternut**

(top) **Powdery mildew** produces a white coating on leaves in late summer and fall. Water regularly and ensure that air can circulate freely around plants to help prevent it.

(bottom) **Store pumpkins and squash** on straw-covered racks or shelves somewhere humid but well-ventilated. If cured to harden their skins, they may keep for six months, or even longer.

(clockwise from top left)
pumpkins—**Atlantic Giant, Rouge Vif d'Etampes**
winter squash—**Sweet Dumpling, Queensland Blue**

Perennial Vegetables

Most vegetables are grown as annuals and are therefore sown or planted fresh each year. However, members of this group—the perennials—are in it for the long haul. Once established, they simply stay in the ground, dying down at the end of each year and then throwing up shoots and producing new growth the next. Asparagus plants may go on in this fashion for up to twenty years. Others are not as long-lasting. After three or four years, globe artichokes and rhubarb, for example, are best lifted and divided into what are called "sets" or "offsets." These can then be replanted as reenergized new plants.

Rhubarb, cardoons, and sea kale all benefit from forcing, the process by which stems are blanched under cover of darkness in order to make them taste more tender and less bitter.

A mature globe artichoke plant should produce a dozen or more large green or purple flower heads each year.

1 **Asparagus** can be grown from seed, but it's easier to grow and success is more likely if you buy ready-to-plant rootstocks, or crowns.

2 **Globe artichokes** are enormous, thistlelike plants, sometimes grown as much for decoration as they are for food.

3 **Cardoons** look much like globe artichokes, but it is the blanched stems or leaf stalks that are eaten, not the flower heads.

4 **Jerusalem artichokes** are grown for their knobby, nutty-tasting tubers, which develop underground among the roots, just like potatoes.

5 **Chinese artichokes** taste similar to Jerusalem artichokes—though crisper and juicier—and are eaten in the same way, either cooked or raw.

6 **Sea kale** looks a bit like an open-leaf, blue-gray cabbage. The young leaves, tender stems, and cream-colored flower heads can be eaten.

7 **Rhubarb** may be one of the earliest crops of the year—perhaps the first if you force it to produce tender, blanched stems.

1

2

Asparagus

Growing asparagus is a long-term project, and one for which you'll need patience. Don't expect much of a crop in the first two years after planting. However, after that, things will improve. Asparagus is a perennial that comes up year after year, so once your bed is established, it could last for as long as twenty years. During that time, cutting your plants down to the ground at the end of each season, and regular fertilizing and mulching, is probably all you'll have to do. Fresh asparagus cooked right after picking is sensational; it tastes quite different from what you buy at the store. Asparagus can be grown from seed, but is more likely to be successful if you buy ready-to-plant rootstocks, or crowns.

If possible, look for one-year-old crowns that come from all-male F1 cultivars. Female plants (which produce berries in among their foliage) do not crop as well.

	spring			summer			fall			winter		
	E	M	L	E	M	L	E	M	L	E	M	L
sow under cover	■											■
sow outdoors		■	■									
plant out			■	■								
plant crowns	■	■	■									
harvest		■	■									

Where to plant

If you're planting an asparagus bed for the first time, bear in mind that the plants can last for up to twenty years, so they are going to remain where you put them for a long while!

Choose somewhere sheltered from the wind and with good drainage. The soil should have a pH of 6.3–7.5 (*see p.21*). If it is light and sandy, you can grow asparagus on a flat surface, but if your soil is heavy, then creating raised beds or ridges will help prevent waterlogging. The plot should be completely free of all perennial weeds before you start planting.

At the height of the season, asparagus should be harvested every few days. Don't let the spears grow any fatter than your index finger.

DIVIDING AN ASPARAGUS CROWN

1 Asparagus can be propagated by division. Dig up the crown in late winter or early spring, then split it in two by carefully prying or cutting it apart.

2 The two halves can then be replanted within a trench. This technique works best with healthy crowns that are at least three to four years old.

(top) **When harvesting**, use a sharp knife to cut each spear diagonally about 1 in (2.5 cm) below the soil surface.

(bottom) **Cut stems down** to 1 in (2.5 cm) above the ground as soon as the foliage turns yellow in fall.

When to plant

If you are buying young plants or crowns, plant them in early spring. If you have decided to raise your own plants from seed, either sow them under cover in early spring and plant out in early summer, or sow them straight into the ground when both the soil and weather are warm enough.

How to sow seeds

Sow seeds indoors in modules filled with fresh seed mix or potting mix at a depth of about 1 in (2.5 cm). Keep them at a temperature of 55–61°F (13–16°C) while they germinate and begin to develop. Harden off the seedlings and plant them out in early summer.

In mid- or late spring, when the soil becomes warmer and drier, plant seeds directly into the ground. There is no point in sowing outdoors too early; if the soil is cold, the seeds simply won't germinate.

How to plant crowns

Asparagus crowns need to be planted in prepared trenches, in either single or double rows. Dig each trench 12 in (30 cm) wide and 8 in (20 cm) deep, in rows 18 in (45 cm) apart, with paths of 3 ft (1 m) between beds. Spread a thin layer of well-rotted manure or compost over the bottom of the trench, then draw up a 4-in- (10-cm-) high ridge of soil all the way along the middle. Place the crowns 12–18 in (30–45 cm) apart, with their roots straddling the ridge, then cover with soil, and water them in.

Routine care

Keep new plants watered and weed-free. Spread a 2-in (5-cm) mulch of well-rotted manure or compost around them to help retain moisture. Scatter a topdressing of general fertilizer on established beds once in early spring and again after you've harvested the last of that year's spears. Established beds should also be mulched every fall with well-rotted compost or manure.

Asparagus produces a mass of fernlike foliage that can easily grow 6 ft (2 m) tall. Stake it up with bamboo poles and string if there is any danger that the wind will blow it over, and in fall, cut down the stems to just above the ground.

Harvesting

Don't harvest new plants in their first year, and do it sparingly in their second year. This will give them a chance to establish themselves. Thereafter, harvest for six to eight weeks from mid-spring onward. Cut the spears every few days, when they are 5–7 in (13–18 cm) long and no thicker than your thumb or index finger.

What can go wrong

Pests

Slugs and snails can attack young spears. You'll need to protect against them, particularly in damp weather (*see pp.324–325*).

Adult asparagus beetles, black and red with yellow spots, and their larvae, gray in color, may cause problems. Both of them strip the foliage from plants and eat the asparagus spears. Unless you spot them early and are able to pick them off by hand, spray with pyrethrum—preferably at dusk so as not to harm any bees.

Diseases

An attack of violet root rot (*see p.323*) is the most serious threat, and at its worst may mean pulling up the plants, burning them, and planting a new bed elsewhere. In addition, foot and root rots (*see p.321*) may cause problems in damp conditions.

Recommended asparagus

Bear in mind that an asparagus bed ought to contain at least 30 separate plants in order to generate sufficient spears for a regular crop.

Ariane, Backlim, Connover's Colossal, Gijnlim, Guelph Millennium, Mary Washington, Pacific 2000, Purple Pacific

(left) **Backlim**
(right) **Connover's Colossal**

Globe artichokes

Globe artichokes are enormous, thistlelike plants, sometimes grown as much for decoration as for food. During the course of the summer, a mature plant should produce a dozen or more large green or purple flower heads. It's these that are picked and eaten—either the soft, fleshy outer leaves or the dense heart that lies right in the center. The globes can even be cooked and eaten whole if harvested young, when they are not much larger than golf balls.

It is quite possible to grow globe artichokes from seed, but the process can be hit-or-miss. It's better if you can start from offsets, which are new sideshoots or suckers cut from a plant that is already established. Initially, these can be purchased or perhaps begged from a fellow gardener. Thereafter, it's easy to propagate new plants yourself by cutting and planting your own offsets.

	spring			summer			fall			winter		
	E	M	L	E	M	L	E	M	L	E	M	L
sow indoors	■											■
plant out		■	■									
plant offsets		■	■									
harvest				■	■	■	■	■				

Where to plant

Globe artichokes like sunshine but not high temperatures, frost, or strong winds. A mild climate and a sheltered location are ideal. The soil should be very fertile, with lots of well-rotted compost or manure dug in to it, and should have a pH of about 6.5 (*see p.21*).

When to plant

If you are raising young plants from sideshoots or offsets, plant them out in spring. If you are trying to grow from seed, sow them under cover in late winter or early spring and plant them out in early summer.

How to sow seeds

Sow seeds indoors in modules or seed flats filled with fresh seed or potting mix. Keep at a temperature of at least 59°F (15°C) while they germinate. Prick out seedlings into larger 4-in (10-cm) pots to harden them off and transplant them in early summer.

The king bud is the globe at the very top of the plant; it's always the one to pick first.

Propagate by cutting offsets (or sideshoots), each with a short length of root, from the base of established plants in spring.

PREPARING FOR OVERWINTERING

1 Cut off any dead stems and remove foliage that is turning yellow or brown.

2 Fork over the soil to keep it from becoming compacted, and spread a mulch of well-rotted compost or manure around the base of the plants. In very cold winters, cover with straw as well.

How to plant offsets

Plant rooted offsets about 3 ft (90 cm) apart and at a depth of about 2 in (5 cm). Water them in and trim the ends of the leaves to about 5 in (13 cm) in length. If the nights are still cold or if there is a danger of frost, cover the plants with fabric.

Routine care

Keep new plants watered and weed-free—do not let them dry out. Brutal as it may sound, in the first year you should cut off the main flower head as soon as it appears. It will stimulate growth and you'll get a better crop the following year.

To help your plants survive the winter, earth them up and cover with straw or dried bracken. In spring, uncover them and either spread a rich organic mulch around them or water with a high-potassium liquid fertilizer.

By the third or fourth year, the plant will be starting to crop less generously, and you should be cutting offsets from it with a plan for phasing it out.

Harvesting

Start by cutting the largest, topmost globe (the king bud) at the moment it turns plump and soft, just before the green scales begin to open out. Leave a short section of stalk attached. Pick the rest of the heads when they ripen in the same way. You should get 10 or 12 from each mature plant—and perhaps even a second crop of smaller globes in early fall.

Just before the scales open, start harvesting the globes from the top of the plant.

(left) **Violetto di Chioggia**
(right) **Green Globe**

What can go wrong

The main problems are likely to revolve around water. Too little in the summer will result in disappointingly small artichokes, while too much in the winter may cause waterlogging and can rot the plants. Otherwise, apart from attacks by slugs and snails (*see pp.324–325*), earwigs, and aphids or blackflies (*see p.326*), globe artichokes are generally pest- and disease-free.

Recommended globe artichokes

Green Globe, Purple Globe, Violetto di Chioggia

Cardoons

Cardoons look a lot like globe artichokes, to which they are closely related. They are equally tall and striking, have similar jagged silver-blue foliage, and produce huge spiky flower heads and purple thistlelike flowers. Unlike globe artichokes, though, it is the stems or leaf stalks that are eaten, not the flower heads. And they must be blanched in order to prevent them from becoming too bitter. This can be carried out by wrapping them up to exclude light in the weeks before harvesting. Cardoons, then, are certainly out of the ordinary—and perhaps should be tackled only by the more adventurous vegetable grower. Yet they're certainly worth a try; even if you don't end up eating them, they look fantastic.

	spring			summer			fall			winter		
	E	M	L	E	M	L	E	M	L	E	M	L
sow under cover	■	■										
plant out				■	■	■						
harvest							■	■				

Where to plant

Cardoons like a sheltered, sunny site and rich, fertile soil that has had lots of well-rotted compost or manure dug in to it. Plants for eating are grown as annuals and are uprooted when harvested. But if left, they will flower and grow as large as globe artichokes—so they might not be the best choice for small gardens.

When to plant

Sow seeds under cover in early or mid-spring and plant out in late spring or early summer. Although it is possible to propagate from sideshoots or "offsets" in the same way as with globe artichokes (see p.243), the new plants tend to flower in their first year and the stems are inedible.

Blanching stems by protecting them from the light reduces their bitterness.

How to sow seeds and plant out seedlings

Sow seeds under cover in modules or seed flats at a temperature of at least 50–59°F (10–15°C). Prick out seedlings into larger 4-in (10-cm) pots, and when they are 10 in (25 cm) tall, harden them off and plant them out 18 in (45 cm) apart in trenches.

Routine care

Water regularly to prevent plants from drying out. Stake up each plant with a strong bamboo pole, and in early fall blanch the stems by gathering them together in a bundle, tying them with string, and wrapping them in paper or black plastic. It's wise to earth up the bases, too, so that no light can get in.

Harvesting

Blanching takes approximately six to eight weeks. When time is up, uproot the whole plant, unwrap it, and cut off both the leaves at the top and the roots at the bottom. Remove any tough outer stems. You should end up with what looks somewhat like a bunch of celery.

What can go wrong

Pests and diseases are the same as those that affect globe artichokes (*see p.245*).

(top) **Cardoon leaves**, though beautiful, are not for eating. They should be cut off and discarded when the blanched stems are harvested.

(bottom) **Cardoon flowers**, which appear in the second year after sowing, are not edible—and are also a sign that the leaf stems will be too tough to eat.

Jerusalem artichokes

Despite its name, the Jerusalem artichoke has nothing to do with the globe artichoke. It is actually a relative of the sunflower, a fact that becomes obvious when you see how tall it grows and take a look at its distinctive yellow flowers. It is grown for its knobby tubers, which develop underground, among the roots, in much the same way as potatoes. Jerusalem artichokes can be eaten either cooked or raw—provided that you (and those close to you) are prepared for the seismic flatulence for which they are notorious.

New plants are grown not from seed but from tubers, either bought from a specialty supplier or saved from your own previous year's crop. Jerusalem artichokes are perennials, so any tuber accidentally left in the ground at the end of one season will result in a new plant the following year.

	spring			summer			fall			winter		
	E	M	L	E	M	L	E	M	L	E	M	L
plant outdoors				■	■	■						
harvest	■	■	■	■	■	■	■	■	■	■	■	■

Where to plant

Jerusalem artichokes are among the least fussy of all vegetables—they will grow almost anywhere. However, they won't thrive in acidic soil, or anywhere that is heavily waterlogged.

Because the plants grow so tall—up to 10 ft (3 m) – they are often planted as natural windbreaks or screens, providing protection for more vulnerable crops.

When to plant

Plant tubers in spring, as soon as the soil has warmed up enough to be workable.

Fuseau

How to plant tubers

Make a furrow 4–6 in (10–15 cm) deep the entire length of your row. Space the tubers 12–18 in (30–45 cm) apart with the main bud uppermost, and cover them with soil.

Routine care

When the plants have grown to a height of about 12 in (30 cm), earth up the stems by 6 in (15 cm) to give them some initial support. As they continue to grow, you may have to stake them, too. In mid- or late summer, cut them down to 5 ft (1.5 m) and remove any flowers so as not to divert the plant's energy away from the tubers. In fall, when the leaves turn yellow, cut the stems down to just above ground level.

Harvesting

Except in very cold weather, the tubers can stay where they are until you need them. Lift them as you would potatoes, taking care not to leave any in the ground unless you want plants in the same place again the following year.

What can go wrong

The most troublesome pests are likely to be slugs and snails (*see pp.324–325*), which will eat both the tubers and the foliage.

Sclerotinia is a fungus that produces white fluffy growth and might rot stems and foliage. It's at its worst in cool, damp conditions. There is no cure—affected plants must be removed and destroyed.

Recommended Jerusalem artichokes

Some tubers are more knobby than others. Smooth varieties such as 'Fuseau' are easier to prepare for cooking.

Fuseau, Gerard

Chinese artichokes

Chinese (or Japanese) artichokes are small, white, ridged tubers that grow underground, like Jerusalem artichokes. In fact, they taste similar—though perhaps a little crisper and juicier—and are eaten in the same way, either cooked or raw. The plants are a member of the mint family and are very easy to grow. Start them off from tubers, not seed.

	spring			summer			fall			winter		
	E	M	L	E	M	L	E	M	L	E	M	L
plant outdoors				■	■							
harvest	■						■	■	▨	■	■	■

Where, when, and how to plant

Choose an open site with fertile, light soil. In early or mid-spring, once the ground has warmed up, plant tubers end-up in a shallow furrow 1½–3 in (4–8 cm) deep and 12 in (30 cm) apart. Then cover them carefully with soil.

Routine care

Weed and water your plants regularly. Snip off any flowers whenever they appear in order to concentrate the plant's energy on developing tubers, and earth up the soil around the stems to ensure that they remain covered.

Harvesting

At any time from fall onward, pull back the soil to check them just as you would do for potatoes, and harvest them if they're ready. However, if you lift them too early, they tend to dry out, so leave them in the soil until you are ready to use them.

What can go wrong

With luck, your only problems are likely to come from slugs and snails (*see pp.324–325*) and possibly root aphids (*see p.332*).

(top) **Growing in containers** restricts the tendency to spread invasively that Chinese artichokes share with all mints.

(bottom) **Washing soil** out of tuber ridges is tough—one reason, perhaps, why Chinese artichokes are not grown as frequently as Jerusalem artichokes.

Sea kale

Sea kale looks a little like an open-leaf blue-gray cabbage, and it is a member of the brassica family. The young leaves, stems, and the cream-colored flower heads can all be eaten raw. Alternatively, the stems can be forced over the course of winter in the same way as rhubarb, and can then can be harvested and cooked in early spring.

	spring			summer			fall			winter		
	E	M	L	E	M	L	E	M	L	E	M	L
plant outdoors	■											
harvest			■									

Where, when, and how to plant
Growing sea kale from seed is difficult, so it's best to start with root cuttings or "thongs." Choose a sunny site with rich, light, sandy soil, and in early spring plant thongs at least 2 ft (60 cm) apart. During the summer, keep plants well watered and cut off flower stems.

Forcing
Before winter sets in, remove any dead leaves and cover the crown with a layer of straw or bracken. Over the top of this, place a traditional forcing pot or an overturned box, pail, or flowerpot at least 15 in (38 cm) deep, and make sure no light can get in. Surround the cover with a layer of leaves, compost, or manure to keep everything warm, and leave it for two to three months.

Harvesting
Cut the blanched stems when they are 6–8 in (15–20 cm) tall. In late spring, remove the pots, spread mulch over the plants, fertilize them, and let them regenerate for the next season.

What can go wrong
As with all brassicas, clubroot can cause problems (see p.62). Flea beetles may also attack the young leaves (see p.329).

(top) **Take root cuttings** in fall, store in sand over winter, and plant in spring as buds start to form.

(middle) **Force sea kale** by covering the crowns with a lightproof pot in early winter.

(bottom) **Harvest** tender blanched shoots in spring.

Rhubarb

Once a rhubarb plant is established, it shouldn't require a lot of attention. Keep it well watered in the summer, fertilize it in the spring and fall, and allow the cold to get to it in winter, and it should reward you with one of your earliest crops of the new year—perhaps the first if you cover it and force it to produce tender, blanched stems in early spring.

Admittedly, rhubarb is greedy when it comes to space. In midsummer, when it is in full leaf, each plant can spread to 6 ft (2 m) across. However, the average family should only need two or three plants. And, if you keep dividing the rootstocks into new sets and replanting them, you should be able to keep those plants regenerating themselves for years and years.

	spring			summer			fall			winter		
	E	M	L	E	M	L	E	M	L	E	M	L
sow indoors		■	■									
transplant				■								
plant outdoors			■	■								
harvest					■	■	■	■				

Where to plant

Rhubarb grows best on an open site in soil that will retain moisture in the summer but will not become too wet in winter. If you're planting it for the first time, dig in plenty of well-rotted compost or manure beforehand.

When to plant

Rhubarb plants are dormant during the cold months between mid-fall and early spring. It's therefore the best period during which to divide established crowns and plant new sets.

Traditional terra-cotta rhubarb forcers have lids that can be removed in order to check when the blanched stems reach the top.

FORCING RHUBARB

Rhubarb can be forced to produce shoots a few weeks earlier than normal by covering the crown—as new stems develop, they are kept in darkness and do not receive any light.

1 During the winter, when the plant is dormant, it should be exposed to a couple of hard frosts.

2 Before the first shoots appear, cover the crown with straw and place a jar or overturned pot on top to exclude any light.

3 The blanched, tender, pink stems should be ready to harvest after about four weeks.

How to sow seeds

It's not easy to grow rhubarb from seed. If you want to try it, sow in pots or modules indoors in early spring, then plant out in late spring; alternatively, sow outdoors directly into the ground in a special seedbed, also in late spring. Thin out seedlings, and transplant them to their final location in fall.

How to divide crowns

Rhubarb can be propagated by dividing the main rootstock or crown of an established plant into separate pieces or sets. It's best done during the winter, when the leaves have all died down and the plant is dormant.

How to plant sets

Plant rhubarb sets in holes about 36 in (90 cm) apart with the main bud just showing above the surface of the soil. If you bury them completely, there's a danger that they will become waterlogged and rot.

Routine care

Weed and water regularly throughout the summer. An organic mulch applied in spring will help to reduce evaporation and keep the crowns as moist as possible. Cut off any stems that go to flower and any leaves that turn yellow and die. In fall, spread more mulch around the plants, leaving the crowns exposed so that frost can get at them—rhubarb needs a number of cold snaps to trigger new growth for the following year.

Harvesting

You should be able to start picking fresh young stems in spring and early summer. Thereafter, as they get older, they become tougher and stringier.

Newly planted sets should be harvested only lightly, if at all, in their first year. Give them until their second year to establish themselves and build up strength.

(top) **Mulch around plants** in fall, avoiding the crowns—exposure to cold will stimulate new growth next season.

(bottom) **Rhubarb is ready to harvest** once the outer stems are about 12 in (30 cm) in height; grip them firmly by the base and twist them off by hand.

Timperley Early

What can go wrong

Slugs and snails (*see pp.324–325*) may attack young buds, and aphids (*see p.326*) are sometimes attracted to new leaves.

    Crown rot and **honey fungus** are two of the diseases that may affect rhubarb. They are bacterial and fungal disorders that can cause the rootstocks to rot and die. You may save them if you're quick and carefully cut out and destroy all infected parts.

WARNING: Rhubarb leaves are poisonous. Do not eat them.

Recommended rhubarb

Champagne, Chipman, Glaskins Perpetual, Livingstone, Raspberry Red, Timperley Early, Victoria

Herbs

No vegetable patch or kitchen garden should be without herbs. They smell wonderful, they're easy to grow, they're essential to just about every kind of cooking, and they have a hundred and one other medicinal, cosmetic, and household uses—some practical and everyday, others mysterious and steeped in folklore. In addition, they attract beneficial wildlife and may even repel pests. Need any more convincing?

Whether your ambitions run to designing a full-scale formal herb garden, growing a few herbs in among your garden flowers, or merely planting a couple of pots on a terrace or balcony, you'll find most herbs very forgiving. Once they're established, they need little maintenance: trim them back from time to time in order to keep them bushy and to encourage new growth. Other than that, simply water them, pick them, and eat them—they taste so much better when harvested straight from the garden.

Group different herbs together and plant them at the front of a flower border to create an attractive informal herb garden.

1. **Basil** is an aromatic, spicy herb, used in salads, sauces, pesto, and flavored oils and vinegars.

2. **Bay** is an evergreen shrub that can be clipped into topiary bushes; it may not survive harsh winters.

3. **Chervil** has tiny, feathery, fernlike leaves and a taste somewhere between anise and parsley.

4. **Chives** are members of the onion family, and have a delicate, mild onion flavor.

5. **Cilantro** is grown not only for its leaves but also for its seeds, which are used as a spice (coriander).

6. **Dill** has delicate, feathery leaves with a mild anise flavor, and seeds that taste slightly stronger.

7. **Fennel** is edible from its flowers to its roots; in practice, it is the leaves and seeds that are most often used.

8. **Horseradish** roots have a pungent, sinus-clearing taste, the essential ingredient in horseradish sauce.

9. **Lemon balm** leaves have a delicate lemon taste, similar to though not as strong as lemon verbena.

10. **Lemongrass** stalks are an essential ingredient in many East Asian dishes.

11. **Lovage** leaves resemble those of flat-leaved parsley, and taste of celery and yeast.

12. **Marjoram** is a familiar ingredient and flavor in Mediterranean cooking.

13 **Mint** spreads so readily that it is best grown in containers in order to restrain it.

14 **Parsley** comes in two different forms—curly-leaf and flat-leaf.

15 **Rosemary** is an evergreen perennial with a distinctive resinous aroma.

16 **Sage** is likely to look as good in the flower border as in the herb garden.

17 **Savory** looks rather like thyme and has a similar though slightly more peppery taste.

18 **Sorrel** has a slightly sharp lemon flavor and is used in soups, sauces, and mixed salads.

19 **Tarragon** has long, narrow, green leaves with a mildly peppery, aniseed flavor.

20 **Thyme** is an evergreen perennial shrub with tiny, wonderfully aromatic leaves.

Basil

A powerfully aromatic, spicy herb, basil is widely used in salads, sauces, pesto, and flavored oils and vinegars. It's a natural companion to tomatoes—a marriage made in the warm climate of the Mediterranean. Basil needs sunshine, so if grown outdoors in cool temperate zones, it's likely to have only a short summer season. However, it's perfect for a brightly lit kitchen windowsill.

Sweet basil has medium-sized, bright-green leaves and is the most common variety. Other forms may have very large leaves (lettuce-leaf basil), very small leaves (Greek basil), colored leaves (purple basil), or multiflavored leaves (lemon basil and cinnamon basil).

How to grow

Sow seeds indoors from mid-spring onward and keep warm. Transplant or sow outdoors only when there is no longer any risk of frost. Water regularly but sparingly in the mornings; plants left wet overnight may rot or "damp off."

Harvesting and storing

Pick young leaves and pinch out growing tips to encourage the plants to become bushy. Remove any flowers. Store basil leaves in a cool place, but not in the refrigerator. Don't attempt to freeze or dry them. Instead, use them fresh or preserve them in olive oil.

(opposite page, clockwise from top left)
Purple basil, sweet basil, cinnamon basil, basil 'African Blue'

(right) **Lettuce-leaf basil**

LAYING OUT AN HERB GARDEN

Since all herbs are best used when fresh—as soon after picking as possible—it's best to site an herb garden as close to your kitchen door as you can. It makes no sense at all to be running back and forth to the far end of the garden every time you want some chives or a handful of mint.

1 Prepare the soil by adding plenty of well-rotted compost or manure. Set bricks into the soil to create different self-contained areas, and to give you something to stand on so that you don't compact the soil.

2 Transplant any pot-grown herbs and seedlings. Firm them down and water them in.

3 Some herbs can be left in their pots, especially if they are attractive terra-cotta ones. This miniature bay, which will eventually grow taller than the plants that surround it, will make a strong centerpiece.

4 Your planting may look a little empty at first, but don't be tempted to overfill the beds; they will quickly fill out as the herbs establish themselves.

Bay

Bay is an evergreen shrub and will grow into bushes (often clipped into topiary shapes) or even a full-sized tree. However, because it comes from the Mediterranean, in cool climates young plants may not survive harsh winters. It's safer to grow them in pots or containers and bring them indoors to protect them from frost and cold winds.

Bay leaves are too tough and hard to eat raw but are widely used as a flavoring in cooked dishes. Along with parsley and thyme, bay is one of the key ingredients in *bouquet garni*.

How to grow

Bay is hard to grow from seed, and although it can be propagated from cuttings (*see p.278*) or by layering, it's easier to buy ready-grown plants. Plant them in fertile soil in a sunny, sheltered location, or in good-sized containers filled with multipurpose potting mix.

Water regularly and fertilize two or three times a year. Shape the plant by clipping the leaves during the summer.

Harvesting and storing

Pick leaves at any time of the year. Use them fresh, or preserve them by drying.

Chervil

Chervil's tiny, feathery, fernlike leaves have a delicate taste that lies somewhere between anise and parsley. It is often added to salads and used in various cooked dishes—particularly omelets and other egg recipes. Chervil is in fact a relative of cow parsley, and though not nearly as large can grow almost as rampantly. In hot, dry summers it flowers and runs to seed readily, although keeping it well watered and growing it in partial shade will slow it down.

How to grow

Sow seeds directly into the ground, starting in early or mid-spring, and then every month or so until early fall. Scatter seeds sparingly and cover with a thin layer of soil. Seedlings should start to appear after about three weeks.

Thin the seedlings out to about 6–9 in (15–23 cm) if they are overcrowded, and remove flower heads when they appear, unless you want the plants to self-seed. Toward the end of the year, use cloches or frames to extend your harvest into late fall and winter.

Harvesting and storing

Chervil tastes best if you pick the small, young leaves before the plants flower. They can be frozen or dried—but they're much better fresh.

(top) **Chives in flower** (bottom) **Garlic chives**

Chives

Chives are members of the onion family, and have a delicate, mild onion taste. They are much smaller, of course—more like green onions in height. Their thin, hollow leaves grow in dense clumps, rather like tufts of grass. Chives are used as a flavoring and as a garnish, most often in salads. Regular chives produce purple or pink flowers in summer—these can also be eaten. Garlic or Chinese chives, which taste mildly of garlic, are a different variety, and have white flowers.

PROPAGATING HERBS BY DIVISION

Division is a technique that can be used to propagate certain perennial herbs, such as mint, thyme, fennel, and chives, which continue to grow from one year to the next.

1 Choose a day in fall when the ground is not too wet, then carefully dig up the rootball of an established plant.

2 Tease apart the roots in order to separate the plant into clumps, and replant the divided sections. Trim the leaves to a height of about 2 in (5 cm).

How to grow

Chives can be grown from seed or by dividing an existing clump. If you are starting with seeds, sow them in spring either in pots or modules or, if the soil is warm enough, directly into the ground. Choose a warm, sunny site with moist, fertile soil. Dig up established clumps and divide them in the fall. Pot or replant the offsets. Chives are perennials and should survive all but the harshest of winters.

Harvesting and storing

Snip a handful of leaves as and when you need them, since they don't keep for long. Regular harvesting promotes the growth of fresh young leaves—even if you cut down the plants almost to the ground.

Cilantro

Cilantro is a relative of parsley; indeed, its lower leaves are much like those of flat-leaf parsley. They have a strong, distinctive taste and are widely used in Mediterranean, Middle Eastern, Asian, and Central and South American cuisines. The finer, wispier upper leaves do not taste the same and tend not to be eaten. The small, round seeds, called coriander seeds, are used as a spice. 'Cilantro' and 'Leisure' are usually grown for their leaves, while 'Moroccan' is grown for seeds.

How to grow

Sow seeds directly into the ground, starting in early spring and then every month or so until late summer. Space rows 12 in (30 cm) apart and thin out seedlings to 6 in (15 cm). Water regularly to discourage plants from bolting. Toward the end of the year, use cloches or frames to extend your harvest or to overwinter seeds sown in the fall.

Harvesting and storing

Pick lower leaves as a cut-and-come-again crop. Collect the seeds when they turn brown, before they drop to the ground, then dry them and use them as a spice. The roots can also be eaten, and are often used in curry pastes.

(left) **Cilantro**

(right) **If allowed to flower**, cilantro may reach 3 ft (1 m) in height.

Dill

Dill is an annual with delicate, feathery leaves and flat clusters of tiny yellow-green flowers. It can grow as high as 4 ft (1.2 m). The leaves have a mild anise flavor—as do the seeds, though they are stronger. Both are widely used to flavor soups, sauces, salads, pickles, and fish dishes, particularly in Scandinavian and other northern European cuisines. The plant is similar to fennel in both taste and appearance, but the two are different. Don't plant them near each other or they may cross-pollinate and self-seed to produce odd hybrids the following year.

How to grow

Dill does not like being transplanted, so don't be tempted to start it off by sowing in pots or flats. Instead, choose a moist, fertile site in an open, sunny location, and sow seeds directly into the ground, starting in mid-spring and then every couple of weeks or so until midsummer. Thin seedlings to about 6 in (15 cm) apart. Dill is very prone to bolting, particularly in hot weather, so water it regularly, and never allow it to dry out.

Harvesting and storing

Pick the young leaves regularly to delay the plant from flowering for as long as possible. Use them as soon after harvesting as you can, since they wilt after just a day or two, even if kept in a refrigerator. They can, however, be frozen.

If you want to collect the seeds for use in pickling or cooking, cut the flower heads as soon as they turn brown and hang them upside down over a sheet of paper or cloth or enclose them in paper bags. When the seeds have dropped, separate them from any pieces of dried stem or husk.

If you leave the flower heads in place, the plant may self-seed for the following year.

Fennel

Unlike dill, to which it is related, fennel is a perennial. It's also larger, growing to a height of 6 ft (2 m) or more, and has green or bronze-colored leaves and yellow flowers. The whole plant is edible, from the flowers to the roots, but it is the anise-tasting leaves and seeds that are most often used as flavorings—in everything from fish and meat dishes through breads and cheeses to Indian spice mixtures. The herb fennel is not the same plant as the vegetable Florence fennel (*see pp.122–123*).

How to grow

Fennel likes to be on a well-drained site and in plenty of sun. Sow seeds directly into the ground any time after mid-spring, and thin seedlings to 18–24 in (45–60 cm) apart. Once established, the plants grow quickly. It's a good idea to remove the flower heads and trim back the plants to a height of about 12 in (30 cm) in early summer: this will stimulate fresh growth and a second wave of new leaves for harvesting.

In fall, cut the plants down to the ground and, unless you want them to self-seed, carefully remove all the flower heads and seeds. At the same time, you can, if you wish, propagate from established plants by digging up the whole rootball, carefully dividing it, and replanting the separate sections so that they continue growing as new plants (*see p.264*).

Harvesting and storing

Pick the leaves regularly and use them fresh or infuse them in oils and vinegars. Seeds can be dried and stored.

(top) **When the seedheads turn brown**, cut them down carefully. Lay the heads on a sheet of paper to collect the seeds, and remove pieces of dried stem or husk.

(middle) **Fennel in flower**

(bottom) **Bronze fennel 'Purpureum'**

Horseradish

Unlike most herbs, horseradish is grown primarily for its roots, not its leaves. Peeled and grated, the roots have a hot, pungent, sinus-clearing taste that is the essential ingredient in horseradish sauce, a traditional partner to roast beef or smoked fish. Homemade horseradish sauce, made with a freshly dug root, makes the store-bought version pale in comparison. Horseradish is a perennial—once established, it will spread and may be hard to get rid of. Its leaves are not particularly attractive, either, so think carefully about where you plant it.

How to grow

It is possible to grow horseradish from seed, but it's more often propagated by dividing an established plant or by taking (or buying) root cuttings called "thongs." Each thong should be about 6 in (15 cm) long, and is planted standing on end, so that its top is about 2 in (5 cm) below the surface of the soil. Plant thongs in spring.

Harvesting and storing

Young leaves can be picked from spring onward for use in salads, but horseradish is essentially all about the roots. You can just dig them up whenever you need them—although it's said that the flavor is at its best in fall.

(left) **A horseradish plant** can grow to 2 ft (60 cm) in height and has leaves that look a little like dock. It is related to the cabbage family.

(right) **The long taproots** are yellow on the outside and white inside. They are finely grated for use as a flavoring.

Lemon balm

The leaves of lemon balm look like a cross between those of mint and a stinging nettle, but they have a delicate lemon taste, similar to lemon verbena if not as strong. The leaves are used in both sweet and savory dishes. Some may even be added to salads, but they are most commonly used to make herbal teas.

Lemon balm is a hardy perennial and can grow to a height of 5 ft (1.5 m). The standard form has plain green leaves, but gold variegated varieties can also be found.

How to grow

Lemon balm will grow pretty much anywhere, as long as the soil is reasonably fertile and does not dry out. The only thing that might trouble it is strong sunshine in the middle of the day.

Sow seeds directly into the ground in the spring, and thin seedlings to 2 ft (60 cm) apart. Alternatively, propagate by dividing existing plants or by taking root cuttings in either spring or fall.

Harvesting and storing

Pick leaves as and when you need them. They can be dried but they are much better fresh. You might want to cut back the whole plant quite hard before it flowers in early summer in order to stimulate new leaf growth.

(top) **Common lemon balm** (bottom) **Variegated lemon balm**

Lemongrass

Lemongrass is a tall tropical or subtropical grass, originally from East Asia. The roots and stems contain an aromatic oil that produces its distinctive citrus flavor. The stalks are too tough to eat whole, so are crushed or thinly sliced and used in Thai, Vietnamese, and other East Asian cuisines, and often in Caribbean cooking, too. In a good summer, lemongrass can be grown outdoors in northern temperate zones, but it is a tender perennial and needs to be inside to survive the winter. Alternatively, cultivate it as an annual and grow from seed each year.

How to grow

In mild areas, sow seeds outdoors in early spring and protect them from frost. In cooler climates, sow in pots under cover or indoors. Germination can be slow, and the plants will need both a minimum temperature of 55°F (13°C) and a humid atmosphere to grow successfully.

Harvesting and storing

Cut the stalks just above the level of the soil, and trim off the leaves. Lemongrass will freeze well.

(above) **Lemongrass stalks** trimmed of their leaves and roots.

(right) **The blue-green leaves** of full-grown plants can reach up to 5 ft (1.5 m) in height.

Lovage

Lovage is a tall perennial with leaves that resemble those of flat-leaf parsley. Within just a year or two of planting, it can grow to be enormous—up to a height of 6 ft (2 m). You might therefore want to consider carefully the best location to grow it—probably not at the front of a border.

The leaves taste of celery and yeast, and can be used in soups, stews, or salads, and to flavor cold drinks or make herbal teas. Other parts of the plant can be eaten, too: seeds, stalks, and even the roots.

How to grow

Sow seed outdoors directly into fertile, moist soil in mid-spring, or—if you are collecting ripe seeds from an established plant—during late summer, although you may have to protect new seedlings from the cold by keeping them under cloches or in frames during the winter.

Alternatively, because lovage is a perennial, you can propagate it by division. In spring, dig up the whole rootball, carefully divide it, and replant the separate sections so that they grow on as new plants (see p.264).

Harvesting and storing

Pick young leaves regularly, as and when you need them. If you cut back the whole plant hard before it flowers in early summer, you can discard any tough older leaves and stimulate a second wave of new growth.

The stems of lovage are hollow and when cut and trimmed can be used as drinking straws; they give a wonderful kick of celery to an ice-cold Bloody Mary!

Marjoram and oregano

There are a number of different varieties within the marjoram family. Pot or French marjoram is a bushy perennial that grows up to 2 ft (60 cm) in height and has white, pink, or purple flowers. Its leaves are often dried. Sweet marjoram is slightly smaller, less attractive, but stronger tasting. Its leaves are more likely to be used fresh. Oregano (also known as wild marjoram) is stronger still. There are also golden, variegated, and crinkle-leaved varieties. Marjoram is an immediately recognizable ingredient in Mediterranean cooking—particularly pizzas.

How to grow

Marjoram needs warmth and sunshine. Sow seeds in spring, either in pots or directly into the ground, but be prepared to be patient, as germination can be hit-or-miss. Thin seedlings or plant them out at least 8 in (20 cm) apart.

Alternatively, dig up and divide establish plants in spring or fall, or propagate them by taking cuttings in summer. You may need to protect plants under cover in severe winters.

Harvesting and storing

Pick the leaves before the flowers start to open, particularly if you plan to dry or freeze them. When fall arrives, cut back the whole bush by two-thirds.

(left) **Oregano** (right) **Golden marjoram**

Mint

Mint is aggressively rampant. It's more of a challenge to restrain it than it is to find ways of encouraging it to grow. Were it not for mint's wonderful taste and aroma, it would surely be regarded as a weed; as it is, mint is almost indispensable. The leaves are used fresh in salads, as a flavoring accompaniment for vegetables, and in sauces, soups, drinks, candies, and desserts.

There are numerous different varieties. Apple mint is considered by many to make the best mint sauce, and peppermint the best tea. Ginger mint is variegated green and gold, Eau de Cologne mint has dark purple and green leaves, and Bowles' mint has large, rounded leaves and grows up to 3 ft (1 m) in height.

How to grow

Mint can be grown from seed—sown in pots or directly into the ground in spring—but you'll probably get a wider choice of varieties if you buy ready-grown plants. It is then very easy to propagate it yourself by division or by taking cuttings. Mint is not picky about sun or shade, but it does like the soil to be kept moist. To keep it from spreading uncontrollably, plant it in a sunken container or raised bed, or grow it in a pot. Change the soil every couple of years.

Harvesting and storing

Pick leaves throughout the summer and early fall, and cut your plants back before they flower. Mint leaves are best used fresh; they can be frozen but don't dry well.

(opposite page, clockwise from top left)
Spearmint, ginger mint, curly mint, apple mint

(right) **This pineapple mint plant** has been confined to a pot to stop it from spreading throughout the garden.

Parsley

Parsley, perhaps the most widely used of all herbs, comes in two different types: curly-leaf and flat-leaf. The latter, sometimes called French or Italian parsley, has a slightly stronger taste. Parsley is a hardy biennial: it produces leaves the first year but only flowers the second. Because the flowers are of no interest, it makes sense to grow it as an annual and sow seeds fresh each year. Harvest the leaves for as long as you can in fall, protecting plants with cloches to prolong the season, but dig up old plants the following spring.

How to grow

Parsley seeds are notoriously slow to germinate, although you can give them a helping hand by soaking them in warm water overnight. Sow in flats or modules, keep them under cover, then transplant later; alternatively, sow outdoors directly into the ground in mid-spring or when the soil is warm enough. Thin seedlings to approximately 9 in (23 cm) apart.

Harvesting and storing

Pick the leaves whenever you need them. The more you pick them, the more they will grow. If you made a second sowing of seeds in late summer, you should get a crop that will last well into the fall. Parsley will keep for a while in the refrigerator, but the leaves can also be frozen or dried.

(left) **Flat-leaf parsley** (right) **Curly-leaf parsley**

Rosemary

Rosemary is an evergreen perennial with gray-green, needlelike leaves, and pale or dark blue, purple, pink, or white flowers. It has a distinctive resinous aroma and is traditionally used to flavor roasted or grilled meats and vegetables. Most forms are naturally bushy, and rosemary is used for formal hedging and even topiary in mild climates.

If grown in large pots, it can be clipped into spheres, mopheads, or conical shapes. Creeping varieties such as 'Prostratus', however, look better tumbling out of a container or hanging basket or crawling over a wall.

How to grow

Rosemary can be raised from seed, but germination may be hit-or-miss. It's easier to buy ready-grown plants, or to propagate from an established shrub by taking cuttings in late summer or by layering in fall. Rosemary likes plenty of warmth and sunshine, and shouldn't be overwatered. Prune it in spring and protect it from extremes of cold during harsh winters.

Harvesting and storing

You can pick the leaves throughout the year if you live in an area with mild winters, although new growth will, of course, stop or slow down over the winter. In cold regions, grow rosemary in a pot and bring it indoors for the winter. Because it's always available, there's little point in taking the time to freeze or dry it.

(top) **Rosemary leaves**

(middle) **Rosemary plant in flower**

(bottom) **Clipped regularly**, a variety such as 'Miss Jessopp's Upright' is ideal for low hedges.

Sage

Sage is an attractive evergreen shrub that looks as good in the flower border as it does in the herb garden. Common sage has gray-green, slightly downy leaves, but there are also numerous other varieties: 'Purpurea' has purple leaves; 'Tricolor' has green leaves splashed with pink and white margins; 'Icterina' has gold variegated leaves; and pineapple sage tastes like... well, pineapple.

Sage leaves are strongly aromatic, and are widely used in meat dishes, stuffings, sauces, and flavored vinegars. They can even be deep-fried in tempura batter.

How to grow

Sage can be raised from seed sown in the spring, although some of the unusual varieties are best bought as ready-grown plants. It's also easy to propagate. Take softwood cuttings in summer or heel cuttings (which include a small section of woody growth from the previous year) in the fall. Pot them up, keep them under cover until they root, then plant them out.

Sage likes a warm, sunny site with well-drained soil, and grows well in containers. To keep established plants compact, prune them fairly hard in spring and pinch out growing tips during the summer. Sadly, sage won't last forever. When it gets too woody or leggy, dig it up and plant fresh.

Harvesting and storing

Because sage is an evergreen, you should be able to harvest leaves throughout the year in relatively mild climates—provided it is not killed off by a cold, damp winter.

Sage can be stored for a few days in the refrigerator by sealing the leaves in plastic bags. If you need to store it for longer, dry the leaves by spreading them out individually on a sheet of cloth or paper, then keep them in an airtight container somewhere out of the light.

(top) **Leaf cuttings** carefully trimmed and pushed into potting mix should quickly develop their own roots.

(bottom) **Pinching out growing tips** will encourage dense, bushy growth.

(clockwise from top left)
Common sage, 'Purpurea', 'Icterina', 'Tricolor'

Savory

Savory is a small, evergreen shrub that has tiny, slender green leaves. It looks somewhat like thyme and has a similar though slightly more peppery taste. There are two types of savory: summer and winter. Summer savory is an annual and has a delicate flavor. Winter savory has a much longer growing season, denser foliage, and a noticeably stronger taste. It should survive most winters, except in very severe conditions.

How to grow

Grow winter savory from seeds sown in spring, or by propagating from established plants. Lift and divide them in spring, or take cuttings in summer or early fall. Grow summer savory from seeds sown between mid-spring and late summer. Both types of savory like well-drained soil and plenty of sun.

Harvesting and storing

Pick the leaves before the plants flower and use them while they are fresh. Once flowering has taken place, the taste deteriorates and the plant is best pruned hard to promote new growth, or cut and hung upside down so that the remaining leaves dry.

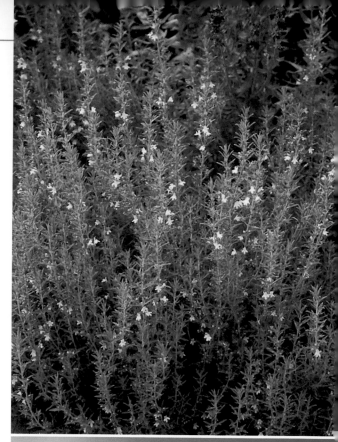

(top) **Winter savory**
(bottom) **Summer savory**

Sorrel

There are two main types of sorrel that are grown as herbs. Common or broad-leaf sorrel is the taller of the two, and has large elongated leaves like dock. Buckler-leaf or French sorrel is shorter and has much smaller, shield-shaped leaves. Both types have a slightly tart, acidic, lemon taste. The young leaves can be used in soups, sauces, and tossed salads.

How to grow

Sow seeds outdoors from late spring onward, or propagate by dividing established plants. Sorrel is happy in partial shade and likes regular watering. If it dries out, it is prone to bolting. Don't let it flower or set seed. If it does, cut it down almost to soil level, and wait for it to shoot again.

Harvesting and storing

Treat sorrel as a cut-and-come-again crop, picking the leaves as and when you need them. Use them fresh, since they don't store well.

(top) **Broad-leaf sorrel**
(bottom) **Buckler-leaf sorrel**

Tarragon

For use as an herb, French tarragon is the variety to grow. It is different from Russian tarragon, which—though it grows taller and is hardier—doesn't taste as good. Both forms have long, narrow, green leaves and, in the case of French tarragon, a mildly peppery, anise flavor. Tarragon is traditionally used in chicken, fish, and egg dishes, and for flavoring wine vinegars, mayonnaise, and sauces such as béarnaise and hollandaise. Along with parsley and chervil, tarragon is a key ingredient in the classic French *fines herbes* mix.

How to grow

French tarragon isn't available as seeds, so you have to either buy ready-grown plants or propagate it yourself by lifting and dividing an existing plant in spring or by taking cuttings in midsummer. It needs a sheltered, sunny location, with rich, well-drained soil. Once established, tarragon tends to spread naturally. Although it's a perennial, it may need covering or mulching with straw or mushroom compost if it is to survive a cold winter.

Harvesting and storing

Cut whole stems and strip the leaves from them—at any time between late spring and early fall. Leaves can be frozen or dried, but they are much better used fresh.

(left) **A large strawberry pot** makes an ideal vertical herb garden. Along with the strawberry plant here are tarragon and rosemary at the top, and golden marjoram and thyme spilling out of the side pockets.

(right) **French tarragon**

Thyme

Most thymes are evergreen perennials that have tiny aromatic leaves, but the family contains scores of different species and varieties. Common thyme grows fairly upright and is the one most often used in cooking. Others have variegated leaves, flowers that may be pink, purple, or white, or even a sprawling or creeping habit. The wonderful lemon-scented thyme does exactly what its name suggests. Along with parsley and bay, thyme is one of the key ingredients in *bouquet garni*.

DRYING HERBS

1 Pick a few bunches of leaves midmorning, after any dew has dried. Tie into bunches and hang upside down somewhere warm, dark, and well-ventilated.

2 Strip the dried leaves, and store in airtight jars.

How to grow

Thyme can be grown from seed, but ready-grown plants are available, and in a wide variety of unusual species, too. It's easy to propagate plants yourself by division, from cuttings, or by layering. Thyme needs a warm, sunny, well-drained site—in other words, the sort of conditions that are found in Mediterranean countries, where it thrives. It's a good idea to cut thyme back hard after it has flowered to prevent it from becoming too straggly.

Harvesting and storing

Pick sprigs of leaves—and flowers—throughout the summer months. Cut as much as you want as often as you want, since regular harvesting will prompt vigorous new growth and encourage plants to become bushy.

Thyme leaves are best used fresh, and will keep for a few days if sealed in a plastic bag in the refrigerator. However, like marjoram or oregano, they can be dried very successfully, too. Entire sprigs of leaves can also be preserved in bottles or jars of flavored oils and vinegars.

(clockwise from top left)
Variegated lemon thyme

Common thyme

Some species spread naturally, putting down roots as they sprawl. Sow seeds in the cracks between the stones of a patio—they'll soon colonize it.

Vegetable Year Planner

Knowing what to do and when is part of the secret of growing vegetables successfully. Sow or plant too early and seeds can fail to germinate or tender seedlings will be killed off by frost. Leave it too late and your growing season may be too short for crops to ripen fully. Getting the timing right is one of the things beginners find most difficult. Yet it's not as much of a mystery as it seems. If you have a community garden, watch what your neighbors are doing, and learn from them. Bear in mind, too, that none of this is a precise science. A great deal depends on where you live, any microclimate factors, and differences in the weather from one year to the next. These are only recommendations.

A summer harvest of eggplant, peppers, zucchini, and fennel.

Midwinter
JANUARY

Preparation
- Unless the ground is frozen, continue your winter digging.
- Spread well-rotted manure or compost over vegetable beds.
- Cover selected areas with polyethylene sheets to start warming up the soil.

Sowing seeds
- Indoors or in a heated greenhouse, sow **onion** seeds.

Planting out
- Plant your first **shallot** and **onion** sets if the ground is not frozen.

Routine care
- Force **rhubarb** if new shoots are beginning to sprout.

Harvesting
- Pick winter **cabbages** and **cauliflower**, Brussels sprouts, **kale**, and **leeks**.
- Lift remaining root vegetables such as **parsnips**, **celery root**, and **winter radishes**.
- Cut any surviving winter salads such as **corn salad**, **land cress**, **komatsuna**, **mibuna**, and **mizuna**.

Other tasks
- Buy seed **potatoes** and start chitting them.
- Buy **onion** and **shallot** sets.
- Order seeds.

(top) **Force rhubarb** by placing pots on top of the crowns.

(bottom) **Chit potatoes** ready for planting in early or mid-spring.

Late winter
FEBRUARY

Preparation
- Complete your winter digging.
- Spread well-rotted manure or compost over vegetable beds.
- Rake early seedbeds and cover them with glass or polyethylene cloches to warm the soil.

Sowing seeds
- Indoors or in a heated greenhouse, sow **onions**, **lettuces**, **tomatoes**, **leeks**, **peas**, and **globe artichokes**.
- Outdoors under cover, sow **fava beans**, early summer **cabbages**, **spinach**, **peas**, and **radishes**.

Planting out
- Plant **shallot** and **onion** sets, and **garlic** if you haven't already done so.
- Plant **Jerusalem artichokes** and protect with frames or cloches.
- Plant new **rhubarb** sets if the ground is not waterlogged.

Routine care
- Topdress overwintering perennial **herbs** (bay, rosemary, thyme, sage, etc.) growing in pots and containers.

Harvesting
- Pick winter **cabbages** and **cauliflower**, kale, sprouting broccoli, leeks, and any remaining **Brussels sprouts**.
- Lift the last of the root vegetables such as **parsnips** and **celery root**.

Other tasks
- Chit any remaining seed **potatoes**.
- Buy **shallot** and **onion** sets.
- Order seeds.

(left) **Cover seedbeds with polyethylene** to prepare the soil for sowing seeds as early as possible.

(right) **Sow seeds** for early crops indoors or under cover.

Early spring
MARCH

Preparation
- Fork or rake over your vegetable patch and break up any large clods of soil. Avoid stepping on the soil, which will compact it if it is still very wet.
- In mild weather, begin hardening off seedlings that have been raised indoors by moving them outside under cover during the day.

Sowing seeds
To give plants the earliest possible start and thus the longest possible growing season, you can start sowing seeds now. But temperatures are still likely to be low, and the soil still cold. Sow outdoors, either in pots or directly into the ground, only if you can protect plants with cloches, frames, or fabric.
- Indoors or within a heated greenhouse, sow **lettuces**, **tomatoes**, **eggplant**, **sweet peppers**, **chili peppers**, **cucumbers**, **celery**, **celery root**, **Florence fennel**, **peas**, **sweet corn**, and **sweet potato** seeds.
- Outdoors under cover, sow **fava beans**, red **cabbages**, summer **cauliflower**, **spinach**, **kale**, **Brussels sprouts**, **onions**, **leeks**, **carrots**, **turnips**, **peas**, **radishes**, early **lettuces**, and **asparagus** seeds.

Planting out
- Plant your first early seed **potatoes**, and any remaining **shallot** and **onion** sets.
- Plant **asparagus** crowns and **globe artichoke** offsets.
- Transplant early summer **cauliflower** seedlings and protect with frames or cloches.

Routine care
- Hoe any new-season weeds that are starting to appear.
- Prune old growth from perennial **herbs** such as rosemary, thyme, and sage. Divide chives.

Harvesting
Sadly, this is perhaps the leanest month of the year for fresh produce.
- Pick **leeks**, **sprouting broccoli**, and **kale**.
- Harvest your first spring **cauliflower**, **spinach**, **Swiss chard**, and **chard**.
- Cut the first of any early spring **lettuces** grown under cover.

Other tasks
- Protect **fava beans** and other young seedlings from slugs and snails.

Plant your first potatoes, setting them upright in the ground so that the end with the most chits is uppermost.

Mid-spring
APRIL

Preparation

- While the ground is still soft, put up canes, wigwams, and other supports for climbers such as **beans** and **peas**.

Sowing seeds

By now, the weather and the soil should be warming up, but there may be frost at night. Snow is possible in some areas. Sowing outdoors may be a gamble, so protect newly sown seeds and young seedlings with cloches, frames, or fleeces—especially at night.

- Indoors or in a heated greenhouse, you could make further sowings of the same seeds you sowed last month—but now add **French beans**, **runner beans**, **zucchini**, and **pumpkins**.
- Outdoors (under cover if necessary), sow **Swiss chard**, **spinach beet**, summer and fall **cabbages**, **celeriac**, **rutabagas**, **cucumbers**, and **land cress**, plus make any additional sowings of vegetables you planted last month.

Planting out

- Plant your second earlies and maincrop seed **potatoes**.
- Transplant seedlings of **eggplants**, **leeks**, **onions**, and early summer **cabbages** and protect with frames or cloches.
- This month is your last chance for planting **onion** sets, **Jerusalem artichokes**, and **globe artichokes**.

Routine care

- Earth up first early **potatoes**.
- Start watering young seedlings and thin them out if necessary.
- Hoe regularly to prevent weeds from establishing themselves.

Harvesting

- The end of the month might just bring the first **asparagus**.
- Harvest your first spring **cabbages**.
- Continue picking **leeks**, spring **cauliflowers**, **spinach**, **Swiss chard**, and **spinach beet**.

Other tasks

- Top-dress vegetables in pots, or transplant to new containers.

(top) **Erect wigwams for climbers**
(middle) **Protect seedlings with a tunnel cloche**
(bottom) **Hoe spring weeds**

Late spring
MAY

(top) **Plastic bottle cloche**
(bottom) **Planting tomatoes**

Preparation
■ Prepare remaining beds for early summer sowings and transplanting.

Sowing seeds
Despite higher temperatures and longer, sunnier days, overnight frost may still be a threat in some areas. If so, protect tender seedlings and young plants with cloches, frames, or fabric.

■ Outdoors (under cover at night if necessary), sow **green beans**, **runner beans**, **carrots**, winter **cauliflower** and **cabbages**, **beets**, **sweet corn**, **mizuna**, **mibuna**, and annual **herbs**, plus make any additional sowings of vegetables you planted last month.

Planting out
■ Harden off and begin to plant out seedlings you have raised indoors or outside under cover—for example, **tomatoes**, **peppers**, **chilis**, **celery**, **celery root**, **Brussels sprouts**, red **cabbages**, and so on.

■ Plant any remaining seed **potatoes**.

■ Plant **sweet potato** slips or seedlings in specially earthed-up ridges or growing bags.

■ Plant containers with ready-grown **herbs**.

Routine care
■ Weed and water regularly—particularly plants in containers or growing bags.

■ Tie in **peas** to sticks or poles.

■ Pinch out tips of **fava beans** in order to discourage aphids.

■ Earth up **potatoes**.

Harvesting

■ Continue picking **asparagus**—but probably only until the end of the month.

■ Harvest the first **garlic** and **globe artichokes**, and any early salad crops grown indoors or under cover—for example, **lettuces**, **arugula**, **radishes**, and **pea shoots**.

■ Pick **rhubarb**. Stems that have been forced will be ready earlier.

■ Continue picking spring **cabbages** and **cauliflower**, **spinach**, **Swiss chard**, and **chard**.

Other tasks

■ Fertilize any vegetables in containers or growing bags.

■ Ensure that brassicas (such as **cabbages**, **cauliflower**, and **Brussels sprouts**) have collars in place to protect them against cabbage root flies.

■ Erect protective barriers around **carrots** to deter carrot rust flies.

(top) **Sow runner beans** directly into the ground if there is no longer any risk of frost.

(bottom) **Earth up potatoes** to protect developing tubers from exposure to the light.

Early summer
JUNE

Sowing seeds

Unless you live in a very cold climate zone—or you are unlucky—frost should be over. Sow remaining seeds or plant out seedlings of everything you hope to harvest during summer and fall.

■ Outdoors, sow **zucchini, pumpkins,** summer and winter **squash, Florence fennel,** and **chicory,** plus anything else that you have not yet had a chance to sow this year.

■ Sow **asparagus** seeds if you want to propagate new plants.

Planting out

■ Plant out **cucumber** and **sweet corn** seedlings, plus anything else raised indoors or outside under cover that has not yet been transplanted into its final location.

■ Plant **herbs** you have grown yourself from seed.

Routine care

■ Weed and water regularly—particularly plants in containers or growing bags. You might want to fertilize them, too.

■ Thin out new seedlings if they become overcrowded.

■ Add an organic mulch around plants to help retain moisture.

■ Tie climbing **green** and **runner beans** in to their cane supports.

Harvesting

■ Depending on the weather, start harvesting **peas, fava beans, green onions,** and early summer **cabbages** and **cauliflower.**

■ You should be able to lift your first new **potatoes, onions, carrots, turnips,** and **beets.**

■ Continue harvesting **rhubarb, garlic,** and **globe artichokes,** as well as salad crops grown under cover.

Other tasks

■ Net **cabbages** and other brassicas to protect them from birds and caterpillar-laying butterflies.

■ Feed **asparagus** plants with a general-purpose fertilizer now you're no longer picking spears, but don't cut them down until fall.

(top) **Plant out seedlings**
(middle) **Water regularly** to prevent seedlings from drying out.
(bottom) **Harvest first turnips**

Use twigs to protect cabbages from birds.

Midsummer
JULY

Sowing seeds

- Outdoors, make additional sowings of successional crops—those for which you want a continuous harvest rather than a glut—in particular, **lettuces** and other salad greens, **radishes**, **green** and **runner beans**, and **spinach**.

Planting out

- Plant out any remaining seedlings raised during the spring and early summer.

Routine care

- Weed and water regularly—particularly plants in containers or growing bags.
- Pinch out sideshoots and growing tips of outdoor **tomatoes**, and feed them with a liquid tomato fertilizer.
- Remove the tip of the leading shoot if climbing **beans** have reached the top of supports.
- Earth up **Brussels sprouts** and other brassicas if their stems are unsteady.
- Blanch curly **endives** before harvesting.

Pinch out sideshoots that appear in the "V" between leaf stems and the main stem of vine tomatoes.

Harvesting

- You should be able to pick your first crops of **green** and **runner beans**, **celery**, red **cabbages**, and **zucchini**, as well as outdoor **tomatoes**, **lettuces**, **eggplant**, **peppers**, and **chili peppers**.
- Continue picking **peas**, **fava beans**, **spinach**, and summer **cabbages**.
- Lift main crop **potatoes** and the first of your storage potatoes.
- Lift further crops of **onions**, **shallots**, **garlic**, **carrots**, **turnips**, and **beets**.

Other tasks

- Cut down any **pea** or **fava bean** plants that are finished cropping, but leave the roots in the soil to disperse the nitrogen they contain.
- Take cuttings if you want to propagate perennial **herbs**.

Take rosemary cuttings and plant them in pots so that they develop new root systems.

Late summer
AUGUST

Preparation

- Sow green manure crops on areas of your garden where you no longer have anything growing.

Sowing seeds

- Outdoors, sow seeds for spring **cabbages**, and make further successional sowings of **spinach**, **corn salad**, **land cress**, and **Asian salad** leaves.

Routine care

- Weed and water regularly—particularly plants in containers or growing bags.
- Top off organic mulch around plants to help retain moisture.
- Pull up any **lettuces** or other salad crops that have bolted.

Harvesting

- Your first **sweet corn** should be ready for harvesting, along with outdoor-grown **cucumbers**.
- Continue picking **green** and **runner beans**, **celery**, red **cabbages**, **zucchini**, **peas**, **fava beans**, **spinach**, summer **cabbages** and **cauliflower**, and outdoor **tomatoes**, **lettuces**, **eggplant**, **peppers**, and **chili peppers**.
- Lift additional storage **potatoes**, **onions**, **shallots**, **garlic**, **carrots**, **turnips**, and **beets**.

Other tasks

- Deadhead flowering **herbs**.

(top) **Harvest main crop carrots**, lifting them with a fork if the roots are very long.

(bottom) **Pick zucchini** every day at the height of the season.

Early fall
SEPTEMBER

Preparation
■ Empty existing compost piles so that you have room to accommodate this season's mass of spent plant material.

Sowing seeds
■ Outdoors, this is probably the last month for sowing **spinach** and **Asian salad** seeds.

Planting out
■ Plant out spring **cabbage** seedlings ready for them to overwinter.

Routine care
■ Remove any dead foliage and clear away plants that are finished cropping.

Harvesting
■ This is probably the end of the season for summer **cauliflower**, **onions**, and **rhubarb**.
■ Continue picking **green** and **runner beans**, **zucchini**, **peas**, **spinach**, summer **cabbages** and **cauliflower**, **leeks**, **sweet corn**, and outdoor **tomatoes**, **lettuces**, **chicory**, and other salad leaves, **eggplant**, **peppers**, **chili peppers**, and **cucumbers**.
■ Lift your first **Florence fennel**, **parsnips**, **rutabagas**, and **celery root**, and more storage **potatoes**, **carrots**, **turnips**, and **beets**.

Other tasks
■ Cut down **asparagus** foliage as soon as it starts to turn yellow.
■ Cure harvested **pumpkins** and **squash** by leaving them in the sun.
■ Cut down the foliage on **potatoes** prior to lifting them.

Cure pumpkins and winter squash by leaving them in the sun so that their skins harden. If the weather turns wet, bring them indoors and store on straw-covered shelves.

Mid-fall
OCTOBER

Preparation
- Sow green manure crops for overwintering.
- Dig in green manure sown in late summer.

Sowing seeds
- Outdoors, sow seeds for next year's early summer **cauliflower**.

Planting out
- Plant **garlic** for next year.
- Divide **rhubarb** crowns and plant new sets.

Routine care
- Clear away the remains of any plants that are finished cropping.
- Take down bamboo poles and supports.
- Remove any yellow or diseased leaves from **cabbages** and **Brussels sprouts**.

Harvesting
- If you are lucky with the weather and have not yet had a frost, you may still be able to harvest **peas, tomatoes, cucumbers, sweet corn, green beans, runner beans, eggplant, peppers, chili peppers**, and **sweet potatoes**.
- Before the first frost, aim to pick all your **zucchini, pumpkins,** and **squashes**.
- Continue picking **spinach, Swiss chard**, fall **cabbages, leeks, Florence fennel, lettuces, chicory**, and other salad greens.
- Lift further crops of root vegetables such as **potatoes, carrots, turnips, parsnips, rutabagas, celery root**, and **beets**.

Other tasks
- Cut **Jerusalem artichokes** down to the ground.
- Lift Belgian **chicory** for forcing and blanching.

(top) **Dig in green manure** to return nutrients to the soil.

(bottom) **Lift Belgian chicory** in preparation for forcing it to produce blanched white chicons.

Late fall
NOVEMBER

Preparation
■ Start digging well-rotted compost or manure into any cleared vegetable beds.

Sowing seeds
■ Outdoors, sow **fava bean** seeds for next year's crop. They should overwinter happily. In areas with mild winters, sow **peas** and keep them under frames or cloches.

Planting out
■ If you haven't already done so, divide **rhubarb** and plant **garlic**.

Divide rhubarb by slicing off sets from the crown of an established plant and replanting them.

Routine care
■ Continue clearing away the remains of any plants that have finished cropping.

Harvesting
■ Start harvesting winter **cabbages**, **kale**, **Brussels sprouts**, and **winter radishes**.
■ Continue picking **spinach**, **Swiss chard**, **leeks**, and **Florence fennel**.
■ Lift further crops of root vegetables such as **carrots**, **turnips**, **parsnips**, **rutabagas**, and **celery root**.
■ You may still be able to pick a few **lettuces** and other salad greens, though they may need protection with fabric, frames, or cloches.

Other tasks
■ Move any tender perennial **herbs** growing in containers under cover or into a sheltered spot for the winter.

Move perennial herbs growing in containers into a spot that is sheltered from excessive winter wind and rain.

Early winter
DECEMBER

Preparation
■ Continue digging over cleared vegetable beds and adding well-rotted compost or manure to improve the soil.

Planting out
■ If you haven't already done so, divide **rhubarb** and plant **garlic**.

Routine care
■ Finish clearing away the remains of any plants that have finished cropping.
■ Do some pH tests on your soil and add lime if necessary.

Harvesting
■ Start harvesting winter **cauliflower**.
■ Continue to pick fall and winter **cabbages**, **Brussels sprouts**, **leeks**, **kale**, and **winter radishes**.
■ Lift **Jerusalem artichokes** and further crops of root vegetables such as **carrots**, **turnips**, **parsnips**, **rutabagas**, and **celery root**.
■ The only salad leaves likely to be left by now are **corn salad**, **land cress**, **komatsuna**, **mibuna**, and **mizuna**.

Other tasks
■ Check fall-harvested vegetables that you have in storage and throw away any that are rotting.

(top) **Enrich the soil** by digging it over and working in plenty of organic material such as compost or manure.

(bottom) **Clear away** any old plant material and add it to the compost pile. It will rot down over the winter.

Vegetable Doctor

At times, growing vegetables can feel like an uphill battle. A barrage of pests, parasites, diseases, and disorders seem intent on killing off the plants on which you have lavished such tender loving care. Any doctor will tell you that good nutrition and a healthy lifestyle help ward off illness. The same is true of plants— strong, healthy ones are less likely to get sick, and are better able to withstand attacks from pests. It may be a cliché, but prevention really is the best cure.

Of course, a diseased plant or one infested with parasites will need treatment. In this chapter you will find a guide to diagnosing what might be wrong with your vegetables, together with details of the most effective and appropriate cures and medicines. Some are organic, and some are not; only you can decide just how ecologically minded you want to be.

All plants need water—but not too much or you'll quite literally drown them. Getting the balance right is crucial.

What can go wrong

Cabbages and leaf vegetables

1 Seedlings dying
If young seedlings wilt and die, the reason may be **damping off** (*see p.320*), caused by a fungus that lives in the soil and thrives in damp, humid conditions. If seedlings fall over, with their stems severed or chewed through at the base, you should suspect **cutworms** (*see p.328*). They are moth caterpillars that live underground but come to the surface to feed at night.

2 Seedlings being eaten
Like almost all tender young plants, brassica seedlings are an irresistible temptation to **slugs** and **snails** (*see pp.324–325*). Try any or all of the traditional deterrents before resorting to pellets. Birds are also particularly partial to brassicas, and you may need nets to keep them off.

3 Small holes in leaves
Leaves peppered with tiny round holes, like perforations, are the telltale sign of **flea beetles** (*see p.329*). You may see the microscopic insects jump into the air if you disturb the leaves on which they are feeding.

4 Large holes in leaves
Big, ragged holes in brassica leaves are most likely caused by **cabbage caterpillars** (*see p.61*), especially between early summer and early fall. There are three types: the caterpillars of large white butterflies, which are yellow, black and hairy; those of small white butterflies, which are pale green; and those of cabbage moths, which are yellow-green or brown. If you spot them before they tunnel into the heart of cabbages, pick them off by hand. The only really effective deterrent is butterfly-proof netting to prevent the adults from laying eggs on your crops.

5 Leaves stripped and torn
Birds are capable of stripping leaves right down to the ribs and veins. Nets are the only certain way of keeping them off.

6 Leaves wilting and plants dying
Check first that your plants don't simply need more water. As plants grow it's not unusual for some of the outer, older leaves to wilt and fall off naturally—if so, clear them away before they rot. However, if young plants are wilting and if they seem loose in the soil, the problem may be **cabbage root flies** (*see p.61*), whose maggots feed on the roots. Worse, the cause could be **clubroot** (*see below*).

7 Pale leaves, stunted growth, plant dies
If brassica leaves discolor, turn pale, and wilt, and if the plant weakens and finally collapses, **clubroot** (*see p.62*) is the most likely cause. You can confirm the diagnosis by checking if the roots are enlarged and misshapen. Clubroot is a serious fungal infection that can survive in the soil for many years.

1

4

8 Yellow patches on leaves

If you can see white fluffy mold or fungal growth on the underneath of the leaves, it's probably an attack of **downy mildew** (*see p.321*). If there are chalky or shiny white spots or blisters on the undersides, then you should suspect **white blister** (*see p.323*). If the leaves curl up and harbor small gray insects covered with white wax, you have an infestation of **mealy cabbage aphids** (*see p.61*).

9 Discolored leaves

If leaves turn pale and perhaps slightly pink, or if they discolor between the veins, the plant may be suffering from a nutrient deficiency (*see pp.334–337*).

10 Leaves covered with insects and black soot

Infestations of **white flies** (*see p.333*) and **mealy cabbage aphids** (*see p.61*) are common. Both excrete a sticky honeydew on which black sooty mold grows. The insects suck sap from the leaves, sometimes causing them to distort and discolor. Severe attacks can weaken plants and make the crops inedible.

11 Cabbages don't form hearts

There are many possible causes: the soil may be poor and lacking in nutrients; the ground may not have been tamped down firmly enough when planting; lack of water; insufficient sunshine.

12 Cauliflower and calabrese don't form heads

The premature formation of small heads (called "button cauliflowers") that rapidly go to seed is a common problem. The most likely causes are: poor or loose soil; temperature too low when seedlings are planted out; insufficient or irregular watering; attack by **aphids** (*see p.326*), **flea beetle** (*see p.329*), or other pests. Try to avoid stressing the plants or checking their growth in any way.

13 Blown Brussels sprouts

Sometimes sprouts form loose, or blown, clusters of leaves instead of tight, round button heads. The cause is likely to be a combination of poor soil, loose planting, and irregular watering. F1 hybrid varieties are less likely to blow.

14 Cabbage heads split

Sudden changes in growing conditions are the most likely cause for cabbage heads splitting, either a downpour of rain after a period of drought, or a sudden frost after a period of warm temperatures.

15 Brussels sprouts and broccoli fall over

All brassicas need planting in rich soil that has been well trodden down. If they are allowed to rock in the wind, they may not form properly and may be blown over. Earth them up, or support them with stakes or bamboo poles.

16 Plants form flowers

Plants bolting by prematurely flowering in an attempt to form seed is usually a sign of stress at a change in growing conditions. Water regularly and try not to expose young plants to cold temperatures if planting out in spring.

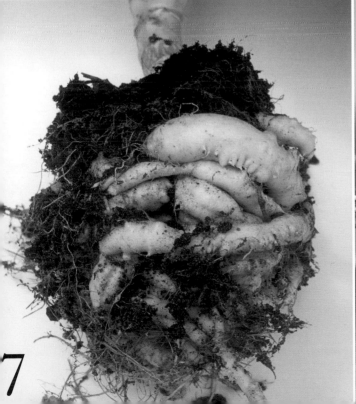

7

10

What can go wrong

Root and stem vegetables

1 Brown, rotting patches on potato leaves and stems
These are the signs of **potato blight** (*see p.93*). It spreads rapidly, particularly in warm, humid weather, when you may also see a fluffy white fungus beneath the brown patches, on the underside of affected leaves. Before rot spreads to the potatoes themselves, cut diseased foliage down to soil level and destroy it—don't put it on your compost heap.

2 Mottled or discolored potato leaves
Late frost can damage the foliage on young potato plants—although they almost always recover. Yellowing of leaves may be the result of lack of water, **magnesium deficiency** (*see p.334*), or a virus infection.

3 Withered potato stems and leaves
If growth is poor and your plants are weak and stunted, the roots may be under attack from **potato cyst eelworm** (*see p.93*). If the stems also turn black at soil level, you should suspect **potato black leg** (*see p.93*).

4 Potatoes are green
The green is caused by exposure to light. It makes the potatoes poisonous and they should not be eaten. Prevent it by earthing them up so that they are always covered with soil.

5 Holes in potatoes
Slugs (*see pp.324–325*) and **wireworms** (*see p.333*) tunnel into potatoes to feed and are the most common cause of holes. Large potatoes are sometimes found to have hollow central cavities in them when cut open—most likely the result of irregular watering, particularly if a period of drought is followed by a very wet spell.

6 Brown patches on potatoes
Dry, brown, corky patches on the skins are signs of **common scab** (*see p.93*). The potatoes are still edible if peeled or scrubbed. **Powdery scab** (*see p.93*) is similar, though not seen as often.

7 Potatoes rot
An attack of **blight** (*see p.93*) may cause potatoes to rot, either while still in the ground or after harvesting. Dry rot or soft rot may set in if seemingly healthy tubers are damaged before being put into storage.

8 Carrot and parsnip seedlings don't germinate or die
If seeds don't germinate at all, they may have been planted too deeply or, in the case of early sowings, the soil may still be too cold. If young seedlings wilt and die, the reason may be **damping off** (*see p.320*).

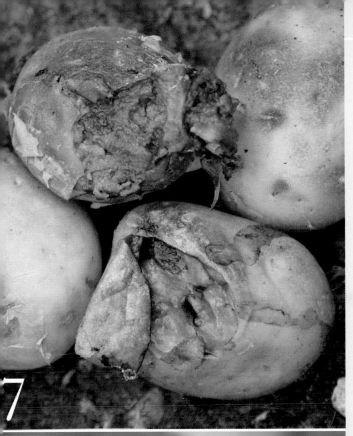

7

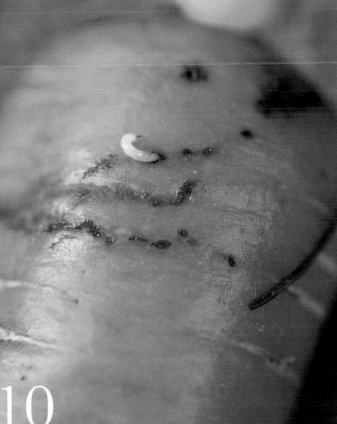

10

9 Forked or split carrots

Carrots tend to fork if they hit rocks in the soil. They prefer deep, fine soil with a high sand or loam content—raised beds are ideal for growing perfect, long, straight roots. They may also split or distort in soil that has been very recently manured or if they suddenly receive a lot of water after a long dry spell.

10 Tunnel-like holes in carrots and parsnips

Carrot rust flies (*see pp.104–105*) lay their eggs in the soil around carrots and parsnips. As soon as the eggs hatch, the small, cream-colored maggots burrow into the roots to feed. The tunnels become infected and the roots begin to rot.

11 Carrots rot

The most common cause of rot is **carrot rust flies** (*see pp.104–105*) but it may also be the result of **black rot,** which is a fungus that can be present in the seeds. Stored carrots are prone to rot, especially if they are damaged before being put away. Black patches are signs of black rot, and fluffy white fungal growth may indicate *Sclerotinia* (*see p.219*).

12 Parsnips have black or colored patches

Black, red-brown, or orange-brown growths on the roots may indicate **parsnip canker** (*see p.108*). It quickly leads to rot and may destroy your entire crop.

13 Turnip and rutabaga seedlings are eaten or die

Young seedlings are often eaten by **slugs** (*see pp.324–325*) or **birds** (*see p.327*). They may also die prematurely due to **damping off** (*see p.320*) or because their stems are severed at soil level by **cutworms** (*see p.328*).

14 Turnips, rutabagas, and radishes are woody or split

Irregular watering is the most likely reason—either too little or a sudden drenching following a drought. Roots also tend to turn woody if left in the ground too long before harvesting.

15 Turnips, rutabagas, and kohlrabi develop distorted roots

These plants are brassicas, so **clubroot** (*see p.62*) is as much of a risk as it is with cabbages. Foliage may yellow and wither, and plants may die. When lifted, the roots will appear deformed and swollen. However, if there are holes in the roots and you spot white maggots among them, you should suspect **cabbage root flies** (*see p.61*).

16 Celery root does not swell up

Celery root needs rich fertile soil and plenty of water. Be careful that plants do not dry out, don't let weeds compete for valuable moisture, and mulch to help with water retention.

17 Plants produce flowers before roots are ready to harvest

Premature flowering, or bolting, is the plant's attempt to form seed, usually in response to stress caused by being too dry, too cold, or having insufficient nutrients. Water regularly and try not to expose young plants to cold temperatures in spring.

What can go wrong

Onions, leeks, and other alliums

1 Leaves curled and distorted
Microscopic **stem and bulb eelworms** (*see p.332*) feeding inside the bulbs are the probable cause. Uproot and destroy affected plants at once.

2 Garlic cloves don't form new heads, shallots don't split into bulbs, and onions don't fatten up
There are numerous possible causes, but the most likely are poor soil, irregular watering, or overcrowding. If garlic doesn't form heads of new cloves, it may be because it has not been exposed to the cold period it needs. Next year, try planting it in fall so that it overwinters in the ground.

3 Orange powdery coating on leaves
This is a fungus called **leek rust** (*see p.139*). It's more common on leeks and garlic than on onions and shallots. If you cut off affected leaves promptly, you stand a good chance of saving your crop. Burn the leaves, don't compost them.

4 Leaves turn yellow and wilt
If as well as yellow leaves you find white fungus and small black growths at the bottom of the bulbs, it is probably **onion white rot** (*see p.128*). If there are maggots in the leaves, stems, or bulbs, the problem is more likely **onion flies** (*see p.128*) or **leek moths** (*see p.330*).

5 Plants produce flowers
If onions, leeks, or other alliums form flower shoots, they have bolted and are trying to set seed. It may be too cold, or too dry. Cut off the flowers, and harvest and use the crops soon, because they are unlikely to store well.

6 Maggots in bulbs and stems
Small creamy-white grubs in the bulbs of onions or the base and stem of leeks may be the larvae of **onion flies** (*see p.128*), **allium leaf miners** (*see p.326*), or **leek moths** (*see p.330*). They make plants inedible and can weaken them so badly that they die.

7 Leeks tunneled with holes
The holes are most likely caused by the creamy-white larvae of either **allium leaf miners** (*see p.326*) or **leek moths** (*see p.330*). Rot often sets in once the plants have been attacked.

8 White or blue mold on bulbs
Fungal growth around the roots and at the base of bulbs is probably **onion white rot** (*see p.128*).

9 Bulbs rot in storage
If the necks of onions turn soft and discolor, they may have **onion neck rot** (*see p.128*) or be infected by **downy mildew** (*see p.321*). Bulbs must be thoroughly dried before storing. Any that are soft won't keep and should be thrown out, not composted.

What can go wrong

Perennial vegetables

1 Asparagus spears being eaten
If young spears are being nibbled, **slugs** and **snails** (*see pp.324–325*) are the most likely culprits. Later in the season, **asparagus beetles** (*see p.241*) can also cause damage.

2 Asparagus foliage being eaten
If the fernlike foliage is being stripped from the stems, there is probably an infestation of **asparagus beetles** (*see p.241*). Look for the gray, grublike larvae or distinctive red, cream, and black beetles.

3 Asparagus rotting
If foliage turns yellow and wilts, and the plant seems at risk of dying, check at the base for signs of **foot** and **root rot** (*see p.321*).

4 Globe artichokes are disappointingly small
These are big plants that need a lot of water in the summer if the flower heads are to fatten up. Cutting the topmost, or king, globe as soon as it is ripe will encourage the heads that follow to grow well.

5 Globe artichokes and cardoons covered in aphids
This can be a serious problem, as a bad infestation of blackflies or **aphids** (*see p.326*) weakens plants and may make the crop inedible.

6 Jerusalem artichokes being eaten
If foliage or tubers are being eaten, suspect **slugs** and **snails** (*see pp.324–325*).

7 Jerusalem artichokes rot
Plants turning yellow and showing signs of white fluffy growth at the base may be infected with the fungal disease *Sclerotinia* (*see p.249*).

8 Rhubarb is flowering
If your rhubarb begins to send up tall flowering shoots, cut them off at ground level to keep it producing stems for eating.

9 Rhubarb wilts and grows poorly
If sticks are thin and pale and if there are signs of rotting in the center of the plant, it may have **crown rot** (*see p.255*), a fungal or bacterial infection.

10 Orange-brown patches on rhubarb leaves
It's common for outer leaves to turn yellow and die. Just cut them off and remove them. But orange patches on the surface of the leaves, coupled with white fluffy mold on the underside, can indicate **downy mildew** (*see p.321*).

What can go wrong

Peas and beans

1 Seeds don't germinate
Mice (*see p.331*) are notorious for eating pea and bean seeds, so what might seem a failure to germinate may simply be that the seeds are no longer in the soil. If green and runner beans don't germinate, the seeds may have been attacked by **bean seed flies** (*see p.327*).

2 Seedlings being eaten
Birds (*see p.327*) and mice (*see p.331*) are very partial to pea seedlings. **Slugs** and **snails** (*see pp.324–325*) can strip green and runner bean seedlings overnight.

3 Seedlings dying
Ragged leaves, tunneled stems, and weak growth of green and runner bean seedlings can indicate attack by maggots of the **bean seed fly** (*see p.327*).Otherwise, the reason may be **damping off** (*see p.320*), caused by a fungus that lives in the soil and thrives in damp, humid conditions.

4 Runner beans don't set
Sometimes runner beans drop their flowers without pods forming. **Birds** (*see p.327*) may be the culprits, or there may have been a lack of pollinating insects. In hot, dry weather, spraying the flowers with a fine water mist is thought to help, as is watering regularly to keep the roots moist.

5 Plants covered in aphids
Blackflies and greenflies are a common problem. An infestation of **black bean aphids** (*see p.327*) can quickly cover fava bean plants, weakening them so badly that growth is stunted and healthy pods do not form. Pinch out the soft growing tips to deter them. They also attack green and runner beans. Peas suffer from **green** or **yellow pea aphids** (*see p.148*), particularly when the weather is warm and humid.

6 Fava bean leaves being nibbled
Semicircular notches eaten in the leaves are the telltale sign of **pea and bean weevils** (*see p.161*). Unless they attack young plants, the damage is unsightly but rarely affects the crop.

8

9

7 Orange powdery coating on leaves

This is a fungus called rust. It is similar to **leek rust** (*see p.139*), which is common on leeks and garlic, but can also affect green, runner and fava beans.

8 Brown spots on fava bean leaves

Round spots and patches on leaves, and dark streaks on stems and pods, are most likely caused by the fungus **chocolate spot** (*see p.161*). It spreads in damp, humid conditions.

9 Yellow or white patches on pea leaves

Yellow markings on leaves can be a sign of **downy mildew** (*see p.321*). If there are yellow blotches on the pods as well, it could be **pea leaf and pod spot** (*see p.148*). A white powdery coating is probably **powdery mildew** (*see p.322*), especially if the weather is warm and dry.

10 Maggots in pea pods

These are the larvae of **pea moths** (*see p.148*), which hatch from eggs laid on the flowers then tunnel into the pods to feed on the peas. Similar tiny grubs can attack fava beans too.

11 Distorted, misshapen pods

Stunted pods that are empty or don't form properly are often the result of pollination problems and are more likely to occur toward the end of the plant's life. If pea pods are stunted and develop white or silvery brown patches, the cause may be **pea thrips** (*see p.148*).

12 Plants wilt and die, leaving signs of rot around roots

If leaves and stems wilt and discolor, the roots turn dark and rot, and the plant dies, it has probably been infected with **foot** and **root rot** (*see p.321*), a fungus that lives in the soil. Dig up and destroy affected plants immediately.

What can go wrong

Salad crops

1 Seeds don't germinate

Lettuces and other salad crops aren't always as easy to grow as you might think. Seeds won't germinate if it's too cold or too hot. Until the soil has warmed up in mid- to late spring, it's best to sow undercover. Outdoors, avoid sowing during spells of very warm weather.

2 Seedlings being eaten

The tender young seedlings of all salad greens are a feast for **slugs** and **snails** (*see pp.324–325*). Even mature lettuce, endive, and chicory plants are targets. Large, ragged holes, stripped leaves, and slime trails are the telltale signs. Try any or all of the traditional deterrents before resorting to slug pellets.

3 Seedlings and young plants dying

If seedlings wilt and die, the reason may be **damping off** (*see p.320*), caused by a fungus that lives in the soil and thrives in damp, humid conditions. If young plants fall over, with their stems severed or chewed through at the base, you should suspect **cutworms** (*see p.328*) or **leatherjackets** (*see p.329*).

4 Plants covered in aphids

Greenflies or other **aphids** (*see p.326*) can be a problem on salad greens, and an infestation can quickly spread, covering plants in sticky honeydew and black sooty mold, weakening them so badly that growth is stunted, and spreading disease.

5 Large holes in leaves

These are most likely caused by **slugs** and **snails** (*see pp.324–325*) but it is not unknown for **birds** (*see p.327*) to feed on salad crops as well.

9

6 Tiny round holes in leaves
Leaves peppered with small round holes, like perforations, are caused by **flea beetles** (*see p.329*). They are particularly fond of Asian salad greens, arugula, and radish tops. You may see the microscopic insects jump into the air if you disturb the leaves on which they are feeding.

7 Leaves are wilting and growth is stunted
The most likely cause is lack of water. Salad crops lose a lot of moisture through their leaves in hot temperatures. Water them regularly and they should recover. If they don't, and if you find a waxy white powder in the soil around the roots, the cause may be creamy white **lettuce root aphids** (*see p.172*).

8 Gray mold on leaves
Fluffy gray, off-white, or gray-brown mold is most likely *Botrytis*, or gray mold (*see p.172*). It can spread quickly in humid weather and can cause plants to rot and die.

9 Older leaves turn yellow or brown
If you also see white fluffy mold growing on the undersides of the affected leaves, it is probably **downy mildew** (*see p.321*). It is worse when the weather is wet or humid.

10 Plants produce tall stems or flowers
This indicates that plants have bolted. In other words, they are flowering—or are about to flower—in an attempt to form seed. It is usually a sign of stress—most often due to lack of water. To prevent it, water regularly and don't ever let plants dry out. Once salad crops such as the arugula shown here have bolted, they are not normally worth saving because the leaves will have turned bitter-tasting.

10

What can go wrong

Tomatoes, peppers, and other fruiting vegetables

1 Seeds don't germinate
Tomatoes, chili peppers, peppers, and eggplant all need heat to germinate. It's best to start them off by sowing them under cover in flats, modules, or pots. You may need a heated propagator. Mice love sweet corn seeds and may steal them before they germinate, so sow more than you need and thin out seedlings later.

2 Seedlings being eaten
Young seedlings grown outdoors are at risk from **slugs** and **snails** (*see pp.324–325*). Try any or all of the traditional deterrents before resorting to slug pellets.

3 Seedlings and young plants dying
If seedlings wilt and die, the reason may be **damping off** (*see p.320*), caused by a fungus that lives in the soil and thrives in damp, humid conditions. If young plants fall over, with their stems severed or chewed through at the base, you should suspect cutworms (*see p.328*) or slugs (*see pp.324–325*). **Foot** and **root rots** (*see p.321*) sometimes afflict tomatoes—check for brown discoloration or mold at the base of the stem.

4 Failure to set fruit
If plants flower but fail to produce miniature fruit, successful pollination has not taken place. Open your greenhouse during the day so that pollinating insects can get inside, and spray or mist plants with water to help pollination.

5 Leaves are sticky and covered with small insects
Outdoors, an infestation of **aphids** (*see p.326*) is probably the cause. In greenhouses, it is most likely to be **whiteflies** (*see p.333*). However, both can attack indoors and out. The insects feed on sap from leaves, and excrete sticky honeydew on which black sooty mold grows. They weaken plants and spread viral diseases.

6 Leaves are pale and mottled, with fine silk webs
If leaves turn dull and colorless, then wilt and drop off, it may indicate an infestation of **spider mites** (*see p.331*). You may just be able to see the tiny insects, and also their white silk webs. The problem is usually restricted to greenhouses but in hot summers, plants outdoors can be attacked, too.

7

9

7 Brown, rotting patches on tomato leaves and stems

These are the signs of **tomato blight** (*see p.210*). It spreads rapidly, particularly in warm, humid weather, and can quickly cause tomatoes themselves to turn brown and rot. Uproot affected plants and destroy them—don't put them on your compost heap.

8 Tomato leaves are curled

Provided that there are no additional signs of mold, rot, or discoloration, this is unlikely to be a serious problem. It is probably caused by temperature variations or irregular watering.

9 Leaves are discolored

Yellowing between the veins, which sometimes turns into dark purple or brown patches, can be a sign of **magnesium deficiency** (*see p.334*), especially in tomatoes. Paradoxically, it may be caused by too much high-potassium tomato food.

10 Split skins

Tomatoes often crack and split. It's not a problem if you eat them immediately, but if you leave them, rot can set in. The cause is usually a growth spurt triggered by fluctuations in temperature or by irregular watering.

11 Tomatoes are not ripening

At the end of the season, tomatoes are notorious for staying green instead of turning red. This is usually caused by falling temperatures and declining light levels. Encourage them to ripen by bringing them indoors or under cover.

12 Tomatoes develop pale rings on their skin

This is known as **tomato ghost spot** (*see p.210*). The rings are fungal gray mold infections caused by water splashes, and they can occur at any time—when the fruit are still green and unripe as well as when they are fully ripened.

13 Dark patches at the base of tomatoes and peppers

These round, sunken, brown or black blotches are called **blossom end rot** (*see p.210*). They indicate calcium deficiency caused by plants being left unwatered and drying out.

14 Sweet corn cobs being eaten

Mice (*see p.331*), squirrels, and birds (*see p.327*) are the most likely culprits, but in rural areas, badgers can be a pest, too.

12

14

What can go wrong

Cucumbers and squashes

1 Seeds don't germinate
The temperature needs to be 20°C (68°F) or higher to guarantee germination, so until the soil has warmed up outdoors, sow undercover in modules or pots, using a heated propagator if necessary. Seeds sometimes fail if they rot before germination takes place; reduce the risk by sowing them on their edge.

2 Seedlings being eaten
Young seedlings grown outdoors are at risk from **slugs** and **snails** (*see pp.324–325*). Try any or all of the traditional deterrents before resorting to slug pellets.

3 Seedlings and young plants dying
If seedlings wilt and die, the reason may be **damping off** (*see p.320*), caused by a fungus that lives in the soil and thrives in damp, humid conditions. In very wet weather or in heavy, water-retentive soil, **foot** and **root rots** (*see p.321*) sometimes afflict young plants—check for brown discoloration or mold at the base of the stem.

4 Failure to set fruit or premature rot
Zucchini, marrows, and squashes sometimes flower but fail to produce miniature fruit, or they are stunted and soon rot or drop off. It means that successful pollination has not taken place, perhaps because it was too cold or because pollinating insects did not visit. You can try hand-pollinating flowers yourself (*see p.226*).

5 Leaves are sticky and covered with small insects
Cucumbers that are grown under cover are prone to attack by **whiteflies** (*see p.333*). The insects feed on sap from leaves, and excrete sticky honeydew on which black sooty mold grows. Outdoors, **aphids** (*see p.326*) can attack both cucumbers and squashes.

3

4

7

10

6 Cucumber leaves are pale and mottled, with fine silk webs

If leaves turn dull and colorless, then wilt and drop off, it may indicate an infestation of **spider mites** (*see p.331*). You may just be able to see the tiny insects, and also the white silk webs they spin. The problem is usually restricted to greenhouses but in hot summers, cucumbers and squashes grown outdoors can be attacked too.

7 White powdery coating on leaves

This is probably **powdery mildew** (*see p.322*), especially if the weather is warm and dry in late summer. Regular watering, feeding, and good air circulation keep plants healthy and help to prevent it.

8 Leaves have a yellow mosaic pattern

Distorted, yellow and green mottled leaves together with small, hard, inedible fruit can indicate **cucumber mosaic virus** (*see p.221*). It affects not just cucumbers but also zucchini, marrows, squashes, and pumpkins. Uproot affected plants and destroy them—don't put them on your compost heap.

9 Zucchini stop producing

Don't let zucchini grow into marrows. If you pick them regularly, the plant will continue to produce flowers and more new fruit.

10 Cucumbers taste bitter

Female greenhouse cucumbers have been bred not to need pollinating. However, if they are accidentally pollinated by male flowers from another plant, the cucumbers will be deformed, bitter, and inedible.

11 Squashes and pumpkins rot in storage

After harvesting, leave winter squashes and pumpkins out in the sun to cure; the drier and harder their skins, the longer they will last in storage. Summer squashes won't keep and should be eaten soon after picking.

Diseases and disorders

Most plant diseases are caused by fungi, viruses, or bacteria. Of the three, fungal diseases are probably the most common and bacterial diseases the least common. In all three cases, microorganisms (or pathogens) invade the plant and trigger a variety of symptoms. Sometimes these are superficial (slightly discolored foliage, or spots on a few leaves, for example) and can be treated if identified in time. In severe cases, where plants are badly infected or the disease has spread widely, growth will be inhibited or disrupted so seriously that they wilt and die.

How diseases spread

Understanding how diseases spread is an important part of learning how to safeguard against them. Fungal infections are usually transmitted from one plant to another by spores (like those that an ordinary mushroom deposits). The spores may be blown in the air or spread by the splashing of rain or water from a garden hose or watering can.

The same goes for bacteria, although they may also be transported by animal or insect carriers. Viruses spread via infected sap, which is often carried by animals and insects. Moreover, if the sap gets on to tools such as pruners, it can turn the process of pruning or taking cuttings into an epidemic. Viruses may also be passed on from one plant generation to the next in infected seeds.

Treating the sick

Certain fungal diseases may be treatable—or at least preventable—by using fungicides. Commercially produced fungicides are either "contact" or "systemic."

Contact fungicides are sprayed or dusted all over the plants and kill fungal spores with which they come in contact as the spores germinate. Unfortunately, that means they may not be of much use in treating fungal growths that have already established themselves.

Systemic fungicides are taken inside a plant and circulate within its system via the sap. They kill fungi that actually live inside the internal plant tissues.

In recent years, many once commonly used fungicides have been withdrawn. Traditional Bordeaux mixture and other copper-based compounds are no longer for sale to home growers, and very few synthetic fungicides available to home gardeners are permitted for use on food crops.

Not much can be done for a plant with a viral disease. It should simply be removed and destroyed, and care should be taken not to let the conditions in which it took hold persist.

With bacterial diseases, prompt action is crucial. If you catch the disease early, and remove any infected plant material, you may be lucky. Otherwise, prevention is the best cure.

(far left) **Crop rotation** is worthwhile even in a small bed.

(left) **Use new or sterilized pots** and fresh potting mix to help prevent damping off.

PROTECTING AGAINST DISEASE

Two things more than any other contribute to the spread of disease. The first is open wounds or damaged tissue in the leaves or stems of a plant. Often this is how diseases enter it in the first place. The second is a damp, humid atmosphere. Most diseases and disorders thrive in warm, wet, stagnant conditions, where they will replicate only too readily.

Here are some simple do's and don'ts that should help you keep diseases at bay.

- Don't overcrowd plants. Give them space so that air can circulate around them freely.
- Weed, water, and if necessary fertilize regularly. Healthy plants are more likely to be able to ward off disease.
- Disinfect tools before and after use if you are working with infected plants—especially those with a viral disease.
- Use clean seed flats and pots for sowing seeds and transplanting.
- Use fresh soil or potting mix.
- Although saving and recycling water is ecologically sound, rain barrels can harbor disease-causing microorganisms. When dealing with vulnerable seedlings and young plants, tapwater is safer.
- Clear away all plant debris at the end of the season, and burn anything that you suspect might be infected. Don't risk putting it on the compost pile.
- Follow a crop-rotation plan (see pp.36–37) to discourage recurrent diseases from building up in the same areas.

Bacterial leaf spot

Affects various vegetables—particularly brassicas and cucumbers.

Symptoms

Leaves develop gray or brown spots or patches of dead leaf tissue, often with a bright yellow halo. As these spread, the leaves die.

Causes and treatment

Bacteria attack the leaf tissue, often entering via damaged areas. They spread via rain or splashing during watering. Caught early, the disease is unlikely to be fatal. Remove and destroy infected leaves, and water the soil around the plant rather than its foliage.

Blight *see* potato blight *(p.93) and* tomato blight *(p.210)*

Blossom end rot *see* tomatoes *(p.210)*

Botrytis *see* lettuces *(p.172)*

Chocolate spot *see* fava beans *(p.161)*

Clubroot *see* cabbages *(p.62)*

Crown rot *see* rhubarb *(p.255)*

Cucumber mosaic virus *see* cucumbers *(p.221)*

Damping off

Affects all young seedlings.

Symptoms

Roots and stem bases darken in color and rot. Seedlings then collapse and die. Some seeds may not germinate at all.

Causes

Caused by a fungus in the soil, which spreads rapidly in damp, poorly ventilated conditions, and can destroy whole seed flats of young plants. Once the disease has taken hold, there is no treatment. Discourage it by not sowing seeds densely, by using fresh potting mix and scrupulously cleaning seed flats or pots, by ensuring good ventilation, and by avoiding overwatering.

(from top) **Bacterial leaf spot, blossom end rot, chocolate spot, clubroot**

Downy mildew

Affects a wide range of vegetables—particularly lettuces, onions, root vegetables, and cabbages and other brassicas.

Symptoms

Yellow or brown patches develop on the upper surface of leaves, with white fluffy mold on the underside, and leaves die. Once the plant is weakened, gray mold (*see p.172*) may follow.

Causes and treatment

Caused by fungi that like damp, humid conditions. Destroy infected leaves immediately. Discourage by sowing thinly to keep air circulating and by watering at soil level, not from overhead.

Foot and root rots

Affect asparagus, celery, tomatoes, cucumbers, zucchini, peas, and beans.

Symptoms

If the plant stem base is infected, it darkens and tissues shrink and die. Leaves and stems will wilt, turn yellow or brown, and die. Infected roots may turn black or brown and break up or rot.

Causes and treatment

Caused by fungi that live in soil and standing water. Once the disease has taken hold, there is no treatment. Remove and destroy infected plants and soil. Discourage by using fresh potting mix and clean seed flats. Crop rotation will help avoid recurrence.

Fungal leaf spot

Affects various—particularly beets, celery root, and celery.

Symptoms

Leaves develop spots of dead tissue, perhaps in concentric gray or brown rings. Spots may spread and join, affecting large areas of leaves. Tiny black or brown growths are the telltale sign that the disease is fungal rather than bacterial leaf spot.

Causes and treatment

A range of different fungi attack the leaf tissues—some target specific vegetables. Caught early, the disease is unlikely to be fatal. Remove and destroy infected leaves. Don't leave any lying around at the end of the year, or the spores may survive the winter and reinfect your crops the following spring.

(from top) **Cucumber mosaic virus, damping off, foot and root rot, fungal leaf spot**

Gray mold *see* lettuces *(p.172)*

Halo blight

Affects dwarf green and runner beans.

Symptoms

Leaves develop dark spots each with a bright yellow halo around it. They then turn yellow between the veins. As the yellow areas spread, the leaves die. Infected pods develop gray patches.

Causes and treatment

Caused by bacteria that may have lain dormant in the seed. It spreads via rain or water from a can or hose splashing from one leaf to the next. Immediately remove and destroy infected plants, including seeds. Carefully water the soil around any plants that appear unaffected rather than splashing the foliage from above.

Honey fungus *see* rhubarb *(p.255)*

Leek rust *see* leeks *(p.139)*

Onion neck/white rot *see* onions *(p.128)*

Parsnip canker *see* parsnips *(p.108)*

Pea leaf/pod spot *see* peas *(p.148)*

Potato black leg *see* potatoes *(p.93)*

Potato blight *see* potatoes *(p.93)*

Potato common scab *see* potatoes *(p.93)*

Potato powdery scab *see* potatoes *(p.93)*

Powdery mildew

Affects a wide range of vegetables.

Symptoms

A white powdery coating of mildew appears on upper (and often lower) surface of leaves. It may turn slightly purple. Leaves turn yellow and fall off. Growth is impaired, and the plant may die.

(from top) **Halo blight, honey fungus, leek rust, onion white rot**

Causes and treatment

The fungi thrive in dry soil: spores spread via wind and rain splash. Remove and destroy infected leaves immediately. Sow thinly for good air circulation, and water the base of plants regularly.

Rhizoctonia *see Florence fennel (p.123)*

Rust *see leek rust (p.139)*

Sclerotinia *see Jerusalem artichokes (p.249)*

Tomato blight *see tomatoes (p.210)*

Tomato ghost spot *see tomatoes (p.210)*

Violet root rot

Affects asparagus, celery, and root vegetables such as carrots, beets, parsnips, and potatoes. Not often seen in the U.S.

Symptoms

Tubers and roots are covered in a mass of purple threads to which soil sticks. Black, velvety fungal growths appear, and roots might rot. Above ground, infected plants discolor and grow poorly.

Causes and treatment

The fungus thrives in warm, wet, acidic soils, often for years. There is no treatment for the disease, and it can be difficult to eradicate. Immediately remove and destroy infected plants and their soil. Practice crop rotation to try to discourage recurrence.

White blister

Affects cabbages and other brassicas.

Symptoms

Chalky or shiny white spots or blisters appear on the underside of leaves, with yellow-brown patches on the upper surface. Leaves and flower heads may become badly distorted.

Causes and treatment

The fungus thrives in damp, humid air. Remove and destroy infected leaves or plants. Choose resistant varieties, practice crop rotation, and sow thinly to ensure good air circulation and low humidity.

(from top) **Parsnip canker, potato blight, powdery mildew, sclerotinia**

Pests and parasites

Most gardeners find a way of coexisting happily with insects, birds, and animals. Not so for vegetable growers. It's a battle to stop the worst of them from eating crops before you do. Pea, bean, or corn seeds are always under threat from mice and birds, while young seedlings are at risk of being felled by slugs, snails, cutworms, or leatherjackets. Fresh green foliage may be riddled with holes where caterpillars and flea beetles have been feeding. Mature plants may be smothered by sap-sucking, honeydew-excreting aphids. Even root crops ready to harvest can be sabotaged by root flies, beetles, and wireworms. Get to know the enemy: the more you know about their life cycle, feeding habits, and behavior, the easier it will be to defend your plants without resorting to potentially harmful chemicals.

Slugs and snails

These leave behind them a telltale, silvery slime trail, and are the bane of many a gardener's life. At their most active at night and after rain, they munch holes in leaves and plant stems, and can devour a row of seedlings in one night. They sometimes eat into celery stalks, leaving discolored patches prone to rot, and they can burrow deeply into potatoes, leaving them riddled with holes.

Eco-friendly control

A simple, foolproof, nonchemical solution to the problem of slugs and snails doesn't yet exist. It's impossible to eradicate them completely from a vegetable patch; the challenge is how best to minimize the damage that they do. Pellets are the most reliable control, but may be harmful to other animals, including pets. There are many ingenious alternatives, some of which are more successful than others.

Plant defenses

Surround vulnerable plants with a circle of something so offputting that only the hungriest slugs and snails will be prepared to cross it. Try sharp gravel, crushed eggshells, bran, or copper bands (which set up a static charge). Of course, the more intrepid will burrow underneath...

Slug nematodes

Phasmarhabditis hermaphrodita is a parasitic nematode that finds its way inside the bodies of slugs (and to a lesser extent snails) when they burrow underground, and triggers a fatal bacterial infection. It is most effective in spring and fall, and in moist, warm conditions.

An anti-slug-and-snail checklist

- Weed regularly, keep grass short, and clear plant debris so they have fewer places to hide.
- Water in the morning rather than the evening so the soil is not damp at night.
- Go out at night with a flashlight and handpick as many slugs as you can find.
- Put out decoy food—like lettuce or comfrey leaves—to tempt slugs away from plants.
- Grow "sacrificial" plants that you don't mind being attacked.
- Protect vulnerable seedlings with cloches—improvised from cut-off plastic bottles.
- Line pots and containers with copper tape.
- Hoe regularly to bring slugs and eggs to the surface where predators may get them.
- Put out overturned orange or grapefruit halves. Slugs and snails will congregate under them, and can then be destroyed.

(far left) **A protective circle of sharp sand** may guard a vulnerable seedling from slugs and snails.

(left) **To make a slug trap**, half-fill steep-sided containers with beer and sink them into the ground so the edges are just above the surface. At night, slugs and snails may fall into the traps and can be picked out and destroyed in the morning.

INSECTICIDES

However energetically you follow eco-friendly procedures, there may be times when an infestation is so severe, or pests and parasites are so resistant to green or biological control measures, that you need to use an insecticide. They work in different ways.

Contact insecticides kill insects that come into contact with the spray or powder. If they eat the poisonous substance, they will also die. Systemic insecticides don't kill so directly. They are absorbed by plants and find their way into their sap. Bugs that feed on the sap will die.

All insecticides are chemical, but some are greener than others. You won't find arsenic, cyanide, or mercury in sheds or garages any more, and infamous insecticides such as DDT have long been outlawed. Modern synthetic insecticides are rigorously tested, and many are highly selective: they target only certain species. Organically approved insecticides include pyrethrum, refined plant oils, and insecticidal soaps, all derived from plant extracts.

Here are some simple rules to follow:
- Wear gloves and, if necessary, a mask and goggles.
- Follow manufacturers' instructions carefully.
- Spray early in the morning or late in the evening when bees and other beneficial insects are less likely to be harmed.
- Take care to spray contact insecticides all over the plant—above and below the leaves.
- Don't resort to spraying insecticides unless you have to.
- Don't spray in windy weather.
- Don't use an insecticide sprayer for fertilizer or weed killer.
- Don't make up more than you need and don't store any leftovers.
- Don't eat vegetables shortly after spraying.

(from top) **Allium leaf miner pupa, black aphids, green aphids**

Allium leaf miners

Also known as allium leaf-mining flies, these tiny flies have maggotlike larvae that burrow into the leaves of onions and leeks. The larvae are creamy-white, about $\frac{1}{4}$ in (5 mm) long, headless, and legless. After eating their fill, they transform into rust-brown pupae, about $\frac{1}{8}$ in (3–4 mm) long, which you might find if you peel back the outer leaves at the base of onions and on the stems of leeks. The damage that leaf miners cause is similar to that of leek moths (*see p.330*) and onion flies (*see p.128*).

Damage

The leaf mines or tunnels made by the larvae harbor bacteria and fungi. Once disease sets in, leaves may become curled and distorted, and the plants begin to rot. They are then unusable.

Treatment

There are no permitted insecticides for the home gardener. Affected plants should be uprooted and destroyed. To reduce the risk, rotate crops and cover plants with horticultural fabric or an insectproof mesh to protect them from adult flies when they lay their eggs in early to mid-spring and again in mid- to late fall.

Aphids

Also known as blackflies or greenflies, they may also be yellow, pink, gray-white, or brown. There are hundreds of different kinds. Most are about $\frac{1}{16}$ in (2 mm) long but some grow to $\frac{1}{4}$ in (5–6 mm). Some have wings and others do not. Aphids breed throughout the summer and their numbers can multiply exponentially. Within a week of birth, young aphids are ready to breed.

Damage

Some types of aphid restrict their attack to a specific vegetable; others are much less choosy. Either way, heavy infestations stunt growth and cause leaves to curl up and distort. Aphids excrete a sticky, sugary substance called honeydew over leaves, on which black, sooty mold grows—this can cause blistering. Because aphids feed on sap, they often transfer viruses between plants.

Treatment

Squash the aphids between finger and thumb, or spray bad infestations with an approved insecticide. Organic treatments include pyrethrum, refined plant oils, and insecticidal soaps. Ladybugs, lacewings, and other insects make natural predators (*see pp.338–339*). *See also* black bean aphids (*p.327*), lettuce root aphids (*p.172*), mealy cabbage aphids (*p.61*), *and* root aphids (*p.332*).

Asparagus beetle *see* asparagus *(p.241)*

Bean seed flies

The small white maggots of the bean seed fly live in the soil and feed on the seeds and seedlings of green and runner beans.

Damage

Attacked seeds may not germinate. Stems of affected seedlings may be tunneled by the grubs, and leaves may be ragged and tattered. Some seedlings recover and survive, while others do not.

Treatment

There are no permitted insecticides for the home gardener. Reduce the risk by sowing seeds in late spring, when temperatures are higher, to speed up germination and early growth, or by raising seedlings in modules or pots before planting outdoors.

Birds

In the kitchen garden or in the vegetable patch, a wide variety of birds can cause headaches.

Damage

The leaves of peas, beans, cabbages, and other brassicas may be damaged or even stripped by birds. Pea and fava bean pods are always at risk, particularly from jays. Newly sown pea and beans seeds and freshly planted onion sets may also be dug up, often by blackbirds. Seedlings are also sometimes pulled up.

Treatment

Scarecrows, mirrors, unwanted CDs, humming wires or tapes, windmills, and even dummy cats or birds of prey may all work for a while. But birds are savvy and they won't be deterred for long. Protecting your plants with nets is the only real answer.

Black bean aphids

Black bean aphids (also known as blackflies) about $\frac{1}{16}$ in (2 mm) in length cover the growing tips and new leaves of fava bean, globe artichoke, and cardoon plants.

Damage

They are attracted to the tender new growth at shoot tips. They eat sap, stunt leaves, and stop bean pods from forming properly.

Treatment

Once the plants are fully grown, or at the first sign of an attack, pinch out the growing tips and discard them. If you spot aphids,

(from top) **Asparagus beetles, blackbird, black bean aphids**

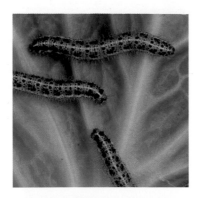

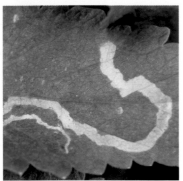

(from top) **Cabbage caterpillars, celery leaf miner, Colorado beetle**

squash them between finger and thumb, or spray bad infestations with an approved insecticide. Organic treatments include pyrethrum, refined plant oils, and insecticidal soaps. Ladybugs and lacewings are natural predators (*see pp.338–339*).

Cabbage caterpillars *see* cabbages (*p.61*)

Cabbage root flies *see* cabbages (*p.61*)

Carrot rust flies *see* carrots (*pp.104–105*)

Caterpillars

These are easy to see feeding on leaves, but harder when boring into plants or in the soil feeding on roots. Many species attack vegetables, and may be various colors and sizes, and smooth or hairy.

Damage

They feed on plant tissue, at best merely perforating the leaves with holes, at worst fatally damaging the heart of the plant.

Treatment

Pick off caterpillars by hand, looking underneath leaves as well as on top. Spray badly infested plants with insecticidal soap, pyrethrum, or an approved pesticide. *See also* cabbage caterpillars (*p.61*), cutworms (*below*), and pea moths (*p.148*).

Celery leaf miner *see* celery (*p.117*)

Colorado beetle *see* potatoes (*p.93*)

Cutworms

These are actually moth caterpillars. They are creamy-brown and grow to about $1\frac{3}{4}$ in (4.5 cm) long. They live in the soil.

Damage

They sever the stems or roots of young plants, causing them to wilt and die. Cabbages, leeks, celery, and lettuces are particularly badly affected. They also feed on leaves near the surface of the ground, and may eat into carrots and potatoes.

Treatment

They come to the surface at night and may be easier to spot by flashlight. Look for them in the soil around a plant that has recently been attacked. Spray plants or treat soil with an appropriate insecticide. Regular weeding reduces their choice of food.

Flea beetles

These are shiny black or blue-black, often with yellow stripes down their backs, and are usually hard to see with the naked eye. Apart from the damage, one telltale sign of infection is that they jump in the air when disturbed. They spend the winter in plant debris and lay eggs in spring, so they can be a problem in summer.

Damage

They eat small round holes in leaves. They are unsightly rather than fatal, but bad infestations can kill seedlings. Vegetables most often affected are arugula, radishes, Asian salad greens, cabbages, sea kale, and potatoes and other root vegetables.

Treatment

Time sowing so vulnerable seedlings grow quickly. Water regularly to stop plants from drying out. Cover with fine mesh or fabric. If necessary, spray badly infested plants with an approved pesticide.

Leafhoppers

Insects that live beneath leaves, feed on plant sap, and jump in the air when disturbed. Of the thousands of species, the problematic ones are mainly green or yellow and $1/16$–$1/8$ in (2–3 mm) long.

Damage

They feed from underneath leaves and cause pale, mottled spots or patches that can be seen from above. Plants affected include tomatoes, eggplant, peppers, and cucumbers—especially if grown in greenhouses—and beans, lettuces, potatoes, and herbs.

Treatment

Spray badly infested plants with an appropriate insecticide. Organic treatments include pyrethrum. Ladybugs, lacewings, and spiders are natural predators (*see pp.338–339*).

Leatherjackets

The larvae of the crane fly. They are gray-brown in color and grow to about $1^3/4$ in (4.5 cm) long. They have no legs, nor anything recognizable as a head. They live in the soil.

Damage

They eat through stems and roots, causing plants to wilt and die—particularly lettuce, cabbage, and other brassica seedlings.

Treatment

They are resistant to most insecticides, but starlings, thrushes, and blackbirds love them. Likely to come to the surface of the

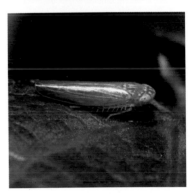

(from top) **Cutworm, flea beetle damage, potato leaf hopper**

(from top) **Leek moth caterpillar, mealybugs, mouse**

soil after lots of rain. A nematode called *Steinernema feltiae* is available; it kills them by infecting them with a bacterial disease.

Leek moths

Small, gray-brown, and rather nondescript, the leek moth lays its eggs twice a year—one generation in mid- to late spring and a second later in the summer. The eggs hatch into creamy-white caterpillars with small legs and a dark brown or black head. As they feed, the larvae can grow to about ½ in (10 mm) until they transform into silk-covered, cocoonlike pupae, usually on the surface of the leaves. The damage leek moth caterpillars cause is similar to that of the allium leaf miner (*see p.326*).

Damage

As their name suggests, leek moths lay their eggs primarily on the leaves of leeks, but they can also attack onions, shallots, garlic, and even chives. The caterpillars tunnel into the leaves or stems of the plant, working their way down toward the base or bulb. Bacteria and fungi colonize the boreholes and rot sets in. White or brown patches appear, leaves may turn yellow, and the plant can become slimy.

Treatment

There are no permitted insecticides for the home gardener. Affected plants might be saved if you spot the caterpillars early and are able to pick them off before they tunnel in too deeply, but plants that have started to rot should be uprooted and destroyed. To reduce the risk in following years, rotate your crops and cover plants with horticultural fabric or an insectproof mesh to protect them from adult flies when they lay their eggs.

Lettuce root aphids *see* lettuces (*p.172*)

Mealy cabbage aphids *see* cabbages (*p.61*)

Mealybugs

Females are flattish, creamy-white insects up to ¼ in (5 mm) long that eat plant sap and secrete a fluffy, sticky white wax to provide a protective covering. Adult males don't live long and don't feed.

Damage

They can weaken plants and restrict growth. In temperate climates, they are likely to be a problem only in greenhouses, where they may attack tomatoes, eggplant, peppers, and cucumbers.

Treatment

They can be "painted" one by one with a brush dipped in methylated spirits. Alternatively, spray with insecticidal soap or, in summer when it's hot, introduce a ladybug called *Cryptolaemus montrouzieri* into your greenhouse—it may eat the mealybugs and their eggs.

Mice

House mice, wood mice, and field mice can all be pests.

Damage

They are very fond of peas, beans, and sweet corn, and will dig up seeds to eat them as soon as they start to sprout, if not before.

Treatment

Traps are more reliable than protecting seedbeds with nets or chicken wire—and they are arguably more humane than poison.

Onion flies *see* onions *(p.128)*

Onion thrips *see* onions *(p.128)*

Pea and bean weevils *see* fava beans *(p.161)*

Pea aphids/moths/thrips *see* peas *(p.148)*

Potato cyst eelworm *see* potatoes *(p.93)*

Root aphids

Root aphids feed on roots rather than leaves. They are usually $1/16$–$1/8$ in (2–3 mm) long and creamy-brown in color, sometimes covered in a white powdery secretion that can be seen on the soil.

Damage

They weaken plants and make them wilt, particularly in warm weather. Different species attack green and runner beans; carrots and parsnips; lettuce; and Jerusalem and Chinese artichokes.

Treatment

They live underground so it's harder to eradicate root aphids than ordinary ones, even with permitted insecticides. Your best bet is to practice crop rotation to prevent next year's crops from being attacked by aphids that survive the winter.

(from top) **Onion thrips, pea moth caterpillar, spider mite damage**

(from top) **Root aphids, slug, snail**

Slugs and snails *see* slugs and snails (*pp.324–325*)

Spider mites
Tiny, eight-legged mites, hard to see with the naked eye; they are yellow-green most of their lives, and turn red in the fall and winter. On badly infested plants you may see fine silk webs.

Damage
Leaves develop dull, pale-yellow flecks or mottling, then curl, turn brown, and may die. In temperate climates, mites are likely to be a problem only during hot, dry summers or in greenhouses, where they may attack tomatoes, eggplant, peppers, and cucumbers.

Treatment
There are no synthetic pesticides for food crops available to the home gardener. You can try spraying with organic plant oils or insecticidal soaps. In greenhouses, employ a predator. From late spring to early fall, when daytime temperatures above 70°F (21°C), introduce into your greenhouse a mite called *Phytoseiulus persimilis* that might eat the spider mites and eggs.

Stem and bulb eelworms
These tiny nematodes live in the soil and feed inside the bulbs of onions and other alliums. They are invisible to the naked eye.

Damage
Leaves become curled, swollen, and distorted. If bulbs are produced, they will not store but will turn soft and rot.

Treatment
There are no pesticides for food crops available to the home gardener. Dig up and destroy affected plants immediately—do not compost them. Reduce the risk through crop rotation.

Whiteflies
There are two types of whiteflies that can attack vegetable crops: cabbage whiteflies and glasshouse whiteflies. The adults of both kinds are about $\frac{1}{16}$ in (2 mm) long with white wings; they fly up when disturbed. They lay eggs on the undersides of leaves, which hatch to release tiny scalelike nymphs that feed on sap. Black, sooty mold grows on the sticky honeydew they excrete.

Damage
They attack cabbages, Brussels sprouts, and other brassicas, plus zucchini and sweet potatoes. Glasshouse whiteflies attack

greenhouse plants like tomatoes, cucumbers, peppers, eggplant, and okra. In hot summers, they thrive outdoors as well as indoors. Heavy infestations may stunt growth and cause leaves to yellow.

Treatment

Organic insecticides are of limited use against cabbage whiteflies. Most synthetic pesticides are not permitted for food crops; check the manufacturer's instructions beforehand and use only for bad infestations. The damage to Brussels sprouts, broccoli, cabbages, and cauliflower is likely to look worse than it is, because only the outer leaves are affected. These can be removed before eating.

Glasshouse whiteflies tend to be resistant to insecticides. They also breed rapidly so that, even if sprays are effective, repeated applications are needed. A better alternative is to hang yellow sticky traps or to introduce a parasitic wasp called *Encarsia formosa* to feed on whiteflies. Don't use both an insecticide and a predator or you may kill both the flies and the wasps.

Wireworms

These are the larvae of click beetles. They have orange-brown bodies and are about 1 in (2.5 cm) long, with six legs at the same end as their head. They live in the soil.

Damage

Like cutworms, they can sever the stems or roots of young plants, causing them to will and die. Lettuces are particularly badly affected. They also eat into potatoes, turnips, carrots, and other root vegetables.

Treatment

Wireworms are resistant to most insecticides. Dig up root crops as soon as they are ready to harvest. If they are attacked, look for wireworms in the soil and destroy them.

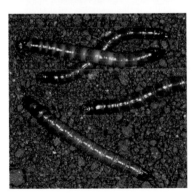

(from top) **Stem and bulb eelworm damage, whiteflies, wireworms**

Unhealthy diets

Just as humans starved of essential vitamins develop diseases such as scurvy and rickets, so plants denied their necessary nutrients may fail to grow properly and will exhibit symptoms of malnutrition. Such disorders can look very like diseases. Actually, most soils contain all the essential minerals and elements that plants need to flourish, but sometimes chemical imbalances occur and plants cannot absorb them properly—perhaps because the soil is too acidic or alkaline (*see p.21*), or because it contains too much fertilizer. Excessive potassium, for example, makes it hard for plants to take up magnesium from the soil.

Major nutrients

The most important three elements for plant growth are nitrogen (N), phosphorus (P), and potassium (K). Plants need a plentiful supply of all of these to grow healthily. They also need calcium and magnesium in smaller quantities. These are all nutrients you should consider adding to your soil.

Calcium deficiency

Affects vegetables listed below.

Symptoms

Cabbages and other brassicas: inner leaves turn brown.
Carrots: discolored spots, cracks, and craters in the roots.
Celery: central leaves turn black.
Lettuce: leaf tips go brown and look scorched.
Potatoes: leaves roll up and shoots get spindly.
Tomatoes/peppers: *see* Blossom end rot (*p.210*)

Prevention and control

In acidic soil, calcium levels may be low; or if the soil is dry, plants may be unable to absorb it. Water regularly and apply a surface mulch to encourage moisture retention. Lime the soil to increase the pH level (*see p.21*).

Magnesium deficiency

Affects potatoes, tomatoes, lettuce, and cabbages and other brassicas.

Symptoms

Leaves are yellow between the veins and around the edges due to insufficient magnesium to produce green chlorophyll. Yellow areas may turn red, purple, or brown.

Prevention and control

Magnesium is easily washed out of light soil by heavy rain. Levels may also be low in acidic soil or when potassium fertilizers have been used to increase the amounts of potassium. Apply Epsom salts (magnesium sulfate) as a foliar spray or spread over the soil.

Nitrogen deficiency

Affects all vegetables, except peas and beans, which absorb their own nitrogen from the air.

Symptoms

Leaves are pale green or yellow due to insufficient chlorophyll. Some may even turn pink, red, or purple. Older leaves near the base of the plant tend to be the worst affected. Plants are smaller than normal, and perhaps spindly or stunted.

Prevention and control

Heavily cropped, light soil that lacks organic matter might suffer, as might container plants. Heavy rain will make the problem worse. Add lots of well-rotted compost, manure, or other organic material, and/or some high-nitrogen fertilizer. Plant some green manures (*see p.24*) that take nitrogen from the air and fix it in the soil. Grow peas and beans, which don't need nitrogen-rich soils.

Phosphorus deficiency

Affects all vegetables.

Symptoms

Phosphorus stimulates quick-growing shoots and roots; without it, plants grow poorly and may be slow to flower and fruit. Leaves may turn yellow, blue-green, or purple and may drop prematurely.

Prevention and control

Phosphorus deficiency is rare. It's most likely in acidic soil, heavy clay, or deep peat after periods of prolonged heavy rain. Add a superphosphate fertilizer or organic bonemeal.

Potassium deficiency

Affects many plants—particularly potatoes and tomatoes.

Symptoms

Potassium helps plants absorb water and photosynthesize. Without enough of it, leaves curl, turn yellow, scorch at the edges, and may have purple-brown spots underneath. Flowering is poor, fruit are small, and plants may be more vulnerable to disease. Tomatoes may not ripen evenly.

Prevention and control

Potassium deficiency is most likely in light, sandy soil that does not contain much clay. Add sulfate of potassium fertilizer. Composted bracken or comfrey will help restore levels, too.

(from top) **Magnesium deficiency, phosphorus deficiency, potassium deficiency, nitrogen deficiency**

Minor nutrients

Sometimes called micronutrients or trace elements, these are just as important as the major ones, but aren't needed in such large quantities. Deficiencies can be serious, but sometimes can be difficult to diagnose.

Boron deficiency

Affects root vegetables, cabbages, cauliflower, celery, lettuce, and sweet corn.

Symptoms

Beets: rough, dead patches on the skin, and the heart may rot.
Cabbages: leaves are distorted, stems become hollow.
Carrots: roots split and core turns gray, leaves turn yellow or pink.
Cauliflower: brown patches appear on heads, and stems and stalks become rough.
Celery: stems start to crack and turn red or brown inside.
Lettuce: hearts fail to form.
Radishes: skin splits and the vegetable becomes woody.
Rutabagas and turnips: roots develop brown heart—they turn brown or gray inside, sometimes in concentric rings.
Sweet corn: kernels may not develop properly.

Prevention and control

Boron can be washed out of light soil by heavy rain. Levels may be low in very dry or recently limed soil. Mix borax with horticultural sand and rake it into the soil before you sow or plant new crops.

Copper deficiency

Affects all vegetables.

Symptoms

Copper deficiency is hard to diagnose. Leaves may turn yellow or blue-green, and the plant may die back.

Prevention and control

Copper deficiency is rare. It's most likely in peaty and other acidic soils. Try adding a multipurpose fertilizer.

(from top) **Copper deficiency, boron deficiency, manganese deficiency, molybdenum deficiency**

Iron deficiency

Affects all vegetables.

Symptoms

Leaves turn yellow or brown, starting at the edges, then spreading in between the veins. New leaves are worst affected.

Prevention and control

It's rare to find soil that is truly short of iron: high levels of calcium in recently limed or very alkaline soils prevent plants from absorbing the iron there is. Increase the soil's acidity by using sulfur or aluminum sulfate and ferrous sulfate before you sow or plant, or spread an acidic mulch of pine needles or chopped conifer bark. Or buy special chelated or sequestered iron mixtures that provide plants with iron in a readily available form.

Manganese deficiency

Affects a wide range of plants—particularly peas and beans, beets, parsnips, onions, potatoes, and spinach.

Symptoms

Leaves turn yellow in between the veins, and brown spots or patches may appear. New leaves are worst affected.

Prevention and control

Most common in acidic, peaty soil or poorly drained, sandy soil. Avoid adding lime to soil where the problem has been identified. Spray affected plants with manganese sulfate solution.

Molybdenum deficiency

Affects cauliflower, sprouting broccoli, and other brassicas.

Symptoms

Leaves turn yellow and are thin, narrow, and stringy—giving rise to the terms brassica "whiptail" and "wire stem." Heads may be very small or may completely fail to develop.

Prevention and control

Acidic soils may prevent absorption, which affects how nitrogen is processed; this will affect growth. Add lime to acidic soil to increase the pH, or avoid growing brassicas there. Spray affected plants or soil with ammonium or sodium molybdate solution.

UNDER- AND OVERWATERING

Too little water, which this spinach is suffering from, causes plants to starve, because they can't absorb soil nutrients. Their growth slows, leaves droop and turn a sickly yellow color, and resistance to pests and diseases drops.

Too much water causes plants to (quite literally) drown. The roots cannot take in air, so they stop working and may rot. Leaves wilt, tissue dies, and the plant becomes susceptible to disease. A sudden increase in water after a prolonged dry period can produce such rapid growth that skins split. Damp conditions will also attract slugs and snails.

Natural allies

It should go without saying that not all insects, birds, and animals are enemies. Many are positively beneficial and, given a chance, will prove to be among your most valuable allies in the battle against pests and diseases.

In any kitchen garden and in any vegetable patch there is a natural order in which pests and predators are balanced against each other. The good guys keep the bad guys under control. Ladybugs and hoverflies eat aphids; centipedes feed on slugs, as do frogs and toads; birds eat snails; and so on. When everything is working properly, the pest population is managed effectively, and the damage they cause is limited.

Working with nature

Two things can throw everything off balance. The first is the use of chemicals. Insecticides, fungicides, and weed killers all carry some risk to wildlife, and their overuse may threaten to kill off as many allies as enemies. The second is monoculture. A plot devoted to growing just one or two different kinds of vegetables is more likely to suffer problems than a diverse one planted with a wide variety of crops, including plenty of flowering plants, too.

Biological controls

Very precise targeting of specific pests can be achieved by introducing biological predators. These are usually nematodes (microscopic worms), predatory mites, parasitic wasps, or even live bacteria. They are released into the soil or onto plants that have an infestation, sometimes in a greenhouse but also outdoors.

Encarsia formosa, for example, is a tiny parasitic wasp that lays its eggs in the larvae of whiteflies. When the young hatch, they eat the larvae. *Phytoseiulus persimilis* is a predatory mite that feeds on the eggs of spider mites. And *Bacillus thuringiensis* is a bacterium that is sprayed on leaves to kill caterpillars by infecting them with a fatal disease. Most of these controls can be bought by mail order.

(clockwise from top left)

Hoverflies lay their eggs in the midst of aphid infestations. When the eggs hatch, the larvae eat the aphids.

Earthworms aerate the soil by tunneling through it, improving drainage, and drawing surface organic matter such as manure and dead plant material underground.

Attract lacewings by giving them a box to hibernate in over the winter, by growing plenty of flowers, or by buying a batch of eggs in the form of a biological control. The larvae feed on aphids.

Ladybugs (bottom middle) and their larvae (bottom right) feast voraciously on aphids, so they should be welcomed.

Attract bees to your garden by planting brightly colored flowers.

BENEFICIAL WILDLIFE

There are numerous ways to encourage an influx of creatures into your garden to help keep pests and predators at bay:

- Plant a mix of vegetables, fruit, and flowers. Diversity encourages a wide range of visitors.
- Keep one or two semi-wild areas at the edges of your yard. Being scrupulously tidy doesn't leave anywhere for creatures to colonize.
- Plant a hedge. It will provide a lot more camouflage and cover for wildlife than a neat wire fence.
- Spray with pesticides and weed killers only when you really have to.
- Create a nesting site for beetles and wasps. Make a small log pile and let it rot naturally.
- Spread organic mulches over the soil. Apart from retaining moisture, they shelter beetles, centipedes, spiders, and so on.
- Put up nesting boxes for birds and bats, and hibernation boxes for insects such as ladybugs, lacewings, and mason bees.
- Dig a pond. However small, it will attract frogs and toads, which will feast on slugs.

Beneficial planting

Natural allies include plants as well as animals and insects. Making sure that your vegetable garden includes a good mix of flowering plants has two clear benefits.

First, flowers will attract a wide variety of beneficial insects—the ones you definitely want, the pollinators and the predators. Bees will of course be drawn to them. And French marigolds are well known for attracting aphid-eating hoverflies.

Second, because certain plants are just as notorious for attracting pests, you may choose to use them as a "sacrifice." Planting nasturtiums, which blackflies find irresistible, close to fava beans may not produce the healthiest-looking nasturtiums but it might keep the blackflies off the beans. You might also try growing some lettuce that you are prepared to lose as a way of baiting slugs in order to attract and then destroy them.

(opposite page, clockwise from top left)
Nasturtiums attract blackflies and may successfully tempt them away from infesting other crops.

French marigold flowers produce a scent that whiteflies dislike so much that it may keep them off nearby tomatoes.

Poached egg flowers (*Limnanthes douglasii*) will attract bees and hoverflies.

Basil is seemingly irresistible to whiteflies and makes a good sacrificial plant for a greenhouse.

Index

Page numbers in *italics* indicate an illustration, while page numbers in **bold** refer to a main entry.

AUTHOR'S ACKNOWLEDGMENTS
Thanks to the team at Dorling Kindersley, especially Katie Dock and Rachael Smith, to Jo Whittingham for all her help and advice, and to Barbara Wood, my plot neighbor at the Royal Paddocks Allotments, Hampton Wick, for so generously sharing her knowledge (and many of her plants!) with me.

PUBLISHER'S ACKNOWLEDGMENTS
Dorling Kindersley would like to thank Zia Allaway for editorial assistance, Michèle Clarke for compiling the index, Trevor Cole for assistance with the US edition, and the following for their kind permission to reproduce their photographs:

(Key: a-above; b-below/bottom; c-center; l-left; r-right; t-top)

1 Dorling Kindersley: RHS Hampton Court Flower Show. **2-3 GAP Photos:** Rob Whitworth / RHS Hampton Court Flower Show / Designer: Paul Stone. **6 Airedale Publishing. 11 Airedale Publishing. 12 Modeste Herwig:** West Dean Gardens (bl). **15 Garden World Images:** F. Davis (c). **28 Airedale Publishing:** (br). **31 Airedale Publishing:** (br). **36 Airedale Publishing:** (cr). **37 Airedale Publishing:** (fbr). **40 Airedale Publishing:** (br). **46 The Garden Collection:** Liz Eddison / RHS Hampton Court Flower Show 200 / Designer: Cherry Burton (bl). **52 Airedale Publishing:** (bl). **56 Garden World Images:** F. Davis (cr). **57 Photos Horticultural:** (br). **62 Le Scanff-Mayer. 63 Dorling Kindersley:** RHS Hampton Court Flower Show (tl). **Garden Picture Library:** Jacqui Hurst (bl). **71 Alamy Images:** Anne Gilbert (bl). **GAP Photos:** Michael Howes (tl). **Garden World Images:** (br). **75 Jo Whitworth:** (br). **76 Garden World Images:** F. Davis. **77 Dorling Kindersley:** RHS Hampton Court Flower Show. **78 Garden Picture Library:** James Guilliam. **82 Airedale Publishing. 83 Jo Whitworth:** RHS Gardens, Rosemoor. **85 Garden Picture Library:** Howard Rice (bl). **87 Airedale Publishing. 88 Airedale Publishing:** (ca). **94 Airedale Publishing:** (tr). **95 GAP Photos:** Jonathan Buckley (br). **Garden Picture Library:** Chris Burrows (cr). **96 GAP Photos:** Jonathan Buckley. **97 Airedale Publishing:** (tl, tc). **105 Alamy Images:** Rex May (clb). **109 Garden World Images:** A. Bagett (br). **110 Garden Picture Library:** Howard Rice (br). **113 Garden World Images:** C. Wheeler (tr). **Photos Horticultural:** (br). **120 Dorling Kindersley:** RHS Hampton Court Flower Show. **121 Garden World Images. 122 Jo Whitworth. 124 Airedale Publishing. 128 Airedale Publishing:** (tl). **Garden World Images:** (cl). **133 Garden World Images:** (tc). **Garden Picture Library:** Chris Burrows (br). **135 Airedale Publishing:** (tl). **136 Airedale Publishing. 139 GAP Photos:** S & O (bl). **Garden World Images:** (r). **142 Photos Horticultural:** HDRA (br). **147 Garden Picture Library:** Stephen Hamilton (tr). **148 Garden World Images:** Jacqui Dracup. **149 Airedale Publishing:** (tr). **GAP Photos:** Jonathan Buckley (br). **Garden Picture Library:** Christi Carter (tl); Michael Howes (bl). **150 Airedale Publishing. 153 Garden Picture Library:** David Askham (t). **Photos Horticultural:** HDRA (b). **157 GAP Photos:** Jonathan Buckley (r). **Photos Horticultural:** (l). **158 GAP Photos:** Jonathan Buckley. **161 Garden Picture Library:** David Askham (br). **162 Airedale Publishing:** (cla). **163 Photos Horticultural:** (tr). **173 FLPA:** NIgel Cattlin (tr). **Garden World Images:** (br). **The Garden Collection:** Torie Chugg (bl). **176 Garden World Images. 183 Photos Horticultural:** (tr, br). **185 Alamy Images:** Martin Hughes-Jones (ll). **Jo Whitworth:** (tr). **195 Alamy Images:** Clare Gainey (bl). **200 Airedale Publishing:** (tl). **Alamy Images:** Rex May (tr). **GAP Photos:** Jonathan Buckley (br). **Garden Picture Library:** Botanica (bl). **205 Photos Horticultural:** (tr). **210 Photos Horticultural:** (lr). **211 Garden Picture Library:** Michael Howes (tl). **Photos Horticultural:** (bl). **217 Garden Picture Library:** Michele Lamontagne (br). **218 Airedale Publishing. 221 Alamy Images:** Tim Gainey (tl). **GAP Photos:** Jonathan Buckley (bl). **222 Alamy Images:** Joel Douillet. **223 Photos Horticultural:** (cr). **227 GAP Photos:** Jonathan Buckley (tl). **The Garden Collection:** Torie Chugg (bl). **232 Airedale Publishing:** (bl). **233 GAP Photos:** Jonathan Buckley (tr). **Garden World Images:** A. Biddle (tl). **Garden Picture Library:** Michele Lamontagne (br). **The Garden Collection:** Andrew Lawson (bl). **237 Garden World Images:** P. McGrath (br). **Photos Horticultural:** (bl). **241 Airedale Publishing:** (bl, br). **245 Airedale Publishing:** (tl, tr). **246 Photos Horticultural:** HDRA. **250 Photos Horticultural:** (cl, bl). **251 Photos Horticultural:** (crb). **252 Garden World Images:** P. McGrath. **255 Garden World Images. 258 GAP Photos:** Visions (tr). **266 GAP Photos:** Visions. **274 Airedale Publishing:** (tl). **279 Airedale Publishing:** (tl). **283 Garden Picture Library:** Botanica. **298 Airedale Publishing. 300 Photos Horticultural:** RHS Chelsea Flower Show 1990 Pembrokeshire Horticultural Society (bl). **303 Airedale Publishing. 318 Photos Horticultural:** MJK (br). **320 Garden World Images:** D. Bevan (tl, clb). **Science Photo Library:** Nigel Cattlin (cla). **321 Garden World Images:** D. Bevan (crb); **P. McGrath** (tr). **Garden Picture Library:** Howard Rice (ca). **322 Garden World Images:** D. Bevan (tl). **Garden Picture Library:** Mark Winwood (cla). **323 GAP Photos:** FhF Greenmedia (tr). **Science Photo Library:** Clive Schaupmayer / Agstock USA (cra). **324 Airedale Publishing:** (br). **327 Science Photo Library:** CSL (tr). **328 Garden World Images:** D. Bevan (cla). **Science Photo Library:** CSL (clb). **329 Garden Picture Library:** Animals Animals / Earth Scenes (crb). **Garden World Images:** D. Wildridge (tr). **330 GAP Photos:** J. S. Sira (cla). **331 Science Photo Library:** Jack Clark / Agstock USA (tr). **332 Science Photo Library:** CSL (tl). **333 Science Photo Library:** Dr. Marlin E. Rice (crb). **335 FLPA:** Nigel Cattlin (cra, br, crb). **336 FLPA:** Nigel Cattlin (cla, clb); **Len McLeod** (bl). Garden World Images: D. Bevan (tl). **337 Garden World Images:** S. Chesterman (tr). **338 Airedale Publishing:** (tl). **Dorling Kindersley:** Ted Benton (bl). **341 Airedale Publishing:** (bl).

All other images © Dorling Kindersley. For further information see: www.dkimages.com

Baker Creek Heirloom Seed Co.
2278 Baker Creek Road
Mansfield, MO 65704
www.rareseeds.com
Large selection of heirloom vegetable, flower, and herb seeds.

Burpee
300 Park Avenue
Warminster, PA 18974
www.burpee.com
Vegetable and flower seeds.

Eden Brothers
34 Old Brevard Road
Asheville, NC 28806
www.edenbrothers.com
Offering thousands of flower seeds, vegetable seeds, heirloom seeds, herb seeds, wildflower seed mixes, and flower bulbs.

Gurney's Seed & Nursery Co.
P.O. Box 4178
Greendale, IN 47025
www.gurneys.com
Vegetable, fruit, herb, and flower seeds and plants.

Forestfarm
990 Tetherow Rd.
Williams, OR 97544
www.forestfarm.com
Large range of plants, including fruits and berries, perennials, and ornamental trees, shrubs, and grasses.

Johnny's Selected Seeds
955 Benton Avenue
Winslow, ME 04901
www.johnnyseeds.com
Vegetable and flower seeds, including heirloom varieties and organic seeds, and tools and supplies.

Park Seed Company
3507 Cokesbury Road
Hodges, SC 29653
www.parkseed.com
Vegetable and flower seeds.

Peaceful Valley Farm & Garden Supply
P.O. Box 2209
Grass Valley, CA 95945
www.groworganic.com
Natural fertilizers, beneficial insects, and seeds, plants, and gardening supplies.

Planet Natural
125 Clydesdale Ct
Grass Valley, CA 95945
www.planetnatural.com
Natural pest controls, composting equipment, hydroponic supplies, and seeds.

St. Lawrence Nurseries
325 State Highway 345
Potsdam, NY 13676
www.sln.potsdam.ny.us
Truly hardy fruit and nut trees for northern gardens.

Sand Hill Preservation Center
1878 230th Street
Calamus, IA 52729
www.sandhillpreservation.com
Heirloom seeds and plants and heritage poultry.

Select Seeds Antique Flowers
180 Stickney Hill Road
Union, CT 06076
www.selectseeds.com
Rare and old-fashioned flower seeds, bulbs, and plants.

Stokes Seeds
P.O. Box 548
Buffalo, NY 14240
www.stokeseeds.com
Vegetable and flower seeds.

Terrior Seeds
P.O. Box 4995
Chino Valley, AZ 86323
www.underwoodgardens.com
Wide range of heirloom, open-pollinated, and rare seeds.

Territorial Seed Company
P.O. Box 158
Cottage Grove, OR 97424
www.territorial-seed.com
Unusual and heirloom flower, fruit, and vegetable seeds and plants.